The
Collected Stories of
**UPENDRAKISHORE RAY
CHOWDHURY**

Also by Lopamudra Maitra

The Owl Delivered Good News All Night Long: Folktales, Legends, and Modern Lore of India

Stories of Colonial Architecture: (Kolkata–Colombo)

India, Sri Lanka and the SAARC Region: History, Popular Culture and Heritage

The Collected Stories of
UPENDRAKISHORE RAY CHOWDHURY

Translated by LOPAMUDRA MAITRA

ALEPH

ALEPH BOOK COMPANY
An independent publishing firm
promoted by *Rupa Publications India*

First published in India in 2023
by Aleph Book Company
7/16 Ansari Road, Daryaganj
New Delhi 110 002

This edition copyright © Aleph Book Company 2023
English translation copyright © Lopamudra Maitra 2023
Illustrations by Upendrakishore Ray Chowdhury are in the
public domain.

All rights reserved.

The translator has asserted her moral rights.

This is a work of fiction. Names, characters, places, and
incidents are either the product of the author's imagination or
are used fictitiously and any resemblance to any actual persons,
living or dead, events or locales is entirely coincidental.

No part of this publication may be reproduced, transmitted,
or stored in a retrieval system, in any form or by any means,
without permission in writing from Aleph Book Company.

ISBN: 978-81-19635-41-2

1 3 5 7 9 10 8 6 4 2
Printed in India.

This book is sold subject to the condition that it shall not,
by way of trade or otherwise, be lent, resold, hired out, or
otherwise circulated without the publisher's prior consent in
any form of binding or cover other than that in which it is
published.

*To Mini and
the sparkly old afternoons of mango pickle and stories of Tuntuni
and the foolish crocodile.*

CONTENTS

Introduction ix

1. The Tailorbird and the Cat 3
2. The Tailorbird and the Barber 6
3. The Tailorbird and the King 11
4. Norohori Das, a Clever Goat Kid 15
5. The Tiger and His Nephew, the Fox 19
6. The Foolish Weaver and the Fox 21
7. The Hunchbacked Old Lady 29
8. The Old Lady Who Had Lice 33
9. The Old Lady Who Ate Fermented Rice 40
10. The Sparrow and the Crow 43
11. The Sparrow and the Tiger 47
12. The Naughty Tiger 50
13. The Tiger Groom 55
14. The Beast atop the Tiger 60
15. The Tiger's Palanquin Ride 66
16. The Old Farmer, Buddhu's Baap 69
17. The Foolish Tiger 76
18. The Tiger's Cook 81
19. The Foolish Crocodile 85
20. The Learned Fox 87
21. The Fox Who Was a Juror 91
22. The Fox Cubs Who Wanted to Feast upon the Tiger 95
23. The Fruit of the Sugarcane 98
24. The Fox inside the Elephant 100
25. The Arrogant Cat, Mawjontali Sarkar 103
26. The Ant, the Elephant, and the Brahmin Pandit's Servant 110
27. The Ant Couple, Mr and Mrs Ant 120
28. Is It Easy to Become Rich? 123
29. How Do You Really Become a Rich Man? 140
30. The Monkey Prince 143

31.	The Elaborate Meal	153
32.	Dukhiram, a Sad Man	160
33.	The Story of Grandfather	174
34.	A Puranic Story from Norway	180
35.	The Grandmother's Bravery	184
36.	Ghyanghashur, Half-bird, Half-beast	188
37.	The 'Intelligent' Servants	198
38.	Byacharam's Servant Kenaram	202
39.	Chanu the Adept Thief	209
40.	The Youngest Brother	221
41.	The Verdict of the Judge	225
42.	Saatmaar Palowan	227
43.	The Hunchback and the Ghosts	233
44.	The Japanese Gods	237
45.	The Three Boons	246
46.	Gupi and Bagha, a Singer and an Instrumentalist	253
47.	The Red Thread and Blue Thread	274
48.	The Naughty Demon	278
49.	A True Incident, Not a Story	281
50.	The Weaver and the Seven Ghosts	285
51.	The 'Clever' Servant	292
52.	The Demons, Phingey and Kunkro	295
53.	Stories of 'Wise' Pandits	300
54.	Big and Small Impossible Stories	305
55.	What Happened after That?	312
56.	The Tale of Bhuto and Ghuto	317
57.	The Strange Sea Voyage of Gilfoy Sahib	322
58.	The Man Who Loved to Criticize	325
59.	New Stories	330
60.	A Ghost Story	332
61.	Why Is Seawater Salty?	339
62.	The Timid Boy Named Kama	342
63.	The Mother Kite	344

INTRODUCTION

ABOUT UPENDRAKISHORE RAY CHOWDHURY

A prolific writer, illustrator, and publisher, Upendrakishore Ray Chowdhury is a well-known name, especially in the genre of Bengali children's literature. He was also the first printer and publisher to introduce modern block-making, including half-tone and colour block-making in South Asia. Apart from his collection and publication of folktales from the erstwhile region of Bengal, Upendrakishore was known for encouraging scientific thought and musical appreciation through his writings for children.

Upendrakishore Ray Chowdhury was born on 12 May 1863 in the village called Moshua, in the Mymansingha district of erstwhile Bengal (present-day Bangladesh). Born as Kamadaranjan Ray to Kalinath Ray, he was adopted when he was five years old by Harikishore, a relative and a zamindar in Mymansingha. Harikishore renamed Kamadaranjan as 'Upendrakishore' and also added the surname 'Ray Chowdhury' as a suffix.

Having successfully completed his entrance examination in 1880 with a scholarship from Mymansingha Zilla School, Upendrakishore travelled to Kolkata for higher studies and studied for a while in Presidency College, before going onto complete his Bachelor of Arts in 1884 from the Calcutta Metropolitan Institution (now known as Vidyasagar College). From a very young age, Upendrakishore had a great love for music and drawing. He further went on to concentrate on publishing, especially inspired by the poor woodcut-line block printing quality for his Bengali book, *Chheleder Ramayana*. Having imported books, chemicals, and equipment from England

and closely studied the process of publishing, Upendrakishore set up his own blockmaking enterprise in 1895 and called it U. Ray and Sons. The office was at 7, Shibnarain Lane, Kolkata. This was his residence as well as his workplace. U. Ray and Sons became the stepping stone for the printing press at 100 Garpar Road, set up in 1914. To date, this is considered to have been the finest in South Asia at that time.

In 1913, U. Ray and Sons began publishing the famous magazine *Sandesh*. Many folktales which became a part of *Sandesh* had found a place in his earlier books, including *Tuntunir Boi* (published in 1910) and *Golpomala* (published somewhere between 1910–12). Unfortunately, within a mere two years after the beginning of *Sandesh*, Upendrakishore passed away in Kolkata on 20 December 1915, at the age of fifty-two.

Upendrakishore was married to Bidhumukhi Devi, the daughter of Dwarakanath Ganguly and the stepdaughter of Kadambini Ganguly. Both Dwarakanath and Kadambini were famous individuals. Dwarakanath was a Brahmo reformer who had contributed immensely towards social enlightenment and the emancipation of women of the time while Kadambini Ganguly was the first female medical practitioner with an Indian medical degree from the Calcutta Medical College. Upendrakishore's eldest daughter, Sukhalata Rao, was a famous social worker. She too wrote for children and edited a newspaper entitled *Alok*. His eldest son was the celebrated writer, illustrator, poet, and publisher Sukumar, who was the father of raconteur par excellence and Bharat Ratna awardee, Satyajit Ray. Upendrakishore's second daughter was Punyalata Chakraborty, his second son was Subinoy Roy, and the youngest was Subimal Ray.

After his death, the responsibility of publishing *Sandesh* was borne by Sukumar Ray. But following his untimely demise in 1923, the task briefly fell upon Upendrakishore's second son,

Subinoy Ray. This continued till 1925 when the magazine came to a standstill because of marketing, distribution, and financial problems. After a long gap, it was resumed in the 1930s, but again shut shop. It was then revived through the editorial desk of Satyajit Ray in 1961.

Tuntunir Boi

THE TAILORBIRD AND THE CAT

TUNTUNI AAR BERALER KOTHA

In the rear garden of the householder's compound, there was an aubergine plant, and on one of its branches, was Tuntuni, the tailorbird's, nest. Neatly stitched together, it was a lovely home for her three little children. The fluffy hatchlings were so small that neither could they see nor could they fly. They only opened their tiny beaks and chirped away all day long.

That householder had a pet cat, Beral, and a very naughty one at that. The only thought which went on in her mind was, 'Oh! Those little birds would make for a grand feast.' Thus, one day, she came close to the aubergine plant, looked up at Tuntuni's nest, and said, 'What are you up to Tuntuni?'

Tuntuni respectfully bowed her head and greeted Beral, 'Pranam Maharani!'

Now, this really pleased Beral and she went away happily.

This continued for many days. Beral would visit the plant and enquire after Tuntuni, who would then greet her warmly and Beral would return happily.

Time passed by, and the nestlings grew into fledgelings with beautiful feathers. They began to see the world around them with their bright eyes and would no longer just sit and chirp in their nest all day. Finally, one day, Tuntuni asked them, 'My dear babies, tell me, can you all fly now?'

They replied in unison, 'Yes, ma. We can.'

'Alright! Show me if you can fly over and sit on the branches of that palm tree.'

The little babies immediately flew over to the palm tree and sat on its tall branches. This made Tuntuni mighty pleased. She said to herself, 'Now, let naughty Beral visit me once again!'

And soon enough, there was Beral, standing near the aubergine plant. The usual banter followed.

'What are you up to Tuntuni?'

Tuntuni had been waiting for this moment. She threw a kick in the air towards Beral and said, 'Go away, nasty Beral,' and flew away immediately towards the palm tree. The mischievous Beral was furious. She snarled, baring all her teeth, and jumped at Tuntuni's nest. But alas, she neither could punish the clever tailorbird, nor feast upon her children. Instead, Beral learned a good lesson when the thorns of the aubergine plant left behind terrible bruises and she limped home, humiliated.

THE TAILORBIRD AND THE BARBER

TUNTUNI AAR NAPITER KOTHA

One day, Tuntuni the tailorbird was dancing merrily on the highest branches of an aubergine plant. Suddenly he was stung by a thorn, and soon, the bruise became a festering boil.

'Oh ma! How will this painful boil ever be cured?'

Tuntuni sought advice from one and all, and everyone had the same solution: 'Get it incised by the barber, Napit.'

So, Tuntuni went over to Napit's house and requested, 'Napit Dada, Napit Dada can you please lance my boil?'

But the haughty barber twitched his nose, cocked his head to one side and said, 'Ish! I am the royal barber. I shave the Raja. Why would I lance your boil?'

This angered Tuntuni. He declared, 'Alright! We'll see if you will help me or not.'

Tuntuni immediately flew to the Raja and complained about Napit's behaviour. 'Your Majesty, why won't your barber lance my boil? Please punish him.'

Upon hearing the tiny bird's complaint, Raja Moshai had a hearty laugh, rolled all over his bed, but did not take any action against the barber. The king's apathy angered Tuntuni even more. He immediately went over to his friend, Indur, the mouse.

'Indur Bhai, Indur Bhai, are you home?'

Upon hearing Tuntuni, the mouse enquired, 'Who is it, Bhai? Is it Tuni Bhai? Please come in, Bhai! Have a seat, Bhai! Let me serve you some rice, Bhai! You must share a meal with me, Bhai.'

'Indeed, I will have a seat and share some rice with you,' Tuntuni answered, 'but you must fulfil a task for me.'

'What kind of task?'

'As Raja Moshai sleeps at night, I want you to go to his bedchamber and nibble and dig a hole in his large, fat belly.'

Indur was shocked.

'Oh dear! I cannot do that.'

The mouse's timid answer made Tuntuni angrier and he set off for his friend, Beral, the cat's house. Upon reaching, Tuntuni called out, 'Beral Bhai, Beral Bhai, are you home?'

Immediately Beral replied: 'Who is it Bhai? Is it Tuni Bhai? Please come in, Bhai! Have a seat, Bhai! Let me serve you some rice, Bhai! You must share a meal with me, Bhai.'

'Indeed, I will have a seat and share some rice with you,' Tuntuni answered, 'but only if you slay the mouse for me.'

Upon hearing Tuntuni's demand, Beral replied drowsily, 'I can't go after any mouse right now. I am very sleepy.'

Beral's answer infuriated Tuntuni, and he left for his friend Lathi, the stick's, house.

'Lathi Bhai, Lathi Bhai, are you home?'

Lathi immediately replied, 'Who is it Bhai? Is it Tuni Bhai? Please come in, Bhai! Have a seat, Bhai! Let me serve you some rice, Bhai! You must share a meal with me, Bhai.'

'Indeed, I will have a seat and share some rice with you,' Tuntuni answered, 'but only if you beat up Beral for me.'

'Why would I beat up Beral?' Lathi replied, amazed at Tuntuni's request. 'He never did me any harm. I cannot do your work.'

Lathi's curtness angered Tuntuni further and he immediately flew over to another friend, Agun the fire, and enquired, 'Agun Bhai, Agun Bhai, are you home?'

Answering Tuntuni's call, Agun replied, 'Who is it Bhai? Is it Tuni Bhai? Please come in, Bhai! Have a seat, Bhai! Let me serve you some rice, Bhai! You must share a meal with me, Bhai.'

'Indeed, I will have a seat and share some rice with you,' Tuntuni said, 'but only if you burn Lathi for me.'

Agun replied looking tired, 'I have been burning a lot of things throughout the day. I am exhausted and cannot help you at this moment.'

Agun's reply left Tuntuni fuming. He scolded Agun and flew over to the abode of his friend, Sagar, the sea and said, 'Sagar Bhai, Sagar Bhai, are you home?'

Upon hearing Tuntuni's voice, Sagar exclaimed, 'Who is it Bhai? Is it Tuni Bhai? Please come in, Bhai! Have a seat, Bhai! Let me serve you some rice, Bhai! You must share a meal with me, Bhai.'

'Indeed, I will have a seat and share some rice with you,' Tuntuni responded, 'but only if you extinguish Agun for me.'

'No, I cannot,' came Sagar's brisk reply. Dejected by the answer, Tuntuni flew over to his friend Hathi, the elephant's house, and said, 'Hathi Bhai, Hathi Bhai, are you home?'

Hathi heard Tuntuni and said, 'Who is it Bhai? Is it Tuni Bhai? Please come in, Bhai! Have a seat, Bhai! Let me serve you some rice, Bhai! You must share a meal with me, Bhai.'

'Indeed, I will have a seat and share some rice with you,' Tuntuni said, 'but only if you empty the sea for me—empty the whole of Sagar.'

Hathi was astonished. 'I cannot drink up all that water. My tummy will burst.'

Now that all his friends proved unwilling to help him, Tuntuni decided to visit the house of Mosha, the mosquito who immediately recognized him from a distance.

'Who is it Bhai? Is it Tuni Bhai? Please come in, Bhai! Have a seat, Bhai! Let me serve you some rice, Bhai! You must share a meal with me, Bhai.'

'Indeed, I will have a seat and share some rice with you,' Tuntuni said, 'but only if you bite Hathi for me.'

'Oh! That's no great task,' the friendly Mosha replied at once. 'I will go right away and bite Hathi. Let me see how thick-skinned he is.'

He summoned his mosquito friends from all over the world. They came buzzing and as they gathered all around him, Mosha commanded, 'Come my brothers, let us all bite Hathi. We'll see how thick-skinned he is.' And as instructed, mosquitoes started flying towards Hathi's house from every direction, humming, 'Peen, peen, peen, peen.'

There were father and son mosquitoes and brother and friend mosquitoes and they flew in a tightly knit formation. A thick shroud of buzzing mosquitoes covered the sky, completely shielding the sun. Darkness descended. The shrill buzzing of a thousand flapping wings terrified everyone in the kingdom.

And after that?

Hathi said, 'Let me go and drink Sagar.'

Sagar said, 'Let me go and extinguish Agun.'

Agun said, 'Let me burn up Lathi.'

Lathi said, 'Let me beat up Beral.'

Beral said, 'Let me slay Indur.'

Indur said, 'Let me nibble at Raja Moshai's fat belly and dig a hole.'

And the angry Raja thundered 'Off with Napit's head.'

Having learned his lesson, the trembling barber approached Tuntuni with folded hands, and implored, 'Save me, Tuni Dada. Come and let me lance your boil.'

Soon, Tuntuni's wound had healed and he was once again back on the branches of the aubergine plant, dancing merrily and singing, '*Tuntuna tun tun tun, dhei dhei!*'

THE TAILORBIRD AND THE KING

TUNTUNI AAR RAJAR KOTHA

Tuntuni had built his nest in a corner of the king's garden. One day, all the taka, money, from the king's treasure chest had been spread on the terrace to be aired. And when the workers returned in the evening to collect the taka, they mistakenly left one taka behind. Tuntuni's eyes fell on the shiny disc. As he scooped it up in his beak and brought it back to his nest, Tuntuni thought to himself, 'I am such a rich man now. The great king and I own the same treasure.'

He began singing:

'Same as the raja's treasure
Tuni has in his home and sings in pleasure.'

At that moment, the raja was holding court. He asked his ministers, 'Listen, what exactly is that tailorbird saying?'

The frightened courtiers replied with folded hands, 'Maharaj, the bird says that he owns the same treasure as the king.'

The raja laughed out loud and then thundered, 'Go and search his nest.'

The courtiers soon returned with the information: 'Maharaj, there is a taka in his nest.'

The king bellowed, 'Well! That is part of my treasure too. Go and bring it back to me.'

Immediately, the courtiers went to fetch the taka from Tuntuni's nest. Now, what else can one do?

Forlorn, Tuntuni began to sing:

'The raja is such a miser
He even took away Tuni's treasure.'

Upon hearing Tuntuni's new song, the Raja said sarcastically, 'That bird is very stubborn. Go and return the taka.'

Once the coin was back in his nest, Tuntuni resumed his happy singing:

*'The raja got scared,
thus, Tuni's taka was spared.'*

Hearing Tuntuni sing once again the raja asked, 'Now what is he saying?'

All the courtiers replied, 'He is saying that the raja returned Tuntuni's taka because he is afraid.'

'How dare he say such a thing?' fumed the raja. 'Bring him immediately. I want to fry him and eat that bird.'

The courtiers immediately marched off and came back to court with Tuntuni as a captive. Clasping Tuntuni tightly in his palm, the raja handed him over to his seven queens and ordered, 'Fry this bird and serve him to me for lunch.'

In the meanwhile, the seven ranis were delighted to see the petite bird. One remarked, 'What a beautiful bird! Do let me see,' and as she took Tuntuni in her hands, the rest gathered around her to have a closer look at Tuntuni. And just as he was being passed to the next rani, Tuntuni slipped out and flew away.

'Oh my goodness! Now what will happen? The Raja will spare none if he gets even an inkling about this.'

Just as the seven ranis sat lamenting about their terrible fate, they spotted a frog hopping away. They caught the frog in a jiffy and whispered amongst themselves, 'Quiet, quiet! No one should get to know about this. We will fry this frog and serve it to the king. He will think that he has feasted upon Tuntuni.'

As decided, the ranis cleaned and cooked the frog, and the king was satisfied with his lunch.

'Now I have taught the little imp a good lesson for life,' the king thought to himself, as he returned to court after a hearty meal. Just then, he once again heard Tuntuni's loud singing:

*'Oh! What fun, what fun,
a fried frog is what the Raja feasted upon.'*

The Raja was livid. He jumped up with disgust, spat and tried to vomit, rinsed his mouth, and did all sorts of antics. 'Off with the noses of all seven ranis!' he thundered with rage.

The executioner immediately chopped off all seven noses. Seeing the pandemonium, Tuntuni started to sing:

*'Tun, tun, a song Tuni composes
As the seven ranis lose their noses.'*

'Go and catch hold of the imp. This time, I will swallow it alive. Let me see how he escapes,' the fuming raja bellowed.

The soldiers once again caught hold of Tuntuni and handed him over to the raja, who then hollered, 'Get me some drinking water.' Someone ran and fetched some water. The raja took a large swig, pushed Tuntuni inside his mouth, closed his eyes, and swallowed the bird with a large gulp.

'Finally, the bird has been taught a lesson,' the ministers thought. But right then, the Raja Moshai belched loudly. The loud noise startled the courtiers. They watched Tuntuni shoot out of the king's mouth and fly away in the blink of an eye.

'There, there. Catch, catch,' the raja shouted. Nearly two hundred people ran after Tuntuni, captured him once again, and brought him to the Raja. Once again, water was fetched, and this time a sepoy stood close by, his sword raised near the king's mouth in preparation to chop Tuntuni into two, lest the mischievous bird tried to escape again. This time, when the Raja gulped down Tuntuni, he covered his mouth with both hands. Poor Tuntuni! He wiggled inside the king's stomach. All that movement made the king feel rather sick. Finally, he couldn't take it any longer. The king screwed his nose and vomited. Out came the bird and his meal.

'Sepoy, sepoy! Catch, kill, kill! It's flying away!'

The bewildered sepoy, flustered by the sudden chaos, couldn't trace the bird's exact location. He raised his rapier and brought down the sharp blade straight on the king's nose.

The raja sprang up in pain. The courtiers shouted in unison. Finally, the royal doctor was summoned. The nose was wrapped in bandages and medicines were prescribed. Watching the scene, Tuntuni sang again:

> *'The noseless raja, what a plight!*
> *Now you see it, serves you right.'*

With these final words, Tuntuni flew far, far away from the kingdom. All the king's men ran to his nest, only to find it abandoned.

NOROHORI DAS, A CLEVER GOAT KID

NOROHORI DAS

There was once a large open field next to a jungle and a mighty mountain beside that. Within a small burrow in that mountain, lived Chhagolchhana, a goat kid, and his mother. Chhagolchhana was still very small and was not allowed to venture out of the burrow on his own. The minute he wanted to step out, his mother warned him, 'Don't go. The bear will catch hold of you, the tiger will snatch you away, the lion will eat you up.' This was enough to strike fear in the heart of Chhagolchhana and he would sit quietly inside his home. After a while, when he had grown up a little, his fear of the outside world began to slowly fade away. So whenever his mother would step out, he would go to the edge of the burrow and have a peep. Finally, one day, he dared to step out on his own.

In the distance, Chhagolchhana saw a huge ox grazing. He had never seen such a giant animal but upon noticing its large horns, he thought the ox was just another goat like him, only bigger from eating healthy grass. So Chhagolchhana went over to the ox and asked, 'Hello, do tell me what is it that you eat?'

The ox replied, 'I eat grass.'

Chhagolchhana said, 'My mother too eats grass, but she is not as huge as you are.'

The ox replied, 'Compared to your mother, I eat copious quantities of good-quality grass.'

Chhagolchhana asked, 'Where can one find this grass?'

The ox pointed to the forest, 'There. It is inside that jungle.'

'You have to take me there.'

So the ox took the little goat along with him to the forest.

Inside, the grass was indeed juicy. Chhagolchhana ate to his heart's content and when it was time to go home, he realized that he had eaten too much and could barely walk. As the evening approached, the ox said 'Come on, let's go home.'

But how could Chhagolchhana go home? He could not even take a step. 'You carry on. I will return tomorrow,' he said. Thus, the ox returned to his cowshed and Chhagolchhana decided to spend the night in a burrow inside the jungle.

Now, that burrow belonged to a fox, Sheyal, who had left to visit his uncle, Bagh, a tiger. When Sheyal returned late that night, he realized there was another animal hiding in his home. The coat of Chhagolchhana was pitch black, so it was difficult to understand what it was in the dark. What if it was a demon? In a trembling voice, Sheyal asked, 'Who hides inside the burrow?'

Chhagolchhana was quite clever. He said:

'I often ruffle my very long beard,
I am Norohori Das, the maternal uncle of the lion. Fear me, for in my single gulp, fifty tigers are severed.'

'My goodness!' Sheyal exclaimed and immediately dashed off at a breakneck speed. He ran until he had reached his uncle, Bagh's home.

'What happened, nephew?' Bagh asked in amazement. 'Why are you back so soon?

'Oh Uncle, what a catastrophe it is,' Sheyal answered, still panting from his sprint 'One Norohori Das is sitting inside my burrow, and it says that it eats fifty tigers in just one gulp.'

This made Bagh very angry. 'Oh really? Is that so? He dared to say that? Let's go, nephew. Even I would like to see what kind of animal eats fifty tigers in a single gulp.'

Sheyal was still petrified. 'I cannot go there any more. If it comes out to gobble us, you can escape in a jiffy with your strong legs, but I cannot run so fast. He will definitely catch me and eat me up.'

'Don't say so! I will never leave you alone and run away,' Bagh said reassuringly.

'Then tie me to your tail and take me along with you,' Sheyal suggested, wanting to be doubly sure that his uncle wouldn't abandon him.

Thus it was. Bagh tied Sheyal to his tail. As they set off for the burrow, the fox thought to himself, 'Now Uncle Bagh cannot run away and leave me behind.'

Inside the burrow, Chhagolchhana could see the tiger and his nephew approaching from a distance. He immediately said aloud, addressing Sheyal:

'You scoundrel, to get me ten tigers you got paid, tied to its tail you got me one instead?'

Upon hearing these words, Bagh nearly collapsed. He thought the nephew had tricked him into coming along so Norohori Das could feast upon him. Horrified, he jumped twenty-five feet into the air and sprinted wildly in the direction of the forest, dragging poor Sheyal along with him. Oh the poor fox! It was hauled furiously and got badly scratched by the thorns of the forest and dykes of the fields. As Bagh frantically crossed the uneven dykes in the agricultural fields, the fox screamed in pain, 'Uncle, mind the dykes. Mind the aal!' Bagh mistook Sheyal's 'aal' for 'elo' (coming), so now Sheyal's pleas frightened Bagh even further. Under the impression that Norohori Das had finally caught up with him, he panicked and doubled his speed. Bagh and Sheyal ran hither and tither all night long.

In the morning, Chhagolchhana returned home.

Sheyal was rightly punished, and ever since, he remains angry with his uncle.

THE TIGER AND HIS NEPHEW, THE FOX

BAGH MAMA AND SHEYAL BHAGNEY

Ever since the painful episode of Norohori Das, Sheyal could only think of one thing about his uncle, Bagh: 'Uncle, you just wait. I will soon teach you a lesson.' Afraid of Norohori Das, he had stopped returning to his old burrow and had now found a new one near a well. One day, Sheyal found a large woven mat by the riverbank. He dragged it home and spread it over the mouth of the well, completely covering it in the process. Then he set off to invite Bagh. Upon meeting his uncle, he said, 'Uncle, why haven't you ever visited my new home?' Caught off-guard by the invitation, Bagh immediately set off to see his nephew's new abode. Upon reaching the well, Sheyal pointed at the mat and said, 'Uncle, do please have a seat. Let me serve you some refreshments.'

Bagh was mighty pleased at the mere mention of refreshments, and hoping to settle comfortably, pounced upon the mat in glee. In an instant, he tumbled into the well!

'Uncle, drink as much water as you would like. Don't spare a single drop,' Sheyal smirked.

Luckily the water inside was not too deep. So Bagh did not drown. He was afraid, but soon managed to scramble out. 'Where have you gone, you scoundrel? Let me catch you just once,' he growled.

Of course, by then, Sheyal had escaped and could no longer be traced. But the situation posed a problem. Now Bagh was always on the lookout for Sheyal, and completely petrified of Bagh, Sheyal could neither return to his burrow nor go hunting. Even if the tiger spotted him at a distance, he broke into a wild chase. No longer able to hunt for food, Sheyal began to starve.

Finally, one day, he told himself, 'It cannot go on like this any more. I will starve to death. Let me make amends with Uncle, and find a way to please him.'

So the fox set off for the tiger's house. He began his loud salutations from a distance.

'Uncle, Uncle,' Sheyal exclaimed, his palms folded respectfully.

Amazed at his behaviour, the tiger answered, 'Oh my! It is my nephew indeed.'

Sheyal immediately prostrated at Bagh's feet and said, 'Uncle, I know you had to go through great troubles to find me. Your suffering brought tears to my eyes. Uncle, I do love you so, and I have finally come to surrender to you. You may hunt me right here, in the comfort of your home.'

Bagh was taken aback at Sheyal's words. Yet he did not hurt the fox but simply scolded him: 'You rascal. Why did you plan to drown me in the well?'

Sheyal appeared visibly apologetic for his actions. 'Goodness! I can never drown you in a well. The spot where you had jumped upon had very soft mud. It collapsed under your weight. How many people have such a brave uncle as yourself?

Bagh was flattered. 'I think you are right. All of this hadn't occurred to me before.'

So Sheyal and Bagh became friends again.

Then one day, while walking across the riverbank, Sheyal spotted a twenty-feet long crocodile, sunbathing. Immediately, he had an idea. He ran to Bagh and said, 'Uncle, I have recently purchased a boat. Please have a look.'

The foolish tiger mistook the crocodile for a boat. The minute he jumped on its back, the irritated crocodile dragged Bagh into the water, ready for a fight.

Finally, Sheyal had had his revenge. He went home, dancing all the way.

THE FOOLISH WEAVER AND THE FOX

BOKA JOLA AAR SHEYALER KOTHA

Once there lived a simpleton named Raja, who was a jola, a weaver, by profession. Unfortunately, he would often be called foolish by all. One day, while working on his farm with his sickle, he fell asleep in the middle of the field. When he awoke, his iron sickle had grown very hot from lying under the sun. But Raja thought that it had contracted a fever. Troubled by the plight of his sickle, he began to cry loudly, 'My poor sickle will soon perish!'

Hearing Raja's loud cries, a farmer working in the neighbouring field, came over, 'What happened?'

'My sickle has a fever,' Raja sobbed.

The farmer chuckled. 'Dip your sickle in water, and the fever will subside.'

Raja did as he was told, and when the water cooled his sickle, he was immensely happy. Then one day soon after that, Raja's mother came down with a fever. Everyone advised him to summon the physician, but Raja said, 'I know the medicine for this.'

He took his mother to the pond and dipped her in the cold water. The more the poor old lady struggled, the more Raja held her head underwater. 'Wait a while, the fever will break away anytime now.' Finally, when the old lady stopped struggling, Raja took her out only to discover that his poor mother was no more. Raja howled uncontrollably. He did not eat anything for three days and refused to budge from the pond.

Now Sheyal, the fox, was Raja's good friend. He came over to the sobbing chap and said, 'Friend, please do not cry. I will get you married to the princess.'

Upon hearing this, Raja wiped his tears and went home. But every day, he enquired after the fox. 'What happened to your promise, friend?'

'When I have given my word, indeed I will,' Sheyal answered finally 'For now, go and weave some fine cloth for me.'

For the next two months, Raja kept weaving. He wove many clothes. Then Sheyal told him to have a thorough bath and scrub himself clean. Finally, the fox left for the palace in the hopes of arranging the union between the raja's daughter and his friend.

Dressed neatly in fresh clothes and clean shoes, a pen, tucked neatly behind his ear, a turban on his head, a shawl draped over his shoulder, and an umbrella in one hand, the fox looked every inch a distinguished gentleman.

As he approached the throne, the king too thought, 'This must be a great intellectual scholar,' and he asked the fox what work he had in the royal court.

Sheyal replied, 'Your Majesty, I have come to enquire if you are interested in having your daughter married to our king.' Indeed the fox wasn't lying. The name 'Raja' does mean king.

The king enquired curiously, 'Describe your raja.'

Thus began Sheyal's narration:

'Our Raja is handsome indeed,
The moonlight illuminates his retreat.
He is a great intellectual—that is straight,
His scholarship is equally great.
He can slay ten at a go,
And with his skills, people survive—both high and low.'

Now, there was a smidgen of truth in what Sheyal was saying. Raja was indeed a handsome chap. He was very poor and lived inside an enclosure without a roof. So, his house was full of moonlight. However, the king presumed the fox was describing another glistening palace just like his. Now Raja barely had formal schooling and the fox was being sarcastic when he described him as 'highly intellectual', but the king believed his daughter's prospective groom was a highly educated man.

Besides being a jola, Raja was also a farmer and he cultivated paddy on his land. When the fox said Raja 'slays ten at a go', he meant ten sheaves of paddy that Raja grew on his field. Alas, the king thought the fox was talking about the boy's strength and bravery that made him capable of defending against ten men at a time. The rice from Raja's paddy field fed hundreds. Thus, when Sheyal said, 'With his hard work people survive—both high and low,' he meant his occupation as a farmer, but the king thought that the groom took care of and looked after hundreds of poor people.

After listening to Sheyal's narration, the king was very pleased. He handed over a thousand rupees to the fox as a token of his appreciation and said, 'I am very happy to hear about your raja. I don't think I will find a better match for my daughter. Please fetch him. The wedding will be held after eight days.'

Sheyal returned, dancing with a sack full of money and handed it over to Raja. As he entered Raja's room, he saw during the past two months, Raja had woven so many clothes that every person in the village could be given one. So the fox took a garment and two rupees for each villager and invited each of them. 'Our friend will be marrying the Raja's daughter after eight days. Do come to the wedding. All are invited.' Though Raja was considered foolish, the villagers adored him for his honesty. Everyone was pleased with the good news.

Then Sheyal visited all his friends in his community. 'Bhai, listen all of you, my friend will be married in eight days. All of you are invited, and you must sing at the occasion.'

The foxes replied in unison, 'Howa howa, yes, yes! We will indeed.'

Then Sheyal went over to invite the frogs. 'Bhai, hear all of you, my friend will be married in eight days. All of you are invited. Do come and sing at the occasion.'

All the frogs replied together, 'Ghont ghont yes, yes! We will indeed.'

Then the fox invited all the rest: the rufous treepie bird, the crow pheasant, the dove, the cuckoo, the fishing eagle, the brain fever bird, and the peacock. They exclaimed in unison, 'Yes, yes! We will go indeed.'

It took seven days to wind up all of this work. The marriage was to be held on the night of the eighth day. On the day of the wedding, the fox rented a gorgeous attire for raja. He looked like a true king. The guests began to arrive and soon, they left for the king's palace.

When the wedding procession was close to the royal residence, Sheyal called his guests and pointed in the direction of the house, 'Bhai, hear all of you, see the light in the palace. Follow that light and arrive at your own pace. In the meantime, let me inform the king about our arrival.' All the guests replied in unison, 'Okay!'

Finally, Sheyal said, 'Now, before I leave, do start singing, all of you. Let me hear your music.' At this request, five thousand foxes began to howl: '*Howa, howa, howa, howa!*'

Twelve thousand frogs started: '*Ghont, ghont, gheao, gheao!*'

Seven thousand sparrows sang: '*Phoring songey, songey, chharijonong, Chokit kat kat kat gurucharan!*'

Two thousand Rufous treepies sang, '*Ghyancha, ghyancha, ghyancha, ghyancha, ghyancha!*'

Four thousand doves said, '*Roghu, roghu, roghu, roghu, roghu!*'

Three thousand crow pheasants joined, '*Punt, punt, punt, punt, punt, punt!*'

One thousand nine hundred fishing eagles chimed, '*Hyan, aa, hyan aa, hyan aa, O ho, ho, ho, ho!*'

The cuckoo, the peacock, and the brain fever bird added their unique musical bits to the cacophony too.

You had to see it to believe the discordant notes that rose from the chaos. Members of the king's palace were petrified upon hearing the din. When Sheyal arrived to inform the king about the guests, he asked, 'Sheyal Pandit, what is that din outside?'

'That's the sound of our guests and the orchestra.'

This worried the king. He couldn't think of a way to accommodate so many guests or even feed them. He asked the fox, 'What do I do now?'

Sheyal replied immediately, 'Do not fear, Your Majesty. I will go right away and make the guests return. I will only bring over our Raja for the wedding.'

This fox's clever idea gave the Raja immense relief and he rewarded the fox with five thousand rupees! With the money, the fox bought puffed rice, fresh fish, and lots of sweetmeats. He then spread them out in the middle of the field and invited his guests.

'Please do eat.'

A commotion broke out as the birds and animals present in the procession began nibbling, snatching, and gobbling. Finally, the fox distributed the sweetmeats amongst the villagers. They ate to their hearts' content and returned home. Then, the fox brought Raja to the palace. On the way, he cautioned him, 'Be warned. Do not utter a single word. You will never get married if you do.'

The king's family was very happy to see the handsome groom. Only one thing seemed strange to them 'What a good-looking groom! Yet why does he not speak?'

Sheyal chipped in, 'You see, his mother passed away two months ago. He is in mourning and wishes not to speak.'

Everyone expressed sympathy. But in reality, the fox was wary of people discovering how foolish Raja was lest he uttered a word.

During dinner, Raja was served rice on a large golden plate. Smaller bowls of silver containing a variety of vegetables were carefully placed around his plate. Raja had never seen nor tasted any of the dishes. He sniffed every bowl, yet none of the food felt familiar. So he took all the sweets and the curries and mixed everything with his rice. He ate a little of this and that, and whatever he could not, he tied in his shawl.

Such actions amused the onlookers. They asked the fox, 'Why is your Raja behaving this way? Has he never eaten anything?'

Sheyal glowered at them and whispered angrily, 'Raja mixes his food so he can finish it in a gulp. He never takes a second bite. He always ties the remaining in his shawl and distributes the food amongst the poor. Do call a poor man.' And a poor person was summoned, who was handed over Raja's shawl, along with the food tied in it.

Bedtime was even more difficult. It was a four-poster ivory bed, with a mosquito net neatly tucked all around. Poor Raja had never seen a proper bed nor a mosquito net. In an attempt to find the mattress, he first crawled under the bed. Then it was the mosquito net that puzzled him. After much inspection, he remarked, 'I get it now! They have built a room within a room, and the entrance is at the top.'

And so Raja gradually started to climb one of the bedposts. When he reached the top, he jumped right in the middle of the mosquito net. In an instant, everything came crashing down: the bed posts, the mosquito net, and the entire ivory bed. Raja broke into loud sobs:

'I farmed paddy and wove clothes and had a good life,

But, now I have a broken back with a princess wife!'

Fortunately, there was no one around. Only Sheyal was sitting outside the door. The princess, who was shocked to see Raja's actions, cried a lot and severely scolded the fox. But she was an astute woman and never breathed a word about Raja's antics to anyone.

The next day, on the advice of the princess, Sheyal went to the king and said, 'Your Majesty, your son-in-law desires to travel far and wide with your daughter and visit foreign countries. He seeks your permission for the vacation.'

The Raja was more than happy to oblige. He blessed the couple with the required amount of money for the trip as well as attendants, bodyguards, and chaperones. Then, the clever princess took Raja to another country. There, she appointed several erudite scholars to teach and guide Raja. Within a couple of years, Raja had transformed into an intellectual and brave man.

And then one day, messengers arrived with the news of the king's demise. Raja was appointed as his successor.

Ever since then, it has been a happy time for all.

THE HUNCHBACKED OLD LADY

KUNJO BURIR KOTHA

There once lived an old lady with a hunchback. They called her Kunjo Buri. She would move about slowly, bend over her walking stick, and her head would wobble from side to side. *Thawk, thawk* went the stick. Kunjo Buri had two dogs, Ronga and Bhonga. One day, as she was leaving for her granddaughter's house, she called her dogs and said, 'Both of you stay here. Don't go wandering off.'

Ronga and Bhonga agreed and Kunjo Buri set off, holding her walking stick, wobbling her head from side to side. She had travelled a short distance when she met a fox.

'There goes Kunjo Buri,' he thought to himself. 'Buri,' he then said aloud, 'I want to eat you.'

'Wait, let me get nice and fat at my granddaughter's house. You may eat me then. If you eat me now, you will only be feasting upon skin and bones.'

The fox liked the proposition. 'Okay! You may go now. Fatten up. After that, I'll eat you.'

Kunjo Buri started off again, holding her walking stick, and wobbling her head from side to side. She hadn't reached far when she met a tiger, who thought, 'There goes Kunjo Buri,' and he told her, 'Buri, I want to eat you.'

She repeated herself: 'Wait, let me become nice and fat at my granddaughter's house. You may eat me then. If you eat me now, you will only be feasting upon skin and bones.' The tiger too thought it was a good idea to wait for her when she would be plumper. He went away saying, 'Okay! You go. Fatten up. I'll eat you then.'

Once again, Kunjo Buri was off, wobbling her head, and bending over her walking stick. In a while, she met a bear who thought, 'There goes Kunjo Buri,' and he told her, 'Buri, I want to eat you.'

Then came the practised answer: 'Wait, let me get nice and fatten up at my granddaughter's house. You may eat me then. If you eat me now, you will only be feasting upon skin and bones.'

The idea of eating a plump old woman appealed to the bear too. He walked away saying, 'Okay! You go. Fatten up. I'll eat you then.'

After walking for a while, Kunjo Buri finally reached her destination. At her granddaughter's house, she was well-looked after and soon gained weight from a healthy diet of curd and payasam, the rich rice pudding. She felt so stuffed that when she wanted to leave for her home, she told her granddaughter, 'Dear, I must leave, but I can barely walk. I will need to roll down the path. The fox, the tiger, and the bear are waiting for me along the way. The moment they see me, they will pounce on me and eat me up. Do tell me what can I do now?'

'Don't fear, granny,' Kunjo Buri's granddaughter said reassuringly. 'I will place you inside the empty shell of this bottle gourd. Then no fox or tiger or bear can find out. They cannot harm you at all.'

Then she made Kunjo Buri sit inside an empty bottle gourd and gave enough flattened rice and tamarind to snack on the way. Finally, she gave the vegetable a good shove.... *Haaaiiiaaaaaa!* Off rolled the bottle gourd down the road.

As it went rolling, Buri sang inside:

'The bottle gourd rolls along garrr, garrr,
I munch upon flattened rice and tamarind,
I spit out the seeds, tul, tul,
Buri travels far.'

On the road, the bear was still sitting and waiting for the old woman to return. But he could see nobody. He only saw a bottle gourd rolling down the way. He stopped it and inspected the vegetable, but realized it was not worth eating. But he heard a voice from within it singing '*Buri travels far.*' Angry at the thought that Kunjo Buri had already left, he gave the bottle gourd a good shove. *Ghhoontt* and it went rolling down the path like a cart on wheels.

Kunjo Buri continued singing:

'The bottle gourd rolls along garrr, garrr,
I munch upon flattened rice and tamarind,
I spit out the seeds, tul, tul,
Buri travels far.'

At a distance, the tiger sat waiting. He too could not understand where the Buri was hidden and thought the gourd to be inedible. Suddenly he heard a voice from within singing '*Buri travels far.*' The tiger thought Kunjo Buri had already gone by. Furious, he too gave the vegetable one great shove. *Ghhoonnttt* and off it started rolling down the road.

Buri continued singing:

'The bottle gourd rolls along garrr, garrr,
I munch upon flattened rice and tamarind,
I spit out the seeds, tul, tul,
Buri travels far.'

The fox sat waiting near Kunjo Buri's house. But unlike the others, he was not fooled. He thought to himself, 'How can a bottle gourd sing? Let me inspect what's inside.'

With a strong kick, the fox cracked open the shell of the bottle gourd, and Kunjo Buri came tumbling out.

'Buri, I will eat you now,' the fox proclaimed.

'Of course, you will eat me. That's why I returned. But how about having a little music before that?'

'Yes, that's a good idea,' the fox agreed, 'I too will pitch in with my renditions.'

'Good then. Let's climb over that mound, and we'll have our musical soiree.'

Then clever Kunjo Buri climbed on top of a mound and sang out, *'Come, come Ronga and Bhonga, tuuuuu!'*

Immediately, her dogs came running. They pounced upon the fox. One caught hold of his neck, and the other one bit his waist. They broke every bone in the fox's body and taught the scheming animal a deserving lesson.

THE OLD LADY WHO HAD LICE

UKUNEY BURIR KOTHA

Once there was an old lady, who had a head full of lice. Thus, she came to be referred to as Ukuney Buri. The lice infestation was so great, that often they would fall into her husband, Buro's plate as she served him his food. Perennially irritated because of the falling lice, Buro beat her with a stick one day. In anger, Buri smashed the pot in which she was preparing their meal and left the house in a huff. She walked all the way to the riverbank and sat there, sulking in silence. Soon, Buro arrived and tried his best to coax Ukuney Buri out of her anger. Alas, nothing helped. She refused to return home and kept sitting in silence.

There was a crane, Bok, near the banks of the river. He asked Buri, 'So, where are you off to?'

Ukuney Buri replied:

'Furious about my husband's thrashings,

I have left my house and everything.'

'Why did your husband beat you? What happened?' the Bok asked in amazement.

'Some lice from my head had fallen into his plate.'

'But a meal of ukun is quite tasty. Why beat your wife for that? Buri, come with me. I have heard that you are a very good cook.'

So off went Ukuney Buri with Bok and began living in the latter's home as a cook. The bird would love the food that she prepared, and just in case he found a few ukun on his plate, it would make him even happier.

One day, Bok caught a large snakehead murrel fish. He instructed Ukuney Buri to cook it well and then left for the river. In the meantime, the poor woman while cooking in the clay oven, caught fire, and met with an unfortunate end. When Bok found out, he was shocked beyond belief. His grief knew no bounds, and he sat sulking for seven days straight on the banks. He didn't touch a morsel of food.

The river, Nodi, noticed the upset crane sitting by the bank. Finally, he asked, 'Well, I can see that you have been here for seven days and have eaten nothing. What is the matter, Bhai Bok?'

'Bhai, what can I say? I've lost everything.'

Nodi insisted, 'Bhai, you must tell me.'

'If I do, your water will froth up.'

Nodi was persistent. Finally, the Bok relented:

'Because Ukuney Buri passed away,

Bok sat fasting in grief for seven days.

And immediately, Nodi foamed up.

In the meantime, Hathi, an elephant, who came to the river

every day for a drink, was rather amused to see the foaming white water and asked the reason.

'I am warning you,' Nodi said, 'if I tell you more, your tail will detach itself and fall off.'

'That's okay,' Hathi replied, 'but you must tell me.'

Nodi thus began:

'Because Ukuney Buri passed away,

Bok sat fasting in grief for seven days.

And the water of the river turned to froth today.'

And right at that moment, Hathi's tail snapped off and fell on the ground with a loud *dhawpaashh*!

As poor Hathi passed under a tree, Gachh, asked, 'What is this? What has happened to you? Where is your tail?'

Hathi replied, 'If you hear the reason, I warn you, all your leaves will fall off.'

'That's okay,' Gachh insisted, 'but you tell me nevertheless.'

'Because Ukuney Buri passed away,

Bok sat fasting in grief for seven days.

And the water of the river turned to froth today.

And Hathi lost its tail in dismay.'

And immediately, Gachh's leaves began to shed.

In that unfortunate tree, a dove, Ghughu used to live. When the leaves fell off, he had gone in search of food. He returned to see the sorry condition of his home and asked the tree, Gachh, 'What is this? What happened?'

'I am warning you,' Gachh said, 'if I tell you more, you will go blind.'

'That is okay,' Ghughu insisted, 'but do tell me.'

'Because Ukuney Buri passed away,

Bok sat fasting in grief for seven days.

And the water of the river turned to froth today.

And Hathi lost its tail in dismay.

And Gachh lost all its leaves and everything was in disarray.'

And immediately, poor Ghughu went blind in one eye. He went hopping into the field where he met a cowherd, Rakhal, who asked in amazement, 'Arey Ghughu, what has happened to your eye?'

'Well, I must warn you. If I tell you that, your stick will get stuck to your hand.'

'That's okay. You tell me nevertheless,' Rakhal said.

'Because Ukuney Buri passed away,

Bok sat fasting in grief for seven days.

And the water of the river turned to froth today.

And Hathi lost its tail in dismay.

And Gachh lost all its leaves and everything was in disarray.

And Ghughu went blind in one eye, I say.'

Right away, Rakhal found his stick stuck to his hand. He shook his hand furiously, but it remained stuck. In the evening, when he returned home with his cows, he was still shaking his hand. A servant, a dashi, from the palace, carrying a winnowing basket full of ashes from the kitchen oven, suddenly met Rakhal. Observing his strange actions, she asked, 'You fool. Why do you shake your hand this way?'

'Well, if I tell you that, I warn you, you cannot keep away the winnowing basket that you hold. It will get stuck to your hands.'

'Isshh, that is okay,' the woman said, 'but you must tell me.'

'Because Ukuney Buri passed away,

Bok sat fasting in grief for seven days.

And the water of the river turned to froth today.

And Hathi lost its tail in dismay.

And Gachh lost all its leaves and everything was in disarray

And Ghughu went blind in one eye, I say.

And stuck to Rakhal's hand his stick stays.'

As soon as Rakhal finished, the dashi began to howl, 'Goodness, now what will I do? What will happen to me?' You see, the winnowing basket was stuck to her hands. However much she tried, it refused to come off. Finally, she started off for the king's palace, cursing Rakhal all the way.

When the servant reached the royal kitchen, the queen was serving rice for the king on a large plate. She smiled upon seeing the woman, tightly clutching the basket.

'What is the matter, girl? Why don't you keep that away?'

'Well, if I answer that,' the servant cried, 'I warn you, my rani, the large plate will get stuck to your hand. You will not be able to put it down.'

'Well, is that so?' the queen asked. 'I'll see to that. You tell me.'

Thus the servant began:

'Because Ukuney Buri passed away,

Bok sat fasting in grief for seven days.

And the water of the river turned to froth today.

And Hathi lost its tail in dismay.

And Gachh lost all its leaves and everything was in disarray

And Ghughu went blind in one eye, I say.

And stuck to Rakhal's hand his stick stays.

And stuck to the hands of the dashi, her basket lay.'

Immediately, the queen saw the large plate that she was holding was now stuck to her hand. What to do now?

Poor rani. She served the rice on another platter and carried it in her other hand to the raja who sat waiting for his lunch. The raja was amused to see his wife carry two plates and asked, 'O Rani, why are you carrying a second plate?'

'If I answer that O Raja,' she answered, 'you will not be able to get up. You will be stuck to your wooden seat.'

Upon hearing the queen's rationale, the king laughed loudly. 'Well, that is okay, but you tell me nevertheless.'

So Rani narrated:

'Because Ukuney Buri passed away,

    Bok sat fasting in grief for seven days.
    And the water of the river turned to froth today.
    And Hathi lost its tail in dismay.
    And Gachh lost all its leaves and everything was in disarray
    And Ghughu went blind in one eye, I say.
    And stuck to Rakhal's hand his stick stays.
    And stuck to the hands of the dashi, her basket lay.
    And stuck to the rani's hand, the platter stays.'

Even before the queen finished her lament, the raja realized he was stuck to the wooden stool he was sitting on. People arrived and surrounded the king, pulling with all their might, but none could help. Finally, it was time for him to attend his court.

What to do?

The palace staff lifted the raja and carried him, along with his wooden seat, to the royal court.

Those who had come to meet the king found themselves in a sticky situation—they were thoroughly amused, but no one could laugh. Nor did anyone dare to ask the king why he was stuck to his seat.

Finally, the Raja spoke up, 'I am sure all of you must be

wondering about why I am sitting here on a wooden stool?'

'Yes, Your Majesty,' everyone answered in unison.

'Well, if I tell you what happened, all of you present here will be stuck to your respective seats.'

'Well, if our raja is stuck, we do not bother about ourselves,' the subjects replied.

So the raja began:

'Because Ukuney Buri passed away,

Bok sat fasting in grief for seven days.

And the water of the river turned to froth today.

And Hathi lost its tail in dismay.

And Gachh lost all its leaves and everything was in disarray

And Ghughu went blind in one eye, I say.

And stuck to Rakhal's hand his stick stays.

And stuck to the hands of the dashi, her basket lay.

And stuck to Rani's hand, the platter stays.

And stuck to his wooden seat, the raja stays.'

And immediately, everybody in court found themselves stuck to their respective places too.

What to do now?

Now in that kingdom lived a very clever barber. He arrived immediately and ordered, 'Someone go immediately and call the carpenter.'

Then the carpenter arrived and sawed off the seat from the raja's back. He then proceeded to release everyone from their respective seats and also removed the remaining pieces of wood from everyone's backs.

Then the carpenter released the plate from the Rani's hand, the winnowing basket from the servant's hands, and the stick from Rakhal's hand. Everyone was relieved.

THE OLD LADY WHO ATE FERMENTED RICE

PANTABURIR KAWTHA

There was once an old lady, Buri, who loved to eat fermented rice, panta bhat. Unfortunately, a thief began to frequent her house to finish off her panta bhat every night. The poor woman was at a loss. She decided to set off to meet the raja, in the hopes that he would listen and lodge her complaint.

As she continued her slow and steady walk along the riverbank, bent over her walking stick, a catfish remarked upon seeing her, 'Where are you off to?'

'A thief has been breaking into my house every night and stealing my panta bhat. So, I am off to register a complaint with the Raja.'

'Do take me along with you on your way back. It'll be good for you,' the catfish said.

'Alright,' Buri said and continued on her walk.

Just as she passed under a wood apple tree, a wood apple, which was lying on the ground asked her, 'Where are you off to?'

'A thief has been breaking into my house every night and stealing my panta bhat. So, I am off to register a complaint with the raja,' the old woman explained her situation again.

'Do take me along with you on your way back. It'll be good for you,' the wood apple replied.

Buri agreed and went on. Soon she passed a pile of dung who asked her where she was off to.

'A thief has been breaking into my house every night and stealing my panta bhat. So, I am off to register a complaint with the raja,' Buri repeated yet again.

Upon hearing her predicament, the pile of dung said, 'Do take me along with you on your way back. It'll be good for you.'

Once again, the old woman said yes and continued on her journey. As she neared the raja's palace, she found a razor in the open field. On being asked where she was off to, Buri repeated herself once more, 'A thief has been breaking into my house every night and stealing my panta bhat. So, I am off to register a complaint with the raja.'

'Do take me along with you on your way back. It'll be good for you,' the razor said. Like the previous three times, the old woman assented.

When Buri finally reached the palace, she was informed that the raja was not at home. Disappointed, she had to return without lodging her complaint. On her way back, she remembered her friends from the field. She collected the razor, the pile of cow dung, the wood apple fruit, and the catfish, and carefully placed them in her bag.

As the old woman was crossing her courtyard, the razor

instructed her to keep him on the grass. Buri left him there.

At the entrance of her home was a low wooden stool. The pile of cow dung wanted to be left there. Buri did as she was told.

When she stepped inside her kitchen, the wood apple asked to be left inside her clay oven. Buri left it there.

Finally, the catfish said, 'Keep me inside your pot of panta bhat,' and so she left the fish inside the utensil.

Night fell. Buri finished her dinner and chores and then went to bed. Late into the night, the thief arrived silently, unaware of the old woman's secret weapons that had been carefully placed around the house. Thus, he entered the kitchen and following his regular routine, dipped his hands into the pot of rice. Immediately, the catfish stung his hands. The thief shouted and cried in pain, holding his bleeding hands. He moved towards the oven to comfort himself with its heat. Inside, the wood apple lay patiently. As soon as the thief approached the oven, the wood apple burst open. It exploded with such force that bits of the hard shell hit the thief's face and eyes.

Howling in pain and discomfort, the thief ran out of the house where he accidentally slipped on the cow dung and landed on the hard wood, right in the midst of the pile. Now sobbing loudly, the thief decided to go and wipe his soiled feet on the grass outside. Right when he began wiping the dung, the razor sliced through his skin.

'Oh ma! Save me!' screamed the thief in pain.

The thief's loud shrieks awoke the neighbours. They came running and immediately identified him as the man who had been stealing the old lady's food.

'Catch hold of him. Beat him up. Tear off his ears!' they exclaimed. Thus, the thief was severely punished.

THE SPARROW AND THE CROW

CHAWRAI AAR KAAKER KOTHA

The crow, Kaak, and the sparrow, Chawrai, were great friends. One day when the householder had spread out chillies and paddy on a large mat for them to dry under the sun, the Chawrai told Kaak, 'Friend, do you think you can finish eating those chillies faster than I can eat the paddy kernels?'

'I will finish those chillies faster than you,' Kaak said confidently.

'No! I will finish the paddy long before you,' Chawrai contested.

'What happens if you can't?'

'If I can't, you may feast upon me. And if you fail, what will happen?' asked Chawrai.

'Then you may feast upon me,' the shrewd crow promptly replied.

So it was decided. Chawrai began to nibble on the paddy kernels, one at a time, while Kaak gobbled one chilly after another. By the time the crow was finished, the sparrow was nowhere close to being done.

'My dear friend, now what happens?' Kaak asked.

'What else is there to say!' Chawrai said sadly. 'Despite our friendship, if you truly want to feast upon me, so be it. But first, you must go and clean your beak as you often eat garbage.'

'I will immediately go and wash my beak,' and Kaak left for the Ganga.

The moment Ganga saw the crow, she refused to let him near.

'You eat plenty of garbage throughout the day. Don't dip your beak in my pristine water. Find another way to fetch water and then you can wash your beak in that.'

'Fine,' the crow said 'I will fetch a clay pitcher,' and he left for the house of the potter. Upon reaching Kaak said:

'Potter, potter, please give me a pitcher
I will draw up some water to wash my beak
Then I will feast upon Chawrai.'

'I don't have any,' came the potter's reply. 'Get me some clay first, and I will make one for you.'

Thus Kaak left to meet the buffalo to ask for his horns to request him to dig some clay for him.

'Buffalo buffalo, lend me your horn,
Will dig up soil, make a pitcher,
Will fill it with water and wash my beak.
Then I will feast upon Chawrai.'

The crow's request angered the buffalo. He came charging at the bird, who barely managed to escape. He immediately flew over to his friend Kukur and said,

'Dog, dog beat the buffalo,
Will take his horn,
Will dig up soil, make a pitcher,

Will fill it with water and wash my beak.

Then I will feast upon Chawrai.'

'First, you must bring me milk,' the dog proclaimed. 'Let me drink it and gain strength, and only then can I deal with the buffalo.'

So Kaak flew over to the cow:

'Cow, cow, give me some milk,

Dog will drink, will gain strength,

Will beat the buffalo,

Will take his horn,

Will dig up soil, make a pitcher,

Will fill it with water and wash my beak.

Then I will feast upon Chawrai.'

However, cow said, 'Before anything, get me some grass. Only then can I give you some milk.'

So the crow went over to the open green field and said:

'Green field, green field give me some grass,

cow will eat and give me some milk,

dog will drink, will gain strength,

Will beat the buffalo,

Will take his horn,

Will dig up soil, make a pitcher,

Will fill it with water and wash my beak.

Then I will feast upon Chawrai.'

The open green field replied, 'There's plenty of grass here. Do take if you wish to.'

Upon receiving the field's assent, Kaak went over to the blacksmith's house.

'Blacksmith blacksmith, give me your sickle,

will cut grass, cow will eat and give me some milk,

dog will drink, will gain strength,

will beat up buffalo, will take his horn,

will dig up some clay to make a pitcher,

will fill it with water and wash my beak.

Then I will feast upon Chawrai.'

'For this, I need fire,' the blacksmith answered. 'I don't have any right now. Find me some fire first.'

Then the crow went to the owner of a household and said:

'Bhai Householder, give me a little fire,

will make sickle, will cut grass,

cow will eat and give me some milk,

dog will drink, will gain strength,

will beat up buffalo, will take his horn,

will dig up some clay, to make a pitcher,

will fill it with water and wash my beaks.

Then I will feast upon Chawrai.'

Upon hearing Kaak's request, the householder stepped out with a large pot of fire. 'Here it is. But how will you carry it?'

Alas, the foolish bird couldn't think of a better idea. He spread out his wings and said, 'Here, pour it over here.'

The householder emptied the pot of fire on Kaak's wings. In a split second, the scheming bird had perished. Now Chawrai was safe. No one would feast upon him.

THE SPARROW AND THE TIGER

CHAWRAI AAR BAGHER KOTHA

At one corner of the householder's kitchen, there hung a clay pitcher in which lived a sparrow couple, Chawrai and Chawrni.

One day, Chawrai said, 'My dear, I want to eat stuffed, sweet pancakes, pithey.'

Chawrni agreed and said, 'You must fetch all the ingredients, and I will cook pithey for you.'

'What all do you need?'

Chawrni stated her list: 'I will need flour, jaggery, bananas, milk, and wood for the fire.'

'Noted. I will fetch all of them,' and Chawrai immediately flew off to the forest and began to break the twigs off the branches.

Now in that forest lived a large and mischievous tiger, Bagh, who called Chawrai his 'friend'.

Upon hearing the snapping of the twigs, Bagh arrived enquiring, 'I could hear the sound of twigs breaking. Is that you, my friend?'

'Yes, it is me.'

'What will you do with the twigs?'

'I need the wood as Chawrni will make pithey.'

'Friend, I have never eaten pithey,' Bagh requested immediately 'You must give me a few.'

'Then you must get me all the ingredients first,' Chawrai answered.

'What all will you need?'

Out came the list: 'I will need flour, jaggery, bananas, milk, and wood for the fire.'

'Okay!' Bagh exclaimed. 'You go back home. I will get it all for you.'

Then Chawrai returned home and Bagh swaggered over to the bazaar. Upon reaching the bazaar, all he had to do was growl. 'Haluum,' and immediately, the shopkeepers ran hither and tither in fright.

'Oh dear! There's a tiger. Run, run.'

They fled, leaving their shops and wares in the open. Bagh searched all over and collected the things that Chawrni needed to make pithey with. Thus, he gathered flour, jaggery, bananas, milk, ghee, a clay pitcher, and wood for the fire. He then took them to the sparrows' house.

Chawrni made some wonderful pitheys and both Chawrai and Chawrni had a feast. Finally, at the end of their meal, they placed a few of them on a leaf for Bagh. Then they went inside their home in the clay pitcher.

When Bagh arrived, he saw the pitheys on the floor and immediately sat down to eat.

He ate the first one and remarked, 'Wow! How delicious!'

He ate the next one and said, 'Nah! This one is not so good. It seems like this one has only been made with flour.'

He ate the third one and said in disgust, 'Chhee! This one only has ashes, bran, and chaff. Friend Chawrai, what did you try to feed me?'

He ate the next one, screwed up his face, and remarked repulsively, 'Uh hu! What a horrible stench. What have they mixed in this? Is it cow dung? Chawrai, you are such a trickster.'

Right at that moment, hiding inside their pitcher, Chawrai told Chawrni rather desperately, 'Chawrni, I want to sneeze.'

'Chup, chup!' Chawrni hushed. 'Don't sneeze now. We'll be in trouble.'

Chawrai tried his best to remain silent. He did manage to hold back his sneeze, but couldn't do so for more than a few seconds. He scrunched up his face, prepared to let out a loud sneeze.

In the meantime, sitting below the pitcher, Bagh was furious after finishing another revolting pithey.

'Tthuu tthuu, this one is only dung and nothing else,' he thundered. 'If ever I get my hands on Chawrai, I will crush him and gobble him up.' And just as Bagh was about to spit out a rotten piece of pithey, came Chawrai's loud sneeze: 'Hyaan choo!'

Petrified at the sudden noise, Bagh jumped up in fright. The pitcher broke from the rope from which it was hung from the roof and came crashing down on Bagh's head, along with Chawrai and Chawrni inside of it.

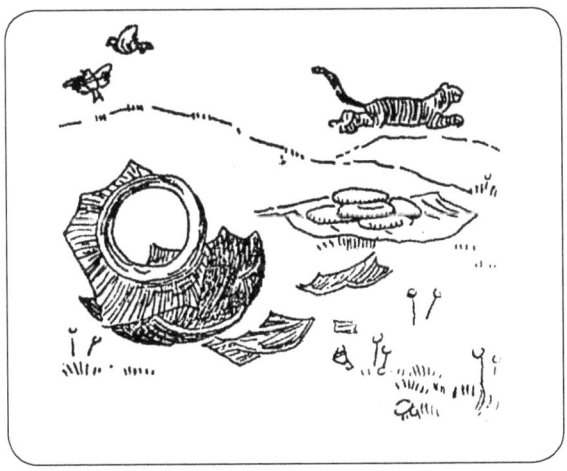

Poor Bagh. He couldn't fathom what had just happened, whether it was the sky or thunder that had come crashing down on his head. Scared out of his wits, he rolled his tail between his legs and started off at full speed, stopping only when he finally reached his home.

THE NAUGHTY TIGER

DUSHTU BAGH

Next to the large central gate of the king's place, stood a big iron cage with a massive tiger inside. And every time someone would pass by, Bagh would implore with folded palms, 'Sir, please do open the gates of my cage just once,' to which everyone had the same reply: 'Yes, indeed. We would open the gates and then you would pounce on us.'

Now one day, there was a feast organized at the palace. Many erudite scholars and priests were invited, and amongst the guests, was a particularly honest Brahmin Pandit, a Thakur Moshai, who was also very meek and humble. The cunning Bagh understood this and immediately folded his palms to feign respect. Thakur Moshai was easily fooled and said, 'Such a well-mannered Bagh. What do you want, dear?'

'Sir, please open the gate of my cage, and let me out just once. I beg of you.'

Feeling sorry for the animal, Thakur Moshai let the tiger out. The minute Bagh came out, he said with a wicked smile, 'Thakur Moshai, now I will eat you.'

If this was someone else, he would have run away in fear, but Thakur Moshai was not one of them. Wanting to reason with Bagh, he said, 'I have never heard or seen something like this. I did help you, and now you're saying that you will eat me. Is this the right thing to do?'

'Of course, Thakur Moshai. People behave in such a manner all the time.'

Thakur Moshai wanted to reason even further: 'No, it is not so. Let us go and speak to three people who can act as our jury. Let's first listen to their respective verdicts. Let us see what they have to say about your behaviour.'

Bagh agreed, 'Okay! Let us go and speak to the jury. If what you say is true, I will leave you in peace. But if they say I am right, I will then feast upon you.'

The duo arrived in the agricultural fields in search of a member of the jury. Separating two tracts of land was a thin, elevated dyke. Farmers make these elevated paths to separate agricultural fields. Thakur Moshai pointed to the dyke and remarked, 'This is my first juror.'

'Okay, do ask him. Let's listen to his opinion.'

'Dyke, please tell me, if I do good for someone, should the person be bad to me?' Thakur Moshai asked.

The dyke immediately replied: 'Of course Thakur Moshai. Just look at me. I lie between two farmlands and benefit both farmers. One cannot steal from the other's land. I even prevent the water from one farmland from flowing into another. I help them in so many ways, yet these scoundrels keep chopping me off from time to time to increase their share of farmlands.'

Bagh chuckled. 'Do you hear that Thakur Moshai? If you are good to someone, do you get bad in return?'

Thakur Moshai was desperate 'Wait! I have two more members of the jury.'

Bagh said, 'Fine! Let's go.'

Standing in the middle was a tall banyan tree. Thakur Moshai declared it as his second juror.

'Ask him,' Bagh said, 'let's hear his verdict.'

Thakur Moshai questioned: 'Brother, you are an elderly person, and you have a lot of experience. Do tell me, if you help someone, do you get evil in return?'

'In reality, that's what people do,' the aged banyan lamented. 'See these people, sitting under my shade to cool themselves? They poke and jab me mercilessly to make me drip sap. Moreover, to collect that sap, they even break my leaves and make bowls out of them. And see, how they are walking away with my broken branches,' pointed the banyan sadly.

'So Thakur Moshai!' the Bagh exclaimed, 'what did he say?'

Now Thakur Moshai was in a fix. He could not figure out what else to say. Right at that moment, Sheyal, a cunning fox, was passing by. Upon seeing the fox, the Thakur Moshai cried out: 'That's my final juror. Let's see what he says. O Sheyal Pandit, do wait. You are my juror.'

Sheyal did stop but refused to come closer. From a distance, he said, 'Goodness! How did this happen? How on earth did I become your juror?'

'Tell me, do you hurt the person who does good for you?'

'If you can tell me who did good for whom and who did bad for whom, only then can I provide an answer,' Sheyal said.

'Bagh was in the cage and I was passing by...' and just as

Thakur Moshai began to tell how he let Bagh out, Sheyal stopped him midway, 'This is very difficult to understand. I need to see that cage and the road. I cannot understand the situation unless I see these things.'

So, everyone returned to the palace's central gate. Sheyal walked around the cage, carefully inspecting it. 'Okay, I understand the cage and the road. Now tell me what happened.'

Once again, Thakur Moshai began narrating the sequence of events: 'Bagh was inside the cage and myself, a pandit was passing by—'

Immediately, Sheyal cut him short. 'Wait, do not hurry while you are explaining. So you are saying that Bagh was the pandit and the road was passing by inside the cage?'

Bagh burst out laughing. 'Dhur, you idiot. I, Bagh, was inside the cage, and Thakur Moshai, a pandit, was walking by.

'Wait! The pandit was inside the cage and Bagh was passing by?' Sheyal interjected again. Bagh once again said, 'You fool! That's not it. Bagh was inside the cage, and the pandit was walking by.'

'This sounds very confusing to me. Are you saying that Bagh was inside the pandit, and the cage was walking by on the road?'

Now frustrated, Bagh snapped, 'I have never met such a silly Sheyal. Bagh was inside the cage, and the pandit was walking by.'

Sheyal scratched his head in deep thought, and finally concluded, 'No! It is too difficult to understand.'

By now, Bagh was livid. 'No!' he thundered at Sheyal. 'You have to understand this. See how simple it is. I was inside the cage, just like this...' and in an attempt to explain himself, Bagh stepped back into the cage. In an instant, Sheyal tightly bolted the door.

Then Sheyal turned to Thakur Moshai and said, 'After understanding what happened, this is my final verdict. Never help a dishonest person. Now, you go off to your feast. It is not too late.'

So Sheyal went back to the forest, and Thakur Moshai headed to the king's grand feast.

THE TIGER GROOM

BAGH BOR

There was once a poor Brahmin pandit who lived with his wife, Brahmni, and their little daughter. Brahmin gathered alms by begging, but what he collected was hardly enough to arrange for one meal a day. Some days, the unfortunate family went without food.

One day, Brahmin's daughter went to the neighbour's house. There she saw the children enjoying a dish of sweet rice pudding, payesh. She too felt like having some. She returned home and asked her mother 'Ma, do prepare some payesh for me. I so do want to have some.' Now, hearing this, Brahmni began to sob. How could she make rice pudding for her daughter when the family could hardly afford rice?'

At this point, Brahmin returned from a round of begging. Seeing his wife crying, he asked her why she was so upset.

'Our daughter wants to have payesh. Now, where will I get that? What else can I do but cry?'

'Let me see what can I do about it,' Brahmin consoled his wife. 'But please do not cry,' and he left for the zamindar's house.

The zamindar of that village was a kind person. The minute he heard Brahmin's little daughter desired to taste payesh, he immediately called for the choicest of Gopalbhog rice, two seer milk, sugar, and spices. He gave the ingredients to Brahmin.

Brahmin blessed the zamindar and ran home to his wife, 'Brahmni, I have all the ingredients. Now you can make payesh.'

Good-natured Brahmni was an equally good cook. The entire neighbourhood was redolent with the sweet smell of Brahmni's cooking.

Now a sly crow, Kaak, was sitting nearby and smelled

Brahmni's cooking. 'What a wonderful smell,' Kaak thought to himself. 'I have to sample this,' and so saying, he perched himself on the thatched roof of Brahmin's hut.

Kaak had been sitting still for a while when he heard a sound from the kitchen. 'Brahmni must have finished cooking,' he thought.

Then came another sound. 'Now she's serving,' thought Kaak.

After a short while, there was another sound. Kaak kept thinking, 'They must be eating.'

And true indeed, Brahmin and his daughter had just sat down to eat. The payesh was so delicious that both father and daughter finished everything. and there was hardly anything left for Brahmni. Finally, when she had finished eating, there was not a drop of payesh left on their plates or on the sides of the pot in which she had cooked.

All this while, Kaak was sitting and waiting. So when he realized he wasn't getting a morsel, he became furious. 'The family has cheated me. I will have my revenge,' he proclaimed.

Very close to the Brahmin's hut was a dense forest, home to a huge tiger, Bagh.

Kaak cooked up a crooked plan and went over to Bagh and told him, 'Bagh Moshai, our Brahmin has a beautiful daughter. You are such a suitable groom. It would be wonderful if you married her.'

Bagh replied, 'But who will facilitate the alliance? If I go with a marriage proposal, they will all run away in fear.'

'You need not worry,' Kaak reassured him. 'I will organize everything. First, you should arrange for some food to be sent to Brahmin's house.'

'Alright, I will hunt down some village dogs and send those.'

Listening to Bagh's plan, Kaak was horrified. 'Oh no! Don't do that. They will never eat meat. Instead, you get me some fresh fruit from your lemon tree. I will take them for you.'

So Kaak took a bunch of lemons to Brahmin's house. Upon his return, he informed the tiger, 'Bagh Moshai, they are very happy with the fruit. If you continue sending these for a few more days, they are sure to accept your proposal.'

Kaak's news made Bagh blush all over. He rolled over the floor in happiness.

So as decided, Kaak continued taking lemons from Bagh's house and every day, he would return and reassure the tiger: 'Yes, Brahmin and Brahmni will have their daughter married to you.'

Of course, this was a lie, but Bagh believed it to be a real promise.

Finally, the day came when Bagh questioned Kaak, 'What happened? I am yet to marry the Brahmin's daughter, and my lemon tree is nearly bare.'

'Don't worry,' Kaak lied. 'They will get her married to you any day you say.'

'Then go and tell them that the wedding must happen tomorrow night. If they do not agree, I will devour everyone.'

This is exactly what Kaak was waiting for. He rushed over to Brahmin's house and declared loudly, 'Listen you all! Bagh will come tomorrow night to marry your daughter. If you do not agree, he will eat all of you.'

This scared the wits out of Brahmin and Brahmni. They beat their chests and howled at the top of their voices. Their loud shrieks brought over curious neighbours. Everyone wanted to know why they were so frightened.

A sobbing Brahmin explained: 'Bagh will come tomorrow to marry our daughter. If we do not agree, he will kill us all.'

The villagers were furious. 'Is it so? We too will see how he manages to marry your daughter. What else did he say? That if we do not agree to his demands, he will feast upon us? Then let him come. You need not worry, Brahmin and Brahmni. We will take care of it all.'

Then the villagers sent a collective message to Bagh: 'Dear Bagh Moshai, you are a most suitable groom. Please come dressed in full regalia, listen to our music, have a grand feast, and finally get married in a nice ceremony before you return home.'

Then began the villagers' preparations. They brought three hundred clay ovens in the Brahmin's courtyard and three hundred pitchers of oil were set up for boiling. Then they spread a nice bed over a well, and finally, fetched many different musical instruments and started creating a din.

Bagh heard the noise from a distance. 'This must be the noise from my wedding ceremony.' So he got dressed in his finest clothing, put a turban on his head, and danced all the way to Brahmin's house.

The minute the villagers saw Bagh approaching, they started to shout: 'Oh! The groom has arrived. Do play the music louder,' and they took him to the bed that had been carefully set atop the well. The minute Bagh pounced on it, he fell headlong into the well with a loud growl. Immediately, the villagers emptied the three hundred pitchers of boiling oil into the well, followed by the fire from the three hundred ovens. And so Bagh perished.

Sitting on a branch, Kaak had been a spectator of the chaos. He was stoned so brutally by the children that the poor chap too breathed his last.

THE BEAST ATOP THE TIGER

BAGHER UPOR TAAG

There once was a Jola, a weaver, who had a darling but spoilt little boy. Always used to getting whatever he desired, the little chap had grown to be very stubborn.

One day, a son of a wealthy man was passing by, riding his horse. The little boy saw this. He went home and demanded from his father, 'Why don't I own a horse? I want a horse. Get me one.'

'It is not so easy,' Jola said. 'I am a poor man. From where will I manage to get a horse for you?' he kept explaining.

But his son was adamant. 'No! I want a horse. You must get me one anyhow!'

So began the boy's tantrums. He stomped and jumped all over the house and cried a little, then he rolled on the floor and howled a little more, and then broke his father's hookah. Finally, when he realized his father was unperturbed by his theatrics, he stopped eating.

Now Jola was in a fix. Watching his son refuse his food, he thought, 'Now what? I have got to get a horse. Let me see how much money I have.'

He searched the nooks and crannies of the house and gathered all the money he had. He put all of these into a bag and went off to see if he could buy a horse at the market.

At the market, Jola asked the merchant who sold horses, 'How much is one horse for?'

'Fifty rupees,' came his answer.

All Jola had was five rupees. Where would he get fifty rupees from?

So having failed to purchase a horse, Jola started off for his home with a sullen face.

On the way, he saw two men fighting. Jola heard one say to the other: 'You will face a lot of trouble!'

'Ghorar dim...nothing will happen,' replied the other in anger.

Now 'ghorar dim', meaning a horse's eggs, is simply a figure of speech; everyone knows that horses do not lay eggs. If someone remarks so, it means they are referring to something absolutely absurd, something that has no chance of happening. But Jola did not know this. With the mere mention of a horse's egg, he got excited and asked the two men, 'Brother, where do I find a ghorar dim?'

One of the two men was a wicked and sly one. He understood Jola's simple mind and decided to entrap him. 'You come with me,' he said. 'The ghorar dim is at my house. I will give it to you.'

In his house was a muskmelon. He handed the fruit over to Jola and said, 'See this is a ghorar dim. See how it is slightly cracked on one side? The baby will spring out any moment. Be careful. Or else, it will run away!'

Jola was ecstatic. 'How much is this for?' he asked.

'Five rupees,' the sly man answered, and Jola immediately gave him all the money he had.

On his way home, Jola peered through the crack on the muskmelon's hard skin. The inside was deep red. He thought that it was almost time for the baby horse to come out. He said to himself, 'If the foal tries to run away, I will grab hold of him, wrap him in my shawl, and then take him home. I will hold onto him so tightly that even if he struggles on the way, he cannot escape.'

Immersed in his thoughts, Jola reached the banks of a river. He was very thirsty. Keeping the fruit on the bank, he went for a drink of water. In the meantime, a fox came wandering. Finding the ripe muskmelon, the fox began to munch on the delicious fruit. When Jola returned, the fox was nearly done. Afraid of the weaver's reaction, he fled in fear. Upon seeing the broken and half-eaten fruit, Jola thought the egg had cracked open and the foal had fled. He mistook the fox to be the horse's baby. 'Oh my goodness,' he cried. 'My baby horse is running away.' He began chasing the fox, but the latter started to run even faster. Jola barely could keep up as the fox ran through fields and forests.

Soon Jola realized that he had lost his way. By then, night had fallen. Jola spotted a small hut nearby. Inside, lived an old woman and her granddaughter. Their hut had only two rooms. They lived in one, and the other was a storeroom. They offered Jola the space in the storeroom to spend the night. Now every night, a tiger, Bagh, would hide behind the old woman's hut, awaiting to prey upon either the old woman or her little granddaughter. The old woman knew this and always forbade her granddaughter from stepping out in the dark. Now, the granddaughter had heard a little about the ghorar dim and was eager to listen to the whole of it. Later that night, when the little girl excitedly asked her grandmother about going to Jola to listen to the story, the old lady stopped her immediately because she knew about Bagh outside, 'No, no don't go! Some bagh-taag will catch hold of you.'

Now, bagh-taag is just a manner of speech. In reality, there is no animal called a taag, but Bagh did not know this. He went deep into thought, assuming taag was another animal, much mightier than him. Maybe a demon or a ghost! Fear gripped the poor tiger. How would he escape the taag? Where would he hide? Bagh spent the night in deep anxiety.

At dawn, Jola stepped out of the hut to see if it was time for sun rise. In the fading darkness of the night, he spotted Bagh and said, 'Oh, there sits my baby horse.' Jola ran with his shawl and wrapped up Bagh's face, neck, and eyes. Then he swiftly climbed on his back.

Poor Bagh was terrified beyond words. He thought 'Oh my goodness. This must be taag. He has caught hold of me!' Thus, Bagh started to run for his life but since his eyes were covered with Jola's shawl, he could barely see. On the other hand, Jola sat tightly, holding onto his shawl, thinking all the while that he would return home when the sun would rise and he could see clearly. Finally, when his surroundings got lighter, Jola was petrified to see that he was riding a tiger and holding his face within his shawl. He was prepared to meet his end. Bagh, on the other hand, continued to run with great fear, mumbling, 'Forgive me Taag Dada. Please get off my back. I will worship you.' But all Jola could think about was a plan to escape safely.

As Bagh kept running, he passed under a banyan tree. Its low-hanging branches were within easy reach, and one could easily touch them while standing on the road. So Jola grabbed onto them and swiftly climbed the tree.

'There! Got saved!' Jola exclaimed.

'There! Got saved!' Bagh thought.

However, Jola could not manage to get down to return home as Bagh sat panting under the same tree, growling all the while, calling out to his friends from all around. Soon, around four or five tigers arrived and surrounded Bagh, and asked 'Look at you! What happened to you? Who tied your face and eyes?'

Still panting from the wild run, Bagh answered 'Brothers, I almost got killed today. Taag had gotten hold of me. It was only when I begged and pleaded and promised to worship him did he let me go. But he has blindfolded me, and now, if I do not perform a ceremony, he will return to catch hold of me.'

The thought of a beast like taag frightened the other tigers, and they began their worship at the base of the banyan tree. Many more joined. They killed several large animals like buffaloes and deer and brought them as offerings.

Jola had never seen so many tigers gathered in a single

place. As he sat trembling in fear, the leaves and the branches around him began to rustle. This made the tigers look up, but they couldn't see through the branches. They wondered what was up there. One of them said 'Brother, what is there amidst the branches?'

'Look! What a large tail it has,' another one remarked, pointing at what was in reality, Jola's shawl hanging through the branches.

'That must be a mighty beast,' an elderly tiger said. 'Probably it is taag!'

And as soon as the tigers heard 'taag', they shrieked: 'He will catch hold of us. Run, run,' and they all fled from the banyan tree. Once they had left, Jola came down and started for his home.

Upon reaching home, Jola's son demanded 'Father, where is my horse?'

Giving the indolent boy a tight slap, Jola said, 'Here. This is your horse.'

He never asked for a horse again.

THE TIGER'S PALANQUIN RIDE

BAGHER PALKI CHAWRA

Bagh, the tiger, and Sheyal, the fox, were great friends. Bagh was Sheyal's maternal uncle, and Sheyal his nephew. One day, Sheyal invited Bagh for a feast but did not prepare anything for him. When Bagh arrived, Sheyal said, 'Uncle, sit down. Be comfortable. I have invited a few others too. Let me go and fetch them,' and Sheyal left. Then he did not return the entire night. Bagh kept waiting and left in the morning, grumbling and cursing Sheyal.

One day soon after, Bagh invited Sheyal. When Sheyal arrived, Bagh served him large bones, each as strong and heavy as iron. Poor Sheyal broke a few teeth, but could not manage to bite off even a tiny piece. But such huge, juicy bones were Bagh's favourite meal. He feasted grandly while mocking Sheyal, 'So dear nephew, did you eat well?'

'Yes, Uncle!' Sheyal answered. 'I enjoyed the feast as much as you enjoyed your meal at my house.' In reality, he was fuming with rage. He thought to himself, 'I will only return home when I have taught my uncle a lesson.'

Sheyal soon came across a field full of sugarcane. Sometimes, he would eat his fill, and at other times, he would simply destroy the crops. Sheyal's antics greatly angered the farmers, and finally, they decided to teach the mischievous animal a lesson. They began by building a khoar, a wooden one-room construction whose door shuts the moment an animal enters inside, thereby imprisoning it.

As the farmers sat building the khoar, Sheyal saw them from a distance and chuckled to himself. 'Who is this for? Me or my uncle? I believe such a lovely house only befits my uncle,' he thought sarcastically.

The very next day, Sheyal went off to invite Bagh. 'Uncle,' he said excitedly, 'we are invited to the prince's wedding. I will sing, and you will play the instruments. After that, we will have a grand feast. They are sending a palanquin to fetch us.'

Bagh was delighted. 'Oh yes, indeed we have to go, and to think that the king will send a palanquin for us.'

'And it is not an ordinary palanquin, Uncle. This is something which you have never seen in your life.'

Discussing the king's feast and the invitation, Bagh and Sheyal arrived in the field of sugarcane where the khoar stood. Seeing the construction, Bagh wondered, 'Has the king sent just one palanquin? Where are the bearers?'

'The bearers will come the minute we step inside.'

Still quite doubtful, Bagh said, 'But there are no poles to carry it.'

'The bearers will get the poles themselves.'

Finally, when Bagh stepped into the khoar, the door immediately slammed shut with a loud noise.

'Oh Uncle, why did you slam the door shut?' Sheyal asked in a rather pretentious tone. 'How will I enter now?'

Bagh, who thought he was being quite clever, answered, 'There is no need for you to come this time. Let me go and have a feast all by myself this once.'

'Okay, Uncle! Do have a grand feast. Eat to your heart's content. You should eat till you drop. Don't return before that,' and with a cackle, Sheyal went back home.

Finally, when the farmers arrived, they saw a large tiger trapped inside the khoar. They were happy to have successfully captured the predator.

'Get your cooking spuds or your spears and anything you can lay your hands on. There's a tiger trapped inside the khoar. We have to teach him a lesson!'

The inhabitants of the village rushed to the spot and attacked the tiger. They beat him black and blue, and Bagh met with an unfortunate end.

THE OLD FARMER, BUDDHU'S BAAP

BUDDHUR BAAP

There was once an old farmer called Buddhu's Baap, who had a field of paddy. Once, just when the paddy was ready for harvesting, they started to be troubled by flocks of weaver birds. The birds would nibble on the ripe crops and destroy them. Buddhu's Baap had made a thakthaki, a musical instrument made of bamboo whose sharp notes he thought would scare the birds away. Alas, it was far from being a complete success. The birds were not scared easily, and this angered Buddhu's Baap even more. He shouted at them: 'Scoundrels! If I can just catch hold of you I'll show you the iri miri kiri badhon.'

The words 'iri miri kiri badhon' were meaningless. Buddhu's Baap was merely venting his anger through these nonsensical phrases. The birds would frequent his paddy field every day and Buddhu's Baap would shout, 'I will show you the iri miri kiri badhon.'

Now one day, a colossal tiger, Bagh, fell asleep in Buddhu's Baap's paddy field. He only woke up past daybreak and could not escape. Bagh remained hidden within the rows of paddy, lest anyone spotted him. That day, like every other day, Buddhu's Baap came to shoo away the birds: 'Scoundrels! If I can just catch hold of you I'll show you the iri miri kiri badhon.'

When Bagh heard the 'iri miri kiri badhon,' he was scared. 'Goodness, what kind of a thing is this? I have to know.' He slowly crept up to Buddhu's Baap and asked, 'Brother, I need to ask you something.'

Seeing a tiger behind him, Buddhu's Baap got the fright of his life. But he was a clever man. Quickly calming his nerves, he answered, 'Yes Brother! What do you want to ask me?'

'You just mentioned about iri miri kiri badhon or something like that. I would like to see it.'

'Well, it is not so easy to show that,' Buddhu's Baap answered cleverly. 'You need a lot of things for that.'

Bagh insisted. 'I will fetch everything for you, whatever you need, but you simply must show it to me.'

'Okay! You first have to get me all the ingredients. I'll decide after that.'

'What do you need?' Bagh asked.

'I need a large and strong sack, a long yard of very strong rope, and a large club.'

Bagh immediately replied, 'That's all? It wouldn't take long for me to get these.'

The Old Farmer, Buddhu's Baap

It was the day of the market. Bagh hid inside a large shrub, in front of which the vendors gathered every week. A while later, three sellers of parched rice walked by. Bagh noticed their sacks; they looked large and strong. The moment the trio passed the shrub Bagh was hiding behind, he sprang out and growled: 'Haaluuumm.'

Immediately, the sellers dropped their bags and fled in different directions.

Bagh took the sack full of parched rice to Buddhu's Baap. Then he left to fetch the rope, and for that, he did not need to go further. In the neighbouring field, a herd of cows stood grazing, tied together with a heavy rope. The minute they saw Bagh approaching, they ran for their lives, tearing away from their ropes. Bagh collected all the torn ropes and handed them to Buddhu's Baap. Finally, it was time to fetch a club.

At a wrestler's den, a group of wrestlers were practising their regular exercises. Many used a club for their exercises. Upon sighting a tiger, the men ran for their lives, screaming 'Oh my goodness. Save us!' Bagh picked up the biggest club with his mouth and carried it to Buddhu's Baap.

'Okay Buddhu's Baap, now that I have gotten everything you had asked for, show me that thing you said you would.'

'Yes. But first, you come and enter this sack.'

Bagh entered the sack and sat down obediently. Immediately, Buddhu's Baap tightly tied the mouth of the sack with the thick ropes. It was so tight that there remained no space for Bagh to move. Then he picked up the club and brought it down with all his might on the sack.

On the very first whack, Bagh was shocked.

'What are you doing?'

'Why? I am showing you iri miri kiri badhon. Are you scared now?'

It was rather embarrassing for Bagh to admit that he indeed

was scared. 'No, of course, I am not,' he lied to Buddhu's Baap.

Buddhu's Baap beat Bagh mercilessly. To prevent himself from coming off as a coward, Bagh bore all the pain and kept quiet. But how long could one endure such an assault? After ten to twelve whacks with the heavy club, Bagh started to growl loudly, 'Gheaooo, gheaooo.'

After shouting for a while, he could barely utter a word and began to whimper. But Buddhu's Baap continued beating Bagh with all his might. Still sometime later, the sack fell silent. Assuming Bagh had died, Buddhu's Baap untied the mouth of the sack and left it in the field. He then returned home.

Bagh, however, did not die from the severe beating. He lay in pain for nearly five hours in the field and gradually managed to stand. Every part of his body was aching, he was running a high temperature, and above all, he was fuming with anger. His rage nearly masked his excruciating pain. He rolled his eyes and bared his teeth, 'That rascal Buddhu's Baap. Wicked, crooked, rogue. Let me teach you a lesson.'

Bagh's words made Buddhu's Baap stop in his tracks. Frozen with fear, he decided not to step out of his house for the next three days. During that time, Bagh paced the grounds around the house. Then he had an idea. Mimicking a human voice, Bagh went to the main door of the house and said, 'Can you lend me your fire, Brother? I need to light up my tobacco.'

Buddhu's Baap was listening intently. The words did sound like that of a human's but the voice resembled a tiger's. He decided to inspect the situation, before lending his fire. So, he peeped through his door. Goodness! Bagh was right outside! Immediately, he had an idea. 'Brother, I am running a temperature. I cannot open the door,' Buddhu's Baap answered. 'Why don't you pass your stick from under the door? I will tie the fire to your stick.'

Now, from where would Bagh get a stick? So he decided to push his tail under the door. The moment Buddhu's Baap saw the tiger's tail under his door, he chopped it off with a neat strike of his kitchen knife.

Bagh sprang up high in the air with a loud 'Gheaooo!' and ran at full speed, curling whatever little tail that remained. That day Buddhu's Baap was saved, but he feared that soon, Bagh would return with his friends to teach him a lesson. True! The very next day, Buddhu's Baap saw nearly twenty-five tigers approaching his hut. Petrified, he ran from his home, climbed a tall tamarind tree behind his house, and hid behind a large clay pot tied to one of the highest branches. Concealed in the thick foliage, Buddhu's Baap sat quietly and observed the ambush of tigers below.

Unfortunately, the tigers spotted Buddhu's Baap and began to pace all around the tree, cursing and swearing at the poor farmer. The horrified man, however, did not utter a word and kept silent. This went on for a while as the tigers concocted a plan. One of them, who thought himself to be quite brainy said, 'The biggest tiger amongst us will sit on the ground. Then the one slightly smaller than him will climb on him and then the one even smaller than him will perch himself on top of the second one. Like that, we will climb on top of each other and reach the highest branch. Then we will catch hold of Buddhu's Baap and feast upon him.'

Amongst all the tigers, the largest and the biggest was that tailless Bagh. The wound from the cut had yet not healed, and every time he tried to sit, the cut would hurt terribly. But now what would he do? The entire plan depended on him forming the base. Finally, he found a small burrow under the same branch on which Buddhu's Baap was sitting. He pushed the wounded stub of a tail inside the small burrow and managed to settle down. Gradually, his friends started to climb on him. A pile of tigers began to form and soon became tall enough to reach the branch where Buddhu's Baap was hiding.

Up there, sitting amongst the branches, a terrified Buddhu's Baap muttered to himself: 'Now I have to face whatever is coming.' He tightly clutched the clay pitcher behind which he was hiding, ready to bring it crashing on the head of the tiger nearest to him.

Now that burrow in which Bagh had placed the wounded stub of his tail belonged to a crab, and that very moment, it had smelled the blood and the wound. The scent of raw flesh enticed the crab; it crawled out of its burrow and snapped hard at the wound with its pincers. The crab's sudden attack sent a chill down Bagh's spine. 'Goodness, there's a Buddhu's Baap in the burrow as well,' and he sprang into the air. Immediately, the column of tigers tumbled and came crashing down. In the meanwhile, Buddhu's Baap had flung the pitcher from his branch. It hit Bagh on the head and smashed into pieces. Right then, Buddhu's Baap began shouting, 'Catch him, catch him, catch him, by his neck!'

Hearing his words, no tiger was willing to stay back. They all bolted in all directions, their tails tucked away between their hind legs. They never bothered Buddhu's Baap again.

THE FOOLISH TIGER

BOKA BAGH

There was a cunning fox, Sheyal, who lived outside the king's palace. His burrow was right next to the walls of the enclosure where the king kept his goats. They were plump and juicy, greatly enticing Sheyal, but he was afraid of the royal goatherds who kept guard. So he refrained from hunting the goats in their shed. However, one day, Sheyal gathered enough courage and began digging through his burrow. Finally, he found his way into the shed. Unfortunately, the goatherds were sitting inside. They caught hold of Sheyal, tied him tightly, and as they left said, 'Let's leave for now. It's almost dark. We will inform everyone tomorrow, and then teach the fox a lesson.'

The goatherds left for the night and Sheyal sat all night long with a sullen face. At that moment, his maternal uncle Bagh, the tiger, was passing by the shed.

'Nephew, what are you doing here?' Bagh asked, surprised to see Sheyal trapped in the shed.

'I am getting married,' Sheyal answered.

'Getting married? Where is the bride then? And what about your guests?'

'The bride is the king's daughter. My guests have left to fetch her.'

Still shocked at the situation, 'Why are you tied up then?'

'You see, I did not want to be married. So, they tied me up in case I ran away.'

'You did not want to get married?' Bagh asked incredulously.

'Yes, Uncle,' Sheyal answered convincingly. 'I am in no mood to get married.'

'Then why don't you leave and tie me up in your place?'

'Right away, Uncle,' Sheyal replied promptly. 'You untie me. I will tie you up and leave immediately.'

Bagh was ecstatic. He happily untied his nephew, who in return, tied Bagh. Before leaving, he said, 'One last word, Uncle. Your brothers-in-law will tease you and have some fun. You should not get angry at them.'

'Of course not,' Bagh said confidently, 'I would never be angry at my brothers-in-law. I am not a fool.' Sheyal laughed at his uncle's excitement and left Bagh thinking about his bride-to-be and her arrival.

In the morning, the group of goatherds arrived. Bagh thought happily, 'There come my brothers-in-law. I should be prepared to laugh at their jokes.'

The boys had come to teach Sheyal a lesson. But when they saw a large tiger tied to the same pole, commotion ensued. The terrified crowd started to run hither and tither. But a few present tried to control the situation. 'Brothers, don't fear,' they said. 'He is tied tightly to the pole and can do us no harm. Grab whatever you can gather—all the weapons you can find—and bring them all over.'

Someone got a large and heavy brick and threw it at Bagh, who still thought all of it to be a part of a playful welcome organized by the bridal party. He simply replied with a hearty laugh. 'He he hee, hee!'

Another person then poked Bagh with a bamboo, and a third one with a spear. To all of these, Bagh replied cheerfully: 'Uh hu hu, ho ho ho ho, ho. I get it. All of you are my brothers-in-law.'

But there is only so much playful poking Bagh was prepared to endure. Once again, when a few of the goatherds prodded Bagh, with spears, he could take it no more. Incensed, he snarled: 'Goodness. I don't want to get married,' and he tore away the ropes, ran fast from the goat shed, and disappeared into the woods.

In the forest, a few carpenters were at work. They were splitting a large log and had left their work half-finished by inserting a small piece of wood at the mouth of the slit. This ensured it would remain open, so the work could be continued the next day. The carpenters had left for the day and the large half-slit log lay unattended. When Bagh arrived at the spot, he saw Sheyal sitting and resting at the very mouth of the slit. The minute Sheyal saw Bagh, he asked: 'So Uncle, how was the marriage?'

'No Nephew,' Bagh replied in a huff. 'I could not take their jokes. They teased me so much that I left.'

'Okay. Never mind. Come and sit here. Let us have a chat.'

Immediately, Bagh jumped on the log and sat down, his tail hanging exactly at the mouth of the slit. Sheyal noticed this and gradually began pushing off the small piece of wood fitted at the mouth of the slit. With a final, heavy shove, it popped out and the slit of the log clamped shut with a loud bang on Bagh's tail.

Pretending to be hurt, Sheyal fell off the log and rolled to the ground, 'Oh Uncle, oh my goodness. I am hurt badly.'

At the same time, Bagh had the fright of his life when the slit of the log slammed shut on his tail. As he jumped up in pain, his tail tore off. Bagh's agony knew no bounds. He fell to the ground and rolled in great pain.

'Nephew, my tail has been snapped off. I am in so much pain,' he howled and growled.

Simultaneously, Sheyal kept crying, 'Uncle, I broke my back. I can't take it any more.'

Finally, both limped into a taro forest and lay there for a few days.

We all know that nothing had happened to Sheyal. He had been pretending all this while, but Bagh was severely injured. In fact, he was so badly hurt that he could not even get up to hunt. But Sheyal could easily gather frogs and other small animals for himself.

Poor Bagh, blinded by pain, he couldn't even spot a frog and grew ravenous by the second. Finally, he asked Sheyal, 'Nephew, did you eat anything?'

'Oh no nothing,' Sheyal lied shrewdly. 'I just ate some wild taro, and now my stomach's bloated.'

What else could Bagh do? He too started munching on some taro, but soon, began to suffer from an allergic reaction to the vegetable, which made his throat and face swell. By this time, Bagh had nearly perished from the pain and the swelling.

'Uncle, what did you eat?' asked Sheyal, pretending to be shocked at Bagh's miserable condition.

'I ate the taro, and now I am suffering,' Bagh replied sorrowfully. 'How come you only had a swollen stomach, but I had such severe reactions all over my face and throat?'

Once again, Sheyal proved how shrewd he was. 'You see Uncle, you are a tiger, and I am a fox. That's why this has happened.'

Sixteen days passed. Bagh could barely move and lay writhing in pain. Because he could not even hunt or eat, he lost weight and was almost starving to death. Then one day Bagh saw that Sheyal was about to leave his side. 'Nephew, how did you get well?' he asked the fox.

'Uncle, I found a new medicine. I munched upon my own limbs and got better. I also got new limbs in place.'

'Oh is it so? Why didn't you tell me this earlier?'

'I thought you could not munch on your limbs as I did, so I did not think of informing you,' Sheyal answered.

Sheyal's answer made Bagh furious, 'You are a fox, and you could do it. I am a tiger, and you think that I cannot do it?'

'But Uncle, you fled the wedding in fear of a few jokes. How would I know that you can manage to munch on your bones?'

'Nephew, you just wait and see if I can do it or not.'

Immediately, Bagh began munching on his limbs. In a few days, the poor animal contracted an infection and did not survive.

THE TIGER'S COOK

BAGHER RADHUNI

Once, a tigress, Baghini, on her deathbed told her husband, the tiger Bagh, 'I am leaving behind two small cubs. Look after them well.'

After Baghini passed away, Bagh thought, 'How will I do it all? Manage the household and also look after the two cubs?'

His friends were quick to advise, 'Remarry. Everything will fall into place.'

Bagh thought it was a good idea too, 'I will not marry a Baghini this time. I will get a human girl for myself. I have heard that they are good cooks.'

So Bagh set off for the village to find a suitable bride for himself. There, in one household, lived a young girl and her brother with their parents. Bagh abducted the girl, brought her home, showed her to his two cubs, and said, 'See now, this is your mother.'

Both immediately retorted, 'No tail, no sharp teeth, no stripes, no fur—how can she be our mother? It will be better if we can kill her and then feast upon her.'

'I warn you,' Bagh growled at his cubs, 'if you talk like that, I will tear you two into tiny pieces.'

Their father's anger forced the cubs to quieten, but in reality, they could never tolerate the girl and would often threaten her, 'Let us grow up a little. We will be stronger, and then we will feast upon you.'

The poor girl. How do I even express her plight? She would howl and cry whenever she was alone at home, remembering her parents and brother at her home in her village. But the moment Bagh entered the house, she would fall silent. She became Bagh's radhuni, a cook.

Time passed.

In the meantime, the girl's parents had been crying foul all the while. Her young brother cried with them too. Finally, he said, 'It is useless to sit and weep at home like this. I am off to search for my sister. Let me try to find her.'

So the boy left his home and began his search through all the jungles. Soon he located Bagh's house amidst the forest. He saw his sister sitting inside. Petrified upon seeing her brother, the girl cried out, 'Oh Brother, why did you come? Bagh will eat you up.'

'We will see about that later. I have come to fetch you and will not leave without you. Now hide me somewhere inside your house.'

The siblings dug a large pit inside the kitchen floor. The boy crept into this pit and his sister put a massive sheel, a grinding stone, to cover the mouth of the pit.

Soon, Bagh returned and sat down to have his lunch with his two cubs, who refused to eat. They kept mumbling:

'Father O Father!
Is he our uncle?
Is he your brother-in-law?
Is he our mother's brother?
Hear him from under the sheel,
Drag him out and we'll feast well.'

Bagh, who was already in a sour mood because of a tiff he had earlier that day, paid no heed to his cubs. Already fuming with anger, he gave them each a hard slap, finished his meal, and left the house. But before stepping out, he told the girl, 'Make some sweet pithey today. I will have them in the evening when I return. Make sure you prepare them well.'

After Bagh was gone, the girl helped her brother out of the pit and served him lunch. Then they put in a large cauldron of oil on top of the clay oven. After that, they killed both the cubs, cut them into small pieces, hung those over the cauldron, and fled from Bagh's house. Blood dripped from the flesh and into the hot oil below. The sound could be heard from a distance.

Towards the evening, as Bagh walked towards his home, he heard the dripping of the blood and thought, 'Lovely, I think that is the sound of the pithey in oil. If she prepares them well, good enough. And if they are not to my liking, I will tear this radhuni into pieces and all three of us will feast upon her.' Finally, when Bagh entered the house, he was shaken to see the kind of 'pithey' that was being prepared. He roared and stormed all over but to no avail. The girl had already run away, and by then, she and her brother had reached the safety of their home, back to their parents.

The villagers rushed to greet and welcome the siblings and celebrated their return most grandly.

THE FOOLISH CROCODILE

BOKA KUMIRER KOTHA

Once Kumir the crocodile and Sheyal the fox decided to do some farming. So the next question was what would they farm? Potatoes. Little did Kumir know that the potato grows under the soil. The leafy part remains above the ground, but it is of no use. Kumir, quite a fool, had not a shred of knowledge about the crop. He had assumed that just like any other fruit, potatoes grew on a potato tree.

In a bid to cheat Sheyal, he said, 'I will take the top half of the plant and you take the part which lies below the soil.'

Clever Sheyal chuckled to himself and instantly agreed to Kumir's proposed division.

When the potatoes were to be harvested, Kumir cut off all the tops of the plant. But it was only after he brought them home did he realize that there were no potato fruits amongst the leaves. He dashed back to the field and saw Sheyal had dug up all the vegetables from under the soil and taken them home. Repenting his silly error, Kumir swore to himself, 'I took a wrong decision this time. Next time, I will choose wisely.'

Next time, the duo decided to reap paddy. This time Kumir was adamant and he prepared himself to not be cheated again. He informed Sheyal beforehand: 'Brother, this season, I will not take the top portion of the crop. I lay my claims on what lies below the soil.'

Once again, Sheyal let out a little laugh. Happy with Kumir's incompetence as a farmer, he agreed to the arrangement.

When the paddy was ready to be harvested, Sheyal cut off the top half of the crop and took it home. Now the stalks and roots of the crop remained for Kumir. Very happily, he dug up the roots only to find nothing for himself. Of course, there was no paddy to take home. What's worse? The stubbles of the paddy stalks, which were left in the fields and could have been used as hay for the animals, also got entirely destroyed because of Kumir's vigorous digging.

Frustrated with his failed farming endeavours, Kumir muttered to himself, 'You just wait Sheyal, you rogue, I will teach you a lesson. The next time, I will take the top-most, leafy part.'

After paddy, the friends reaped sugarcane. As decided, Sheyal cut the top-most part of the plant and gave them to Kumir. He then took the stalks home and feasted upon the juicy fruit to his heart's content. On the other hand, Kumir tried biting into the leaves and found them salty and inedible. Furious, he threw away all the sugarcane leaves and told Sheyal, 'No Brother. I do not want to farm anything else with you. You cheat a lot.'

THE LEARNED FOX

SHEYAL PANDIT

The crocodile, Kumir, tired of being cheated, had realized that under no circumstances could he outwit his friend the fox, Sheyal. One day, he had an epiphany: 'Sheyal is very educated. That's how he outsmarts me every time. I am indeed an imbecile and can never put up a fight or provide a befitting reply ever.' Finally, Kumir decided that he would take his seven chhanas, the hatchlings, to Sheyal and ask him to tutor them so they too could become learned one day. The very next day, he took his children to Sheyal's house. When they arrived, Sheyal was enjoying a meal of crabs inside his den. Kumir called out, 'Sheyal Pandit, Sheyal Pandit are you home?'

Sheyal came out and said, 'Hello Brother. What do you want?'

'Kumir, I brought my seven sons to you. I fear that they will have a very hard life if they grow up to be dimwits. It would be wonderful if you can teach them, and see that they receive a good education.'

'Of course,' Sheyal assented. 'I will teach them and get them ready within seven days.'

Kumir was mighty pleased with the answer and happily left for his home, leaving his children behind. Then Sheyal took one of them aside and said:

'Come dear, read kaana, khaana, gaana, ghaana, how is it kumirchhana?'

And immediately, he gobbled up the hatchling.

Next day, when Kumir came to visit, Sheyal brought out all six kumirchhanas once and the last kid twice. Kumir did not understand the trickery. He thought he had seen all seven hatchlings and went home happily. Soon, Sheyal took one of the kids to one side and said,

'Come dear, read kaana, khaana, gaana, ghaana, how is it kumirchhana?' and so saying, he ate the second kid as well.

The day after, when Kumir arrived enquiring about his children, Sheyal repeated his cunning tactic, bringing out the last kid thrice. Kumir was satisfied and returned home happily once again. Soon, Sheyal gobbled up the third kid as well.

Thus a pattern was formed. Every day, Sheyal would feast upon one of Kumir's hatchlings and would make a fool of Kumir when he came to meet them. Soon, there was only one kid left. Sheyal showed the same kid to Kumir seven times and devoured him after Kumir left. Seeing this, Sheyal's wife, Sheyalni, said, 'Now what will you do? What will you show Kumir? If he doesn't get to meet his kids, he will spare none of us.'

'He can only eat us if he finds us,' Sheyal answered. 'There is a dense forest on the other side of the river. Let us all go there. Kumir will never be able to find us there.'

Sheyal and Sheyalni left their old burrow immediately. Soon after they left, Kumir arrived, and though he called out 'Sheyal Pandit' many times, there was no reply. He searched the area. There was no trace of the fox, his wife or their cubs, but he discovered the unfortunate bones of his children.

Kumir was livid with anger. He ran helter-skelter in all directions, searching for the foxes, and finally arrived at the riverbank to discover that they were in the middle of the river, swimming at top speed to reach the other side.

'Wait, you rascal,' Kumir said and jumped into the water. Now no one can swim faster than a mighty crocodile. With swift strokes, Kumir reached just in time to grab Sheyal's hind leg as the animal was about to get out of the water and onto the riverbank. The minute Sheyal realized that Kumir had caught up with him, he called out to his wife, 'Sheyalni, Sheyalni.

Somebody has gotten hold of my walking stick and is not letting go. I think he will snatch it away from me.' Hearing Sheyal, Kumir doubted himself, 'Oh no. What a mistake. I have grabbed his walking stick instead of his leg,' and just as Kumir let go of the Sheyal's leg, the fox jumped onto the bank and ran as fast as he could into the depths of the forest. Kumir could not catch Sheyal.

Kumir continued his attempts to get even with Sheyal, but the latter was too shrewd. Finally, Kumir devised another plan, and accordingly, he lay down motionless on the banks of the river in an upturned position. Soon, Sheyal and Sheyalni came to hunt for turtles. Both of them saw Kumir lying in a strange position.

'It seems he is dead,' Sheyalni remarked. 'Let's feast upon him.'

The cunning Sheyal was more careful than his wife. 'Wait, let me see,' he warned and so saying, he inched closer towards Kumir and said aloud, 'This looks too dead. We don't eat animals which are dead for long. We only eat animals which are half-dead. Our food must be somewhat alive, wriggling and slightly moving.'

Listening to Sheyal and Sheyalni's conversation, Kumir thought, 'I should start wriggling or else Sheyal will not come closer to eat me.' So he started to wriggle the tip of his tail.

That was all the confirmation Sheyal needed. 'Look,' he told his wife, 'he's wagging his tail, and you said that he's dead.'

So what happened after that? Of course, the foxes did not wait by the river for a second longer, while Kumir kept lamenting, 'I was fooled again. Wait for the next time.'

Now there was a section of the river where Sheyal would come to drink water every day. Kumir knew the spot. He hid there, thinking he would catch hold of the wretched fox the minute he would arrive. The same day, Sheyal came to the river and discovered all the fishes were missing. This was a strange departure from most other days when he found plenty of fishes in that part of the water. 'Now where did all the fishes go?' Sheyal wondered to himself. Then it dawned upon him. Kumir must be hiding in the same spot, thus, all the fishes must have fled.

'The water here is too clear,' Sheyal declared loudly. 'No one can drink such clean water. It needs to be slightly muddy. Come Sheyalni, let's go and find a different river.' Instantly, Kumir began to disturb the mud so the water would appear murky. Laughing aloud at Kumir's foolish attempts, Sheyal and Sheyalni fled.

One day soon after that, Sheyal returned to hunt crabs near the river. Kumir was already hiding there. The fox, shrewd as he was realized it was Kumir's hiding spot, and said aloud, 'I don't think there are any crabs here, otherwise they would have been floating on the surface.' Hoping to draw Sheyal into the water, Kumir lifted a part of his tail to resemble a floating crab, and immediately, Sheyal understood and refrained from proceeding any further. Once again, he ran away.

Outsmarted by Sheyal for the umpteenth time, Kumir felt quite ashamed. Humiliated, he decided to not show his face to anyone else and spent his days sulking indoors.

THE FOX WHO WAS A JUROR

SHAKKHI SHEYAL

Once Saudagar, a merchant, was travelling on his horse. After a while, as he felt drowsy he decided to take a restful nap under a tree. He tied his horse and went off to sleep. When Saudagar was asleep, a thief came along, untied the horse, and was about to silently escape, when the rustling noise of the horse's hooves woke up Saudagar. He sat up and asked, 'What are you doing? Where are you off to with my horse?'

Feigning anger, the thief said, 'Which is your horse?'

The answer amazed Saudagar. 'What do you mean? You are walking away with my horse, and you have the audacity to ask me such a question?'

The thief continued to feign anger. 'Be warned!' he huffed. 'You cannot refer to my horse as your horse.'

Saudagar's surprise knew no bounds. 'What? I got the horse from my home and now you're saying it is your horse?'

'This is the child of this tree which belongs to me. It has just been born, and I am taking it home. Be careful about what you're saying or else you will land in trouble,' said the thief pointing to the tree that the horse was tied to.

Angry, Saudagar lodged a complaint with the king. 'Your Majesty, I had tied my horse to a tree and was resting when this thief arrived and tried to walk away with it.'

'So, why were you walking away with his horse?' the king questioned the thief.

The thief implored with folded palms, 'Forgive me, Your Majesty. This can never be his horse. This is the child of a tree which belongs to me. I was taking it home after it was born. Now he claims that this is his horse.'

'This is highly unjustified,' the king told Saudagar. 'If the tree had a baby, how can you call it your horse? You are indeed a wicked man. Leave my palace at once,' and with that order, the king permitted the thief to return with the horse.

Sobbing, Saudagar headed home. On the way, he met a fox, Sheyal, who, at the sight of his sullen face, asked him the reason, 'What happened to you, Brother?'

'It is a sad story, Brother Sheyal,' Saudagar answered. 'A thief stole my horse. But when I approached the king, the wretch said my horse was in reality the cub of a tree that belonged to him. Hearing his lie, the king handed over my horse to the thief.'

After listening to Saudagar's story, Sheyal said, 'There is one thing you can do.'

'What exactly?'

'You return to the king and tell him you have a juror whom you would like to bring for an opinion. Tell him, that if he does not have any dogs at his residence, he would come over.'

Once again, Saudagar returned to the king and pleaded, 'My Lord, I have a juror, but he is scared of your pet dog and so is hesitant to approach you. If you permit your dog to be taken away, I will then bring my juror.'

'Okay, let the dog be taken away,' the king agreed. 'Now tell your juror to come over.'

The minute Saudagar informed Sheyal, the latter came swaggering to the king's court, his eyes drooping. Within seconds of his arrival, Sheyal sat down, leaned against a pillar, and started nodding off, pretending to go off to sleep. The king was amused. He chuckled and remarked, 'Sheyal Pandit, are you feeling sleepy?'

Acting as if he could barely open his eyes, Sheyal answered drowsily, 'Your Majesty, I was busy eating fish the whole of last night. So, I am feeling sleepy now.'

'Where did you get all these fishes from?'

'Yesterday, the river caught fire, and all the fishes jumped out of the water and onto the banks. We gathered and feasted the whole night long and still could not finish all of them.'

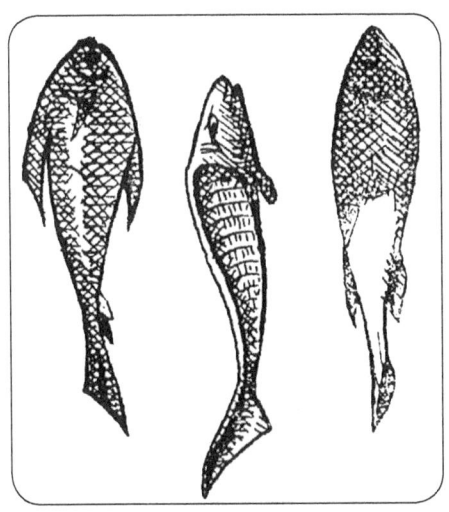

Listening to the story, the king burst out into a fit of laughter that continued for a while. Finally, after composing himself with much difficulty, he said, 'I have never heard anything like this before. How can water catch fire? Is this even possible? These are words of a madcap.'

'Your Majesty, have you ever heard that a horse is the child of a tree? If those are not the words of a madcap, how can you say so?'

The king fell silent and went into deep thought. Finally, he agreed, 'Right you are! How can a tree give birth? That scoundrel is a true thief!'

With that, the king ordered his guards to fetch the thief, tie him up, and bring him to court.

Immediately, ten soldiers marched off and returned with

the thief.

'Beat him up fifty times with a shoe,' the king proclaimed.

So the soldiers took off their shoes and furiously beat up the thief. *Chaatash, chaatash, chaatash* came the sound of the soles of their shoes landing on the thief.

He had only received twenty-five lashings, when the thief howled, 'Save me! Let me fetch the horse for you. I will never commit a crime again!'

Nobody was ready to listen to him. It was only when he had received all fifty strikes did the king permit him to fetch the horse.

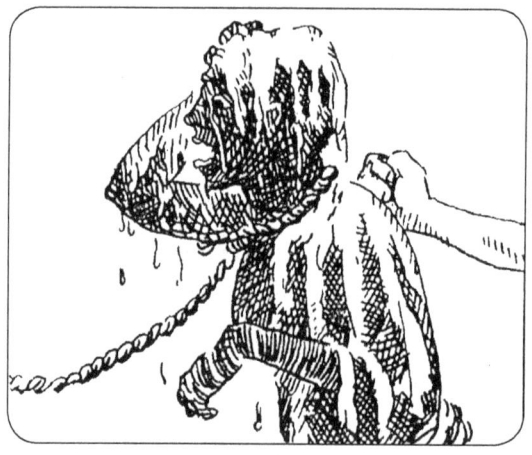

The thief dashed and came back with the horse. After that, as per the king's orders, his head was shaved and a great amount of whey was poured on his scalp. Then his ears and nose were boxed, and he was driven out of the kingdom. Saudagar got his horse back and blessed Sheyal for his help.

THE FOX CUBS WHO WANTED TO FEAST UPON THE TIGER

BAGHKHEKO SHEYALER CHHANA

There was once a family of foxes: Sheyal, his wife Sheyalni, and their three cubs, the sheyalchhanas. However, they didn't have a proper place to stay. The parents were always worried thinking where they would keep their children. 'We need a burrow or else they will get wet in the rain, fall sick and die,' they said. Sheyal and Sheyalni searched far and wide and finally managed to find an empty burrow. However, they were frightened to see that the burrow was surrounded by the pugmarks of a tiger, Bagh.

Sheyalni was worried. 'This looks like a place where Bagh lives,' she told her husband. 'How can we live here?'

'You know well for how long we've searched for a home. We cannot find a more suitable place. This is it. We simply must live here.'

'But what if Bagh comes?'

'Then you start to pinch all the cubs. When they scream in pain, I will ask you why they are crying. Then you will reply that they are hungry to feast upon a tiger.'

Sheyalni was somewhat consoled. So all of them entered the burrow and started to live there.

Time went by, and then one day, Sheyal and Sheyalni saw Bagh approaching from a distance. As planned, Sheyalni immediately went inside and pinched her cubs hard. They screamed. As per the plan, Sheyal asked 'Why are the little ones crying?'

Sheyalni replied in an irritated tone: 'They want to feast upon a tiger. So they are crying.'

Bagh, who was close to his large burrow, immediately overheard a part of the conversation.

As he listened to the new occupants of his home demanding to eat a tiger, he froze in his place. 'Goodness!' he thought. 'What is hiding in my burrow? They must be demons. Or else which baby animal would want to eat a tiger?' Then he heard Sheyalni tell her husband, 'You simply must arrange for a tiger,' and the cubs shrieked even louder as their mother pinched harder.

'Wait, wait,' Sheyal said. 'I can see one tiger approaching. Give me my jhhawpang. I will immediately bhawtang him.'

Now there is nothing in this world called a jhhawpang or a bhawtang—it was all made up by Sheyal. But poor Bagh was petrified listening to all of it. 'Goodness,' he exclaimed. 'I should run away at once or else, I don't know what they are planning on doing to a tiger and with what.'

So he began to run. Sheyal saw Bagh taking off and running away past the trees and shrubs and into the dense forest. Both Sheyal and Sheyalni breathed a sigh of relief, 'We are saved!'

In the meanwhile, as Bagh was running through the forest, a monkey saw him from atop a tree. Curious as to why the animal was fleeing in such a troubled manner, he stopped Bagh and asked, 'Brother Bagh, why are you running so?'

'Don't even ask,' Bagh answered, panting heavily. 'There was no other way but to run for my life or I would have been gobbled up'

'You are telling me that there is something which can even gobble up a tiger? I have never heard of such an animal. I don't believe you.'

Bagh was offended. 'Hah! You would have understood if you were there. Anybody can talk like yourself when you are not faced with a grave situation.'

'If I was there, I would have told you that there is nothing to be scared of. You are simply foolish, and so you get easily scared.'

Now Bagh was doubly offended. 'Really? I am a fool?' he retorted. 'And you have all the wisdom in the world? Come, I'll take you to the burrow.'

'Yes I will go with you,' the monkey agreed. 'But you must carry me on your back.'

'Okay,' Bagh said. 'Ride on my back.'

Once again, Bagh set off for his burrow, but this time with the monkey on his back.

In the meantime, Sheyal and Sheyalni had just calmed their cubs when they saw Bagh approaching the burrow once again, this time with a monkey on his back. Sheyalni rushed to her babies and began to pinch them. The mad howling resumed.

Sheyal added to the din. 'Please be quite. Don't shout so much, or else you will fall sick.'

'I told you they will not stop till you fetch a tiger for them to feast upon,' came Sheyalni's practised reply.

'I have just sent their uncle to fetch a tiger. He will be here anytime now. Now you'll be silent,' was Sheyal's clever answer. He paused momentarily and then added, 'There, there! I can see their uncle, the monkey, walking towards us with a tiger. Don't cry, my babies. Give me my jhhawpang. I will immediately bhawtang him.'

All this while, the monkey wasn't scared. But now the mention of 'jhhawpang' and 'bhawtang' worried him. He leapt into the air and perched himself on the highest branch of a nearby tree. He then disappeared into the dense jungle in a flash.

What about poor Bagh? What else can I say about him? He ran at full speed from the burrow and kept running for two days.

And the family of foxes? From that day forth, they were never troubled by anyone and happily lived in their newfound burrow.

THE FRUIT OF THE SUGARCANE

AAKHER PHAWL

Sheyal Pandit, the learned fox, loved to munch on some juicy aakh, sugarcane. He would often enter the plantations to enjoy his fill of the syrupy treat. One day, he saw a hornet's nest. Now, Sheyal Pandit had never seen something like that before. He thought it was the phawl, the fruit, of the sugarcane.

A scholarly gentleman, Sheyal Pandit would often use Sanskrit words and refer to sugarcane, 'aakh' as 'ikshu', the agricultural field which is otherwise referred to as 'khet' as 'kshetra', and the walking stick, which is otherwise called 'lathi', a 'danda'. When he caught a glimpse of the hornet's nest, he exclaimed: 'Aha! This is such a ripe ikshu phawl. I am sure it will taste just as wonderful as it looks,' and just as he was about to bite into the nest, the hornets came rushing out to sting Sheyal Pandit.

Goodness! What a racket that was!

Sheyal ran hither and tither in great fear, shouting in pain, all the while screaming, 'I will never enter an "ikshu kshetra" again!'

When the hornets dispersed, Sheyal Pandit was back to his scheming ways. 'It is rather strange,' he thought, 'I visit the kshetra every day and nothing has ever happened before. The problem occurred when I tried to eat the "ikhshu phawl". Now I get it. I should refrain from touching the phawl. That's all. Why should I stop going to the kshetra altogether?' And for the next two days, he kept muttering to himself, 'If I visit the ikshu kshetra, I will not eat the ikshu phawl.'

Soon, Sheyal Pandit's pain reduced, and he began to think afresh.

'I believe the ikshu phawl was infested with insects. If only I had shaken the phawl vigorously before biting into it, all the insects would have flown away, and none of them would have bitten me. Ah, the phawl must be very sweet indeed. I just need to be more careful and shake it well before eating.'

Then he added, 'When I munch upon the ikshu phawl, I will give it a good poke with my danda' and with that, Sheyal Pandit entered the plantation and gave the hornet's nest a sturdy poke with his walking stick. And that was it. The hornets came buzzing out, full of wrath, and they began stinging Sheyal furiously. After that, Sheyal Pandit never visited the ikshu kshetra again.

THE FOX INSIDE THE ELEPHANT

HATHIR BHETOREY SHEYAL

The king's royal mount, the Pathasti, was the biggest and largest of all the elephants that he had. He was a beautiful animal, and the king sat regally on its back and travelled everywhere. The king adored the animal. Unfortunately, one day, the beloved elephant passed away. Grief-stricken, the king gave orders for it to be carried to an open field. Five hundred men arrived and tied thick ropes to the elephant's four feet and dragged him along. Then they left for the day. In the meantime, a fox, Sheyal, who lived in those fields, saw the dead mount. Sheyal was starving for several days and was overjoyed to see meat in front of him. Seeing that the elephant was left unattended, he came and started devouring the dead animal. Soon, it had burrowed a hole into its stomach and yet, it kept nibbling and eating.

Two days passed and Sheyal was still gnawing and pecking away inside the stomach of the dead animal. At the same time, tanning and drying under the sun, the dead elephant's skin began to wither and wrinkle. Slowly, the mouth of the burrow which Sheyal had dug to enter inside, started shrinking. Sitting inside the large belly and feasting incessantly for several days, Sheyal had put on so much weight that it was now difficult to squeeze himself out of the burrow's narrow opening. What would happen? He had to find a solution!

Sheyal saw three farmers walking by. An idea struck him. He shouted out to them, 'Brothers! Can you convey my message to the king? If you apply fifty pitchers of clarified butter, ghee to my stomach, I will stand up again.'

The farmers were amazed. 'Listen to what the royal mount

is saying. Let us immediately go and inform the king,' and the trio ran to the palace. 'Your Majesty, your Pathasti says that if you apply fifty pitchers of ghee to its stomach, it will once again stand up straight. Do send fifty pitchers of ghee right away.'

Overjoyed, the king exclaimed: 'If I can see my beloved elephant alive once again, not only a mere fifty pitchers, but I am sending one thousand pitchers of ghee to be rubbed on its stomach.' At once, a thousand men with A thousand pots of ghee arrived in the field, and then two thousand men began to rub ghee onto the Pathasti's stomach. For the next seven days, the field was only abuzz with the king's men who kept shouting: 'Bring the ghee' and 'Pour the ghee.'

After seven days, Sheyal saw that the mouth of the burrow had been lubricated enough to help him slip through. At that moment he had another idea. He called everyone and said: 'My dear men, now it is time for me to rise. I insist all of you to stand aside and make some room, just in case I lose my balance and topple over, I should not fall on anyone.'

A massive commotion ensued. People started to push each other to make their way out of the area. Shouts of 'Move aside, quickly! Move! The elephant is getting up. It will fall on me' was heard all around.

Each person shoved the one next to him. Nobody wanted to be in the field for a minute longer. They ran, leaving their pitchers of ghee behind. Nobody remained to witness whether Pathasti rose or not. Sheyal had been waiting for this opportune moment to escape. Soon, when there was no one around, he wriggled out of the hole in the elephant's stomach and ran straight back into the woods.

THE ARROGANT CAT, MAWJONTALI SARKAR

MAWJONTALI SARKAR

In a village there lived two cats. One used to live close to the milkman's house and enjoyed feasting on a regular supply of delicious and nutritious milk, curd, cottage cheese, butter, and clotted cream. The second one often hovered around the fisherman's house. He would be regularly beaten up, kicked around, and shooed away. The cat which used to live close to the milkman's house was plump and walked around with a swagger and a chest swollen with pride. His counterpart in the fisherman's neighbourhood was skinny, merely flesh and bones. He could barely walk straight, and the only thought that circled his head was how to become plump like the milkman's cat. Finally, one day, he went over to the chubby cat and said 'Brother, I came to invite you to my house for dinner today. Please do come.' But this was all a lie. He could barely find anything to eat himself; how could he possibly invite a friend? He knew that the plump cat would also be beaten up, just like himself, if he too lingered near the fisherman's house. The real scheme was to somehow shoo him away and then take his place at the milkman's house.

True indeed, the minute the milkman's cat arrived, the people in the fisherman's house shouted: 'Look that's the thieving cat from the milkman's house. He will steal all our fish. Catch him, and give him a good thrashing,' and they beat the poor cat such that he succumbed to his injuries.

And what about the other cat? Well, he had long escaped and had now found a spot close to the milkman's house. In his new home, the wicked cat feasted regularly upon rice pudding and clotted cream, and within a very short time, became healthy and plump. In his new avatar, he turned so vain that he stopped speaking to common cats on the streets, and if anyone asked him his name, out came his proud reply: 'Mawjontali Sarkar.'

One day, Mawjontali Sarkar went gallivanting all over the place with papers and a pen. He travelled into the jungle and discovered three tiger cubs at play. He shooed them away, and asked in an angry tone 'Eiiyyoo, pay your taxes.'

Seeing Mawjontali Sarkar's pen and papers, the small cubs were frightened. They ran to their mother, and called out to her, 'Mother, come out quickly. Someone is here, and he is saying something.'

The tigress, Baghini, came out and asked politely, 'Who are you, sir? Where have you come from? What do you want?'

The cat replied authoritatively, 'I am Mawjontali Sarkar. I manage the king's treasury at the palace, and I am in charge of collecting taxes. You stay on our king's land. You have to pay your dues for that. Where is your payment? Pay up right away.'

Baghini was worried. 'But I have no idea what taxes are. We live in the jungle, and if somebody trespasses on our land, we catch hold of them. Why don't you have a seat and wait for my husband, Bagh?'

Then Mawjantali sat on the top branches of a very tall tree and had a good look all around. He spotted Bagh approaching his den from a distance. Immediately, he left his pen and papers and climbed higher up, sitting on a branch that was out of easy reach.

When Bagh arrived, his wife told him everything. Furious at Mawjontali's audacity, he growled, 'Where is that rascal? I will break his neck immediately.' Bagh understood that Mawjontali was a trickster.

'What happened, my dear tiger?' Mawjontali shouted and teased from atop the tree. 'Wouldn't you pay the tax? Come and get me.'

Fuming, Bagh uttered a loud growl, 'Halum,' and pounced, trying with all his might to reach Mawjontali. But being small and light, he climbed higher and higher, out of the tiger's reach. Bagh kept following Mawjontali, reaching out for the higher branches, but the thin branches could not take it any more, and they collapsed. The tiger came crashing down but was caught midway between the ledges of two massive branches. Stuck there, the poor animal lost his life.

Mawjontali saw everything from where he was sitting. When he realized that the tiger was dead, he came down, scratched its face a few times, and rushed to call Baghini, He then pointed to the dead tiger and said, 'See, how I have punished your husband. I will not tolerate any misbehaviour.'

Baghini was petrified. Seeing the mighty Bagh in such a condition scared the living daylights out of her. She begged Mawjontali with folded palms, 'I beg of you Mawjontali Moshai. Spare us. We will forever remain your slaves.'

'Well then, I agree,' Mawjontali replied. 'But do your work and feed me well.'

From that day, Mawjontali began to live in the tigress's den, along with her three cubs. He was pampered and fed throughout the day, and sometimes, he would roam all around, sitting atop the cubs. The poor children would always be terrified of Mawjontali; they thought he was a big honcho.

One day, the tigress approached Mawjontali and said beseechingly, 'Mawjontali Moshai, there are only small animals to hunt in these parts of the jungle. They will not be enough for you. There is a dense forest on the other side of the river. which has large animals living in it. Let us go there.'

'This is a good suggestion. Let's go,' and immediately, the tigress set off with her cubs. They reached the other side of the river soon and looked back to find Mawjontali. But where was he?

Oh, there he was, gasping for breath midstream. The waves and the current of the river were too strong for Mawjontali and kept pulling him downstream. Poor cat knew well that his end was near. A sweep of a few more waves, and he would die. Right at that moment, one of the tiger cubs grabbed Mawjontali and pulled him ashore. Thanks to the cub, the cat was saved. But being pompous, he did not show any gratitude. Upon reaching the bank, Mawjontali feigned anger, slapped the cub a few times, and began cursing him. Goodness, how much he cursed. One cannot even write all that.

'You imbecile,' snapped Mawjontali. 'See what you have done. I was midway with my calculations. It was all going so well. You pulled me out before I could complete it. I was counting the quantity of water in the river and the number of waves and the number of fishes. You are a moron. You ruined everything. If I fail to answer the king, I will teach you a lesson.'

Once again, Baghini begged, 'Spare us Mawjontali Moshai.

My son is just an illiterate cub. He has no knowledge of right and wrong and didn't know he was creating such a blunder. Please excuse him.'

'Only this one time, but I am warning you,' Mawjontali said. 'This should never repeat itself,' and the obnoxious cat went off in search of a sunny spot to dry his wet coat.

It was a dense jungle, difficult for any light to penetrate through the thick forest cover. So Mawjontali climbed a tall tree to sun himself. There, sitting on the top branch, he saw a dead buffalo lying at a distance. He rushed to the spot, scratched the buffalo a few times, went to Baghini, and said, 'Quickly fetch the buffalo I have just killed for lunch.'

The tigress and her cubs reached the spot in no time and dragged the dead buffalo to their den with much difficulty. All the while they thought to themselves, 'Isshh! Mawjontali Moshai has such remarkable strength to have slayed a buffalo as large as this one.'

One day after that, Baghini said, 'Mawjontali Moshai, there are large animals in these parts, like elephants and rhinoceroses. Let us go and kill these one day.'

'True indeed. I should kill elephants and rhinoceroses. Why should I feast upon anything smaller? Let us go straight away,' and Mawjontali left with the family of tigers to kill bigger animals. On the way, Baghini enquired, 'Mawjontali Moshai, will you hunt in khap or in jhap?'

What does hunting in khap and jhap mean? Well, while hunting, if one waits silently for the animal to arrive, it is called hunting in khap. The hunter will sit still for the animal to come. On the other hand, when one jumps around a jungle, makes a lot of noise, and drives all the animals towards the hunter, that is referred to as hunting in jhap. These people help the hunter by driving the animals towards him.

Mawjontali thought to himself, 'I am sure no animal will be

frightened by me.' So he told the tigress aloud, 'I think you three will be unable to kill the kind of animals I will drive towards you. So you all hunt in jhap, and I will hunt in khap.'

Baghini was worried. 'I understand,' she told Mawjontali. 'We will be unable to hunt such large animals. Let us go kids, we will hunt in jhap.'

So the tigress reached the other corner of the jungle and began making a great deal of noise, growling and trampling across a large area. And the rest of the animals? Goodness! How much noise they made. The loud shrieks of the animals made Mawjontali tremble in fear. He sat under a tree, shivering and shuddering.

Soon, a porcupine came running towards the spot where Mawjontali was sitting. To avoid him, he took refuge inside a pit, near the roots of a tall tree. Immediately, a massive elephant came rushing in the direction, trampling upon the roots and grazing lightly against Mawjontali's stomach. Poor chap. The slightest brush of the elephant's foot caused his stomach to burst open. Mawjantali lay dying.

After some time, Baghini returned with her cubs. She had assumed that by then, Mawjontali Moshai must have already killed a herd of animals. So when she found him near the roots of a tall tree, she was surprised to see him wounded and dying.

Shocked, the cubs said, 'What has happened to our Mawjontali Moshai?'

'What else did you expect?' Mawjontali groaned. 'You sent such small animals my way that it made me laugh out loud. I laughed so much that my tummy burst. Now, see my condition,' and with that Mawjontali Sarkar passed away.

THE ANT, THE ELEPHANT, AND THE BRAHMIN PANDIT'S SERVANT

PINPREY AAR HATHI AAR BAMUNER CHAKOR

There was once an ant couple, Pinprey and Pinpri, and they were very fond of each other. One day, Pinpri said, 'Pinprey, if I die before you, you must promise to immerse me in the Ganga river. You will, wouldn't you?'

'Yes, Pinpri. I will, of course,' Pinprey said. 'And you must promise me, that if I die before you, then you will also give me immerse me in the Ganga. You will, wouldn't you?'

'Yes, of course. Without any doubt,' Pinpri assented.

One day soon after that, Pinpri passed away. Pinprey wept and mourned and reminded himself of her promise. 'Now, I have to take Pinpri to the Ganga for her cremation.'

So Pinprey started on the journey, carrying his wife's corpse on his shoulder. But Ganga was very far away. Pinprey walked the whole day, and when dusk arrived, he saw he had reached the royal elephant shed. Exhausted from the long journey, Pinprey decided to rest for a while. Inside the shed, there stood the king's colossal royal mount, Hathi. He was so large that his mere breathing sounded like a gale. '*Phonsh, phonsh*' he went, and with each exhale, Pinpri and Pinprey were almost blown away. This continued for a while, greatly troubling Pinprey. Finally, he could take it no more and snapped at Hathi, 'Beware, I must warn you!' but Hathi could not hear the tiny ant. It continued to breathe, and once again, Pinprey nearly flew off with the gust of air. In anger, Pinprey shouted a few times more, 'Beware you scoundrel, mischievous animal!'

Now, Hathi thought to himself, 'I believe I can hear someone cursing me in a very soft voice. But I can barely hear, neither

The Ant, the Elephant, and the Brahmin Pandit's Servant 111

do I see anyone around me.' Deep in thought, the elephant rubbed one of his front paws on the ground.

Pinprey froze with fear. He was prepared to meet his end but was saved when he managed to lodge himself and Pinpri into one of the grooves on the elephant's paw.

Relieved at his narrow escape, Pinprey settled down in the groove and began to nibble at the elephant's paw. He continued to eat his way and finally made a channel right through Hathi's massive body till he reached his head.

Poor Hathi fell sick, very sick. He shook his head from side to side, would unexpectedly emit a loud trumpet, and then run hither and tither. His erratic behaviour alarmed everybody, and the king's men wondered what had happened to the royal mount. They had no idea it was Pinprey who was nesting inside the elephant's head and causing it so much pain. If they knew, they could have easily extracted the ant by applying sugar to the wound on the elephant's paw. The smell of sugar would have enticed Pinprey to crawl out of Hathi's body. But no one understood what had happened. The physician was summoned and many medicines were given to Hathi. Ultimately, the poor animal perished.

That same night, the king saw his favourite elephant in a dream. The elephant told him, 'Your Majesty, I have worked hard for you and served you well. Make sure you immerse my body in the Ganga.'

Early the next morning, the king issued clear instructions, 'Immerse my elephant in the Ganga.'

Three hundred people tied ropes to the Hathi's feet and chanting 'Haiiyoo, Haiiyoo,' slowly proceeded towards the Ganga. But it was too difficult to drag the animal any faster. So the men would pull for a while, stop and rest, and then start again. This is how they continued.

In the meanwhile, a Brahmin Pandit, Bamunthakur, and his servant were passing by. The servant saw the men struggling with the elephant and remarked caustically, 'It is funny to see so many people struggle with an elephant the size of a mouse. I can carry it all by myself.'

The servant's sly remark incensed the men. 'How dare you claim such a thing?' they retorted. 'We are struggling to pull this heavy animal, and yet you say you can do it yourself? This is insulting, and we refuse to pull the elephant any longer till the king rightly punishes you. You consider yourself to be so smart and strong. We will see to that. Come with us to the king. He will decide.'

The Ant, the Elephant, and the Brahmin Pandit's Servant 113

'Fine, let's see if I am as strong as all of you or not,' the servant answered.

The group left for the palace. They met the king and said, 'We seek your help, Your Majesty. There are three hundred of us, and we are all fatigued from pulling your elephant. But this fellow over here says that he can pull it alone. We are highly offended. You have to decide what is to be done now. Or else, we will not touch your elephant.'

After hearing the account of the men, the king asked the Pandit's servant, 'Are you telling the truth? Can you carry the elephant all by yourself?'

With his palms folded, the servant answered, 'If Your Majesty orders me to, I indeed can carry the animal. But I must be fed well before that.'

'Feed him well,' hollered the king. 'Fetch him one seer of rice, pulses, and vegetables. Let him feast well. Then, he has to carry my Hathi.'

Laughing at the king's orders, the servant added, 'Your Majesty, that is too little for me; the amount of food you have asked for is more suitable for a sweeper. You cannot expect me to carry an elephant with that.'

'Then what do you want?' asked the king.

'Two maunds of rice, the meat of two goats, and one maund of curd.'

'Well, so be it,' the king agreed. 'But remember, you must finish all of it.'

After finishing that scrumptious meal, the priest's servant drifted off into a deep sleep. The servant had a gamchha, a fine cotton towel, tied firmly around his waist. When he awoke, he spread it out, put the massive elephant inside of it and wrapped it up into a small bundle as if he were wrapping up his belongings. Then he hung that bundle containing the dead elephant from the tip of a stick and flung it over one of his shoulders. Finally, he stuffed around ten ganda[1] betel leaves into his mouth and started on his way, humming a merry tune.

The king sat staring, with a gaping wide mouth, along with his three hundred men, while the rest hurried home to inform everyone about this extraordinary feat.

By then, that servant had travelled quite a distance, but it was a sunny day, and he soon had to stop for a drink of water. It was then that he spotted a pond with a neat shelter near it consisting of a cottage and a few trees. The servant kept his small bundle under the shade of the trees and approached the hut. Finding a young girl sitting inside, he asked her warmly, 'Dear, I am very thirsty. Can you please give me some water?'

---

[1] An old unit of land measurement used in the region of Tripura and some other parts of eastern India; 1 ganda= 871.2 sq ft.

'But I only have one large pitcher of water,' the girl said. 'If I give you that, there will be nothing left for my father when he comes back home.'

This made the servant livid. 'Well, is that so?' he snapped at the girl. 'You wouldn't give me even a tiny drop? We'll see where will you get any water to drink from this day onwards,' and he stormed into the pond and began to gulp down its water. *Choon choon.* Soon, the pond was empty. Not a single drop remained in it, and the servant's tummy grew so large that it resembled a mountain. The servant realized it was difficult for him to keep all the water inside of him, so he quickly uprooted a banyan tree and swallowed it. The tree lodged itself midway between his throat and tummy like a cork, stopping the water from rushing out.

Happy with this decision, the servant lay down next to the empty pond for a nap, but his tummy remained bloated, like a large mountain and could be seen from a distance. The girl's father, working in a faraway field, saw the colossal mound and wondered what it was. He ran home to find out what had happened.

As soon as the farmer arrived, the little girl complained, 'Father, see that naughty man outside our home? He had asked for some water. When I had told him that we had only one large pitcher left and that if I gave it to him, there would be nothing to serve you, he finished all the water in our pond.'

Father and daughter set out for the spot where the servant was resting. As they approached him, the girl screwed up her nose; there was a rotten smell all around.

'Father, there must be a rotting mouse inside this,' she said, pointing to the little bundle and picked it up with only two fingers and flung it towards the horizon. That bundle flew from the girl's hand and landed straight into the Ganga.

And what did the girl's father do? He tightened his waistband, drew up a massive kick, and hit the sleeping servant's bloated stomach. It was so strong a kick that all the water from inside pushed out the banyan tree stuck in the servant's throat and came rushing out. The force of the water was so strong that it inundated everything in its wake, carrying away the hut and everything inside of it, including the little girl. All that was left was the servant and the farmer. The two men embraced each other, praising each other's strength

'Brother, I have never seen a mightier man such as you,' the girl's father praised the servant. 'How did you drink our entire pond?'

'I too have never seen such a mighty man as yourself. You managed to empty my tummy with just one kick,' the servant answered.

Soon, a heated argument broke out between the two men about who was mightier. Now who would decide as to who is right? Finally, they decided to go to a large market and test their strengths in a wrestling match.

On their way, they met a fisherwoman heading in the direction of the market, carrying a large basket of fish.

'Where are you going?' she asked the duo.

'We are off to the market to have a bout of wrestling.'

Hearing the servant and farmer's plan, the fisherwoman proposed, 'Well, the market is quite far away. How will you travel so far? Why don't you step into my basket and wrestle in there while I walk to the market? I will understand who among you is losing when the basket will tilt to one side because of the person's weight. That way, the winner will be decided.'

The two men immediately agreed, 'Bah! This sounds great. We can get to wrestle, and we need not walk all the way to the market.'

So they stepped into the fisherwoman's basket and began

their game, while the fisherwoman started for her destination.

Now in that kingdom lived a sly kite who would swoop down and pick up just about anything that it could lay its eyes on—cows, buffalos, elephants, horses...anything! It would lunge at the unsuspecting animal, snatch them in its talons, and gobble them in one go. However, the kite had always been afraid of the fisherwoman. Every time he would swoop down to take fish from her basket, the fisherwoman would rebuke him so severely that he would fly away in fright. Frustrated at his thwarted attempts, the kite was always thinking about ways to get to the fish.

On that day, the kite was out searching for his prey when he spotted a cowherd who was out grazing his seven hundred buffalos. Upon hearing the distant *shoon shoon* of flapping wings, the man exclaimed, 'Goodness! It's that kite. It will definitely gobble my herd. What do I do now?' and he rounded all his seven hundred buffalos, tucked them away in his waistband, and made a run for his home, *bhoon, bhoon*.

'What is the matter? Why are you running so?' everyone asked when he arrived.

'What else to do? That kite was almost there. It would have gobbled up all of my buffalos.'

'So, where did you leave your herd?'

'Why will I leave them somewhere else? I got them along.'

'But where are they?'

'Well here they are,' the cowherd answered, and saying so, he released his waistband. Instantly all the seven hundred buffalos came jumping out.

Everyone was mighty pleased with the cowherd's quick thinking that saved their animals from the clutches of the evil bird.

In the meantime, the kite was still hovering in the sky as the fisherwoman walked towards the market, the two men still fighting inside her basket. So engrossed was she in her thoughts about the fight that she had completely forgotten about the menace in the sky. Taking advantage of the situation, the kite swooped and snatched the basket before flying away.

Now at that very moment, the royal princess was enjoying her time on the palace terrace. Her attendant sat with her, gently combing her hair. As the princess sat looking up at the sky, she suddenly felt something fall into her eyes. She screamed out to her maid, 'Come see quickly. Something seems to have fallen into my eyes.'

The attendant gathered the loose end of her sari, rolled it into the shape of a thin stick, licked it a few times, and then dipped the tip of the cloth into the princess's eye. She managed to pull out a rather funny-looking, black object.

The princess was ecstatic. 'How beautiful! But what exactly is this?'

Nobody in the palace could identify the black object, not the royal staff, neither the ministers of the court, nor the king himself.

Then the king called for a group of erudite scholars. These wise men had plenty of amazing machinery, and using one of them, they could see an enlarged picture of an ant, so much so, that the machine would make the little ant look as big as an elephant. The scholars peered through that wonderful apparatus, and finally ascertained, 'Your Majesty, this is just a mere basket with some fish in it, and next to these, there are two men, busy over a bout of wrestling.'

THE ANT COUPLE, MR AND MRS ANT

PINPREY AAR PINPRIR KOTHA

There once lived an ant couple, Pinprey and Pinpri.

One day, Pinpri said, 'Pinprey, I want to travel to my father's house. Do fetch a boat for me.'

Pinprey got a paddy husk.

Overjoyed at the sight of the makeshift boat, Pinpri exclaimed, 'What a beautiful boat. Come dear, take me to my father's house.'

Thus, both Pinprey and Pinpri sat on the floating paddy husk, and it gradually moved down the river. After travelling a little distance, the husk suddenly became stuck at a corner of the bank. So Pinprey said to Pinpri:

'I will push it now. You come and push too.

My stories end here, on this cue.'

Golpomala

IS IT EASY TO BECOME RICH?

SHOHOJEY KI BOROLOK HOWA JAI?

More or less, all of us were stubborn as kids. I do not want to sound offensive, nor do I want to hurt anyone's sentiments as I know there are many who are easily upset upon hearing the truth. Let me explain it further using my personal experiences.

Children are often afflicted with a sense of judgement that is solely their own. They choose to do things which they are not supposed to and, in the process, frequently upset others. But if they are instructed to do the same thing, then they suddenly lose interest in doing the task altogether. When Dada, my elder brother, was learning the English alphabet, he had a colourfully illustrated textbook to study from. But whenever it was time for his lessons, he could never find it as the book would be with me, and I would be sitting in a place where no one could find me. Finally, the day arrived when I was told that I too would have to learn from that same textbook. I was overjoyed. I immediately ran to inform all my friends. The next day, when the teacher arrived, I immediately went to him with the book in my hand. I was hopeful that the teacher would be discussing the first picture in the book which I knew well, but alas, he did not even look at it, nor did he read from the page. He skipped many pages and finally reached a pictureless one and started off by rattling names which made no sense to me 'ABCD....' That was it. Ever since that disappointing day, I never liked that book again.

Sometimes, when Dada went to school, he would take me along with him. He had a wonderful teacher who made me believe that all teachers are as perfect. At the start, I was homeschooled for three years, and within this period, I had finished a number of textbooks for beginners. Then when I was sent to school and spent a few years there, I stopped harbouring any fondness towards teachers. The only thought that occupied my mind was when will I grow up and leave school.

Once, when I was in the third standard, I had an English textbook with a story about an Englishman. It was a tale of how he left home as a boy, travelled to a far-off land, and though he suffered, he finally became a borolok, a rich man. I calculated and was overjoyed to discover that I was the exact same age as the Englishman when he had left home. That was it. At once, I decided my next course of action. I had a friend who was very close to me—Satish. He was in my class, and I confided in him. I told Satish all about my secret plans which he was delighted to know. In fact, he jumped up in joy. To us, it seemed that one is bound to become wealthy if they leave home and travel abroad.

'Let's go tomorrow,' Satish decided.

Easier said than done. 'Tomorrow' seemed a little difficult, but we were determined that we could not delay our plans for much longer.

One day, soon after that, we left school early and returned home. Satish came along with me. Baba, my father, wasn't home and the rest of the family were enjoying their afternoon siesta. I picked up a few clothes and tied them into a small bundle. Then I took some money from Baba's money box, and then we silently crept out like light-footed thieves. Once outside, we ran for a distance, then we walked a little, then we ran a little more. We continued this way till we felt we were far away from my home. Towards evening, we reached near a large house.

Looking at our scruffy condition, the head of the household was visibly worried. He began to enquire after us, but we were careful not to provide proper answers and went on inserting a lie here and there, making up various fabricated versions of the real picture.

After hearing our story, the man took us for two children who'd lost their way. Finally, he said, 'Tomorrow morning, one of my men will accompany both of you home. He'll drop you off safely.'

While having dinner, he sat right in front of us and did not leave till we were finished. Later, he made arrangements for us to sleep in a guest room which had nobody other than us. I realized that if the owner of the house was intent on taking us back home, that would completely ruin our chances of becoming a borolok. So I decided to leave amidst the still of the night, even without thanking the man of the house for his kindness. I had to wake up my friend.

'Satish! Satish!' I called.

No answer. Satish was lying still. It was then that I understood he was sobbing silently.

What happened? Did the man's words make Satish feel sorry for his actions? Indeed, it turned out to be so. In spite of several requests, Satish remained adamant: 'I will not go further with you.'

Now you readers may wonder about my emotions at that moment. You see, I was very stubborn in my decision to be wealthy. I had mistaken the brief moments of freedom which came from running away from home to be something closer to being a borolok. In my determined mind, Satish became a coward. Both of us had left our parents behind. But the only difference was Satish was not as self-centred as I was. So, all the sad thoughts and emotions brewing inside Satish at that moment did not affect me at all. I failed to understand how he was feeling. Of course, I did not intend to hurt my parents, but I was too engrossed with my own thoughts to even think about them. I watched Satish drift off to sleep. Rummaging through my self-absorbed notions for a while at some point, I too fell asleep.

I had a dream that night where I had a tiff with my mother and she was trying her best to counsel and cajole me, but I remained adamant and refused to give in. Finally, Ma stood with tears in her eyes. Her sadness seemed to fan my egotistical and arrogant mind, and I started to rebuke her at the top of my voice. She came forward to hold my hand. I jerked it away and began to climb a nearby tree. But then I saw myself slipping and falling down. Right then, I woke up. Tears filled my eyes as I recollected my dream, but the thoughts of amassing wealth overpowered me once again. I understood that Satish's decision was doubtful. He might wake up and not want to go any further. In fact, he may even want me to return with him. The night was young, and it was still pitch dark. I thought it was the opportune time to slip out silently, even without informing Satish. I took my clothes and money.

Though it was the middle of the night, the fear of dawn breaking at any moment made me panic. I chose the widest road ahead of me and kept walking. After a while, when the sunrise still seemed distant, I saw the wide road had reached a big river. The road ended there. I too stopped.

Now what? The road must be continuing its journey on the other side of the river, but how would I cross the water? Darkness stretched in every direction; there was no trace of dawn. Probably morning was still very far off. Right then, I saw a boat tied to the bank. It was empty without a covered seating area. I had once seen a man row such a boat. In fact, it seemed so easy. I felt I could easily manoeuvre such a thing. Without any trouble, I easily climbed into the boat and untied the ropes after a little struggle. Then I gave it a shove and off it went into the river.

It was then that a sudden realization crept in, never did I imagine the strength of water to be so mighty. Water lashed against the sides of the boat. And the more they struck, the more the little boat rocked violently from side to side. Then it started to spin, moving away from the bank. The jerk snatched away the rope of the boat which I was holding till then. That was it; swiftly, the little boat with me in it, began to be pulled midstream. The ferocity with which the boat was being swept away left me overwhelmed and speechless. As I sensed the disaster, my head started to reel, I couldn't take it any more. I sat down, covering both my eyes in fear. The waves were climbing high against the sides of the boat, making it rock and sway wildly from side to side. And right at that moment, it struck me: Why, oh why, did I ever leave home? I remembered Ma's face, my house, my room, and my comfortable bed. Tears rolled down my cheeks uncontrollably. I began to weep, calling out loudly for my mother. Why did I not return with Satish? Oh! Why did I ever leave him?

I can't say for how long this continued but suddenly, I saw that the boat had stopped. I turned to see several larger boats gathered in one place. Mine had floated and latched itself to the side of a large one from amidst the group. I felt a sense of relief but soon was alarmed at the sound of shrill voices. A few men jumped out of the boat. In the dark, they appeared half-naked and were shouting at the top of their voices. I could not understand anything as it was a different language but knew that they were hurling abuses and cursing me. I tried to explain but understood that they were unable to comprehend me either. They did not know my language and their shrill voices rose higher. Soon, a few others from another nearby boat arrived. They could comprehend my predicament and began to scold the other group of men. There was one nice gentleman in the crowd who took pity on me and took me along with him on his boat. With great care, he took my little bundle and kept it in a corner.

'I am going to Ka...' he said 'If you do not mind, you may come with me. You will have no trouble in my home.' I agreed and started off with the gentleman.

Ka... is a small city. It had many people, and many were borolok as well. The gentleman I accompanied, let me call him Kalidash Babu here onwards, he too was a borolok. Seeing all this, my old thoughts returned to haunt me. Was it possible to stay here and become a borolok? Of course, it is possible. If it wasn't, how come these people ride so many cars? I thought that just by staying with Kalidash Babu, I would become a borolok. One day Kalidash Babu called me. By then, I had grown very fond of him. He would often call me and give me nice gifts, and I liked receiving them. I know this comes across as rather a childish behaviour in comparison to several of my other friends who would have perhaps behaved more maturely. I guess, Kalidash Babu too, understood it. I went and stood in front of him.

'Girish, how are you liking it here?'

'Quite well.'

'Good. But you never feel like going somewhere else?'

'Where will I go? I want to stay here.'

'Okay, fine!' and with that, he removed his spectacles, which were perched atop his forehead, and continued reading his newspaper. The very first page of the newspaper had a photograph. It was that of the same Englishman from my school textbook. I was a little amazed. I thought I had found a long-lost friend. Overwhelmed, I exclaimed, 'Arey!'

Kalidash Babu was amused. He put away the newspaper and looked at me inquisitively.

'Actually, this picture...' I began to explain..

'He was once a rich and famous man. You too want to be a borolok, right?'

The suddenness of Kalidash Babu's question made me

uneasy. 'Can just about anyone become a borolok?' I asked hesitantly.

'Oh yes. Even you.'

'I can?'

'Of course, you can! I have decided to send you to school from tomorrow. You cannot become borolok if you don't study. I wanted to explain this to you and thus called for you. Is that alright?'

The palace of my dreams came crashing down. I had run away from home to avoid this scenario—and now, it is back once again. I withheld my answer and didn't say anything. Kalidash Babu did not suspect anything—so he didn't press any further. You see, Kalidash Babu, would often ask me questions about my adventures on the boat: 'How did you get into that boat that night?', 'Where do you stay?', 'Don't you have your parents at home?', and I mostly remained quiet. Perhaps Kalidash Babu had always thought of sending me back home, but my answers discouraged him. Maybe that was the reason, he decided it was best if I returned to my studies.

I joined school soon, but was far from being happy. I managed for a few days, but soon it became intolerable. I decided it was time to leave Kalidash Babu's home. But where will I go? And even if I do go, I decided not to go on foot. From Ka..., two steamers used to ferry passengers to Dhu... twice a week. It took three days to reach Dhu.... Most people would tie puffed rice in a small bundle and board the vessel. The steamer departed in the early hours of the morning.

One day, as I was strolling by the banks of the river, I noticed a steamer arriving. I decided to depart the next day at dawn. I was overpowered by the urge to travel to Dhu.... I returned home and gathered my few clothes, but was careful to be discreet, lest anybody became suspicious. The money that I had was all I had brought with me from my home. Till then,

I had spent nothing. Over the days, I had also collected a few pennies which Kalidash Babu had given me. All the money in my possession made me feel wiser. I had heard that the rich don't spend their money easily.

I organized everything for my escape at the next dawn. If there's something in your mind, you would often have a disturbed sleep. I, too, suffered that night and could barely get any rest. Finally, when the clock struck four, I took my bundle that had my clothes, a pair of shoes, the money, some gifts from Kalidash Babu, a few photographs, a big knife, and some of my school textbooks. I did not know why I took those textbooks with me; perhaps Kalidash Babu's words had scared me: 'You cannot become a borolok if you don't study.' I wrapped the bedsheet around my bundle, took an umbrella, and quietly left the house. It did not take me long to reach the ghat, a set of steps, leading down to the river. There, I bought some flattened rice and stored it safely in my bundle. Then a man who seemed to be working in the steamer showed me a spot. I climbed in and silently sat there. Nothing much happened during the long trip, but the little money which I had was almost over. The steamer reached Dhu... on time.

Ramlochan Babu, who was a resident of Dhu..., belonged to our town. He was a very famous advocate. I thought he would be very happy to see me and would treat me well. So the minute I got off the steamer, I asked for his address. Somebody showed me the way, and I soon reached. Upon reaching, I thought of asking somebody I met at the entrance. He looked like the guard of the house. 'Is this Ramlochan Babu's home?' I enquired. Forget about an answer, the man did not even look at me. He scrunched his face and walked past me, straight into a large room in the house. I had to ask another man, and it was from him I got to know that the man I had spoken to earlier, thinking him to be Ramlochan Babu's gatekeeper, was Ramlochan Babu himself! No wonder he was so angry at my question.

With trepidation in my heart, I went and stood near the door of the room where Ramlochan Babu was sitting. He sat leaning against a bolster, dressed in a dhoti, tied up to almost his chest. Dark complexioned and medium in stature, his moustache stuck out straight from his face, and most of his hair had turned grey. There was a pen tucked behind his ear, and his dhoti was pulled up to his knees. There was a large book on his lap, and from time to time, he was thoroughly inspecting its pages, grumbling to himself, and what looked like, even cursing someone. A part of his bolster had ink stains, and it looked like Ramlochan Babu had used it to wipe the ink bleeding from his pen. Soon I realized the stains were not from the bleeding pen. He was dipping his pen into the ink pot which was placed next to the bolster, writing in the large book on his lap, tucking the pen behind his ear, and then wiping his fingers on the bolster. Hence the blotches.

Suddenly, Ramlochan Babu stopped writing and looked up. Once again, he leaned against the pillow, propped himself up on one elbow, and put his leg on the table.

'Bhau,' he barked, making me jump. 'What do you want?'

'Sir, I have come from quite far....'

'Even I have come from far away!'

'I am from Shu....'

'Even I am from Shu... so what?'

'Sir, if you please...'

'Sir, if you can *pleeeassse heeelp*? No, I cannot. I do not encourage these kinds of unscrupulous activities. Leave this instant.'

I left without a moment's delay. But where would I go? Anywhere but here. I would never step back inside Ramlochan Babu's house. I asked a passerby for help and he directed me towards a grocery store.

'Ask any grocer on the road. If you pay him, he will give

you food and a place to stay.'

Finding a grocery store was not difficult. I stayed there for a couple of days but soon enough realized, that I could no longer afford it. The thought of running out of money kept me awake at night. So early morning, on the third day, I paid the grocer his dues, packed my bundle of belongings, and left.

After walking for a while, I came across a colossal house. I thought, maybe the owner wouldn't be like Ramlochan Babu. Emboldened by the idea, I climbed its large steps and met the householder, who was sitting and chatting in his large drawing room with another man. They looked like dear friends.

The owner turned to look the moment I stood near the doorway. 'Who are you?'

'I am a traveller in trouble,' I answered.

'Then you must be hungry,' the other man remarked.

I did not reply, but the man continued. He pointed towards the north, shook his head from side to side, and said rudely, 'There's a hotel right there, you see... a hotel. The chef there is an excellent cook. Fresh food is prepared every day. You only need to pay five rupees.'

His words disappointed me. I looked at them with hopeless eyes. The owner of the house grew furious at this interchange.

'You may not be able to feed an individual in your home, but you need not come over to my house and dictate what I can or cannot do. Don't come visiting me again,' he retorted at the top of his voice.

Needless to say, my fondness, affection, admiration, reverence—every emotion that arises from love and respect increased by leaps and bounds towards the householder.

'If you deem it fit, you may stay here. I will arrange for your food and stay,' he said.

'But I do not want to stay for free. I can work for you... any work. It would be very kind if you give me some food in

Is It Easy to Become Rich? 133

exchange for my services.'

'Excellent! Can you write in English?'

'Little, very little as I have not studied far.'

'How far have you studied?'

I answered him

'That's okay. That will do.'

I stayed back at Babu's house. My work entailed making copies of various letters and other documents and keeping them securely. While working, I would often think about my home. I had undergone so much pain in an attempt to become a borolok, but as I could see, I was still so far from becoming one. Is it true at all then? Do you really become wealthy upon leaving your home? But you must be needing something else too, which I felt, I did not have.

Gradually my longing for home increased. A time came when I decided I must go back. With the little money I had left, I could not travel by steamer. I decided to join a group of pilgrims. For this, I had to travel to Boi..., a holy town not very far from Dhu... where I was staying. If I could travel there, I might meet other travellers. I confided in Babu, bid him goodbye, and left for Boi... in search of fellow travellers.

It did not take long to reach Boi.... It was a beautiful place. The site of the pilgrimage was atop a small hill. Several flights of steps led to the hilltop, and it took a while to reach the summit. During the climb, I rested thrice and asked the first person I met, 'Where can pilgrims stay?' He said there was no adequate place for pilgrims to rest. Most people stayed in the houses of the pandas, the priests who performed religious ceremonies in the temple on the top of the hill. It did not take me long to find one. The very first panda I met took me to his home, almost dragging me by my hand.

Within a couple of days at the panda's residence, I realized how I had made another mistake. I had arrived at a time which was considered as 'off-season', and if I had to meet pilgrims, I would have to wait for another three months. Forget about staying for three months, an incident happened on the very third day which made me decide to leave at once

In the morning, the panda came and told me, 'You want to see something? Come!' I followed him to a large temple. Inside the temple was a cave, and inside the cave, was a waterfall.

'You will need to do a puja here,' the panda said pointing to the spot. Then he revealed how much the ceremony would cost. If I agreed to perform the puja, I would have no money to go home.

'I am just a kid. How can I do such a thing?'

My reply greatly angered the panda, and he refused to take me back to his home.

That was it. I left the place, but had only travelled a little distance from the temple when a group of small boys came running and surrounded me, shouting and asking for money, 'Paisa, paisa.' I refused, and they grew angry. They began to harass me; a few abused me, some pinched and scratched, and others pulled at my clothes. Another group threw stones at me from a distance. I had had enough. Furious, I picked up a small stick lying nearby and began chasing the boys. They disappeared within seconds. I attempted to calm myself and started to run downhill. Alas, I was barefoot! My shoes had fallen off somewhere. The horror of my experiences in the mountains sent a shudder down my spine. I remembered having a pair of flip-flops in my bundle. I took them out and continued on my way.

With every step downhill, the pangs of hunger grew more intense. I knew if I had to reach the nearest grocery store to eat, I had to at least walk for three hours. That seemed impossible in the tremendous heat. Completely exhausted, I felt like lying down to rest under a very tall tree that came my way, but my tremendous thirst and hunger forced me to trudge ahead.

Drowning in worry, I stopped at the nearest house and decided to go inside.

Inside I found two young boys chatting with each other. I asked them for some food and their reply immediately showed me that they misunderstood me.

'Are you a Bengali?' one of them asked. 'Who are you? You must be a thief, we will not give you anything.'

'I am from a respectable Brahmin family. I am not a thief.'

'Go away from here. Crip crip, dash, dash!'

They pretended to converse in English to scare me away, but in reality, the words meant nothing.

I was in no mood for a joke but laughed in spite of my exhaustion. I too mumbled a few English words. I was too young to form a proper sentence in English, but it was enough to prove my point.

'What did you say?' the boys asked.

'That was English—Ram is ill. I will not let him run in the sun.'

But the boys continued to act, constructing more and more nonsensical sentences in their make-believe English. 'All Bengalis are thieves. Shoo, away from here.'

'Do you go to school?' I asked them.

Now, the boys sat up straight, but to frighten me they said, 'Our teacher reads very big, fat books.'

'I am not very far off from your teacher. See this,' and I took out an English book from my bundle, *Lamb's Tales*.

Seeing the book, the boys fell silent. The older of the two went inside, scratching his head as if in doubt. I began chatting with the younger one and found they were brothers. Their father had passed away, and they lived in the big house with their mother, several servants, and attendants. Needless to say, after the little chat, my stay at their residence was duly arranged.

They gave me a small room to stay. When I arrived, everyone

had already finished their lunch. So they arranged for fresh food for me. One of the attendants told me to take a bath. I went to a nearby pond where I quickly washed myself. When I returned, I saw the older boy waiting in my small room with a plate of rice and a few sweetmeats. The rice looked strange, as the raw rice was dipped in hot water to fatten and cook it. But I had seen some other people have the same kind of rice in that region. So, I was familiar with it. I sat down to eat.

Just as I began to eat, I felt the boy wanted to tell me something. Suddenly, he put his arms around me and embraced me, took my hands in his, and pleaded, 'My mother has scolded me. She said you are a Brahmin and would curse me as I have treated you wrongly.'

'I am not angry at you at all. I would pray that you have a good and blessed life.' It took a long time to console him.

Finally, he was convinced 'Well then, let me go and inform my mother.'

I bid goodbye to the two boys and started off from their home just when dusk was creeping in. That night, I stayed at a grocer's shop. The next couple of days went like that. I would walk the whole day and approach a grocer for lunch and dinner and then sleep in his house. The problem arose on the third day when I could not find a shopkeeper who would give me food and a place to sleep. I had to find another house and approach its owner. He did not refuse a meal and a stay for the night, but after dinner, pointed to the area where all the dirty kitchen utensils were kept, and sternly instructed me, 'Before you leave tomorrow morning, wash all of them. You are a Bengali. We will not touch your utensils.'

Washing all the utensils of the household after dinner only because I had partaken a single meal was too much for me. 'I did not touch any of those, but only ate from this plate and a bowl,' I said, pointing to the plate I was eating from and the bowl which had my dal. The man of the house relented. He showed me the closest pond near the house. I walked to it and spent the next half an hour rinsing and cleaning my dishes. Then I fell into a deep slumber from the exhaustion.

Next morning, I was awakened by the owner. The sun was already up, and I picked up my bundle and asked for directions to Fa.... It was not far off, and the man of the house told me to follow a single, straight road.

After walking a distance, I reached an open field where there was an inn for travellers. I met someone who offered to take me on his horse.

'Come with me,' he said. 'I was looking for a fellow traveller.'

'Why would you need a fellow traveller?'

'You don't know these parts. They'll eat you alive if you travel alone.'

His words frightened me. Travelling with a companion did give me a sense of relief. The road was very narrow, and the open field was so vast that one could not see its borders. It was an endless stretch, interspersed with clumps of poppy shrubs here and there. There were no animals in sight, only a particular kind of bird, slightly bigger than a sparrow, hopped around from one bush to another. It was green with a thin beak, and a very unique tail—long and slim, with a needle-like protrusion that extended till its very tip. A very restless bird, it chirped the same song: 'Tiririn tiririn tiririn' as it leapt along. My companion remarked in jest, 'That bird must've stolen a needle from its in-laws. So, it was punished this way.' With no other animals in sight, I keenly observed the bird as we continued on our journey.

Around four in the afternoon, we reached an inn. My companion said, 'We will spend the night here.'

'It is only four. Why must we stop so soon?' I asked, amused at his suggestion.

'If we travel now, it will be dark soon and we will be still in the middle of these fields. We'll be hunted by tigers.'

I had no desire to be hunted by tigers. So it was settled that we would rest at the inn. That night, I heard a lot of strange sounds from all around. I was told, those are noises of elephants. We were lucky that none of them decided to pay us a visit.

The next morning, we met a mahout, riding atop an elephant and on his way to Fa... I told him I would pay four annas if he took me along with him When we reached Fa... I refrained from paying a visit to Kalidash Babu. I spent the night at another grocer's and left early the next day.

Many small incidents took place along the way, and I would specifically speak about one. One afternoon, as I was walking, I found myself amidst a vast field. There was not a soul in sight. Soon, I found a thin strip of a road with stretches of cogon grass, a type of wild reed, interspersed with a few tall trees on both sides. I kept walking. But as dusk grew nearer, everything changed. By night, I had reached a jungle. It was fearsome and I began to run. The road became narrower. Trees brushed against me. My heart raced as I quickened my pace and just then, I felt as if someone touched my back. I jumped and turned around to see a tall man. He looked like a local resident from the mountains.

'Where are you off to? No fear of life?' he questioned. He had a thick accent.

The man signalled me to follow him, and I accepted his instructions without a question. Within seconds he was running, swiftly making his way through the tall cogon grass. I ran after him in a state of frenzy.

'Come fast or you'll die,' he kept calling out to me.

I don't know for how long we continued the mad rush. Finally, we reached the banks of a very large river, where a few others just like the man I was following, sat in a circle. They motioned me to join them till a boat arrived. The men removed titbits from their respective bundles and began eating.

The man who had brought me along with him, let me call him a Pahari since he was from the mountains, had a few oranges and he offered me some. I ate and immediately felt drowsy. I covered my head and neck with my shawl and was preparing to sleep when suddenly all the men started to shout, 'Don't sleep, you'll be eaten alive.'

I needed their shouting to keep me awake as I was almost numb with exhaustion. That night, their loud voices saved me. I understood it all when I heard the loud growling of tigers after dusk from the surrounding jungles. The terrific cacophony of wild animals grew louder as the night darkened and this continued throughout the night. I will never forget that night of terror. The boatman was on the other side of the river, waiting for passengers to arrive and fill his boat so he could set sail and reach our side. So the only option was to wait for him and spend the night in fear.

Three days later, I reached the market closest to my home. The first thing I did was eat a hearty meal of curd, flattened rice, and sweetmeats. The food immediately eased my hunger and extreme exhaustion. I reached home around two in the afternoon. There was no one in the living room at the front of the house. Suddenly, a chill took over me, and I began to shiver. I dragged myself to my room, wrapped my body in layers of thick, handwoven quilts which I could find nearby and slumped down on my bed. I had a very high fever.

Thus ended my dreams of becoming a borolok through easy means.

HOW DO YOU REALLY BECOME A RICH MAN?

BOROLOK KISHEY HOI?

While I was finishing the story on 'Shohojey Ki Borolok Howa Jai?', we wanted to also mention exactly what happened to Girish later in his life. But sadly, his life turned out to be so miserable that the thought of penning it down greatly upset me. However, it is important to say here that he never succeeded in becoming a borolok. He lived a life of great misery and nearly destroyed his own life.

Everything that I have mentioned about Girish is true. In fact, because they are true, they are even more serious. If we follow his path and emulate what he did to gather riches, soon there will come a day when there will be others who will write stories about us as a warning…just like how we are telling Girish's story. It is important to be forewarned than to suffer later on.

Indeed, it is not easy to become a borolok. One cannot become rich simply by wishing. If that were the case, I would have seen many others achieve such a feat. You see, doesn't everyone wish to be one? Including you and me? Alas till today, I remain a small fry. Just wishing is not enough, you need something more.

You see, Girish had wished enough, and he even tried as much as he could. But why was he not successful? For to become a rich man, one needs to know exactly what to do. If you do not know what is to be done, you will forever be an imbecile like Ramkanta. Let me tell you about this Ramkanta fellow. He was a bad student, always at the bottom of the class. He never aspired to improve. His teacher in his pathshala would often rebuke him, 'I have no hope for you. To improve, you need to burn the midnight oil. You need to work hard, in spite of all odds.' One day, while returning home from school, Ramkanta bought two seers of oil. He dipped some cloth in it and set the cloth on fire. Then he fashioned a swing out of a piece of rope and sat swinging from the roof of his house. Unfortunately, the rope snapped, and Ramkanta fell right into the fire. You can imagine how badly burnt he was. My goodness! He was bedridden for two weeks, and all the while, he kept thinking how wrong his Master Moshai was. The very day he joined the school, he had a heated argument with his Master Moshai. You see, both Ramkanta and Girish made the same mistakes. If we do not succeed in our endeavours to gather riches, it is because of our own faults.

So if you still desire to be a rich man (for I would laugh if you say that you do not), then carefully listen to me, and I will tell you how to become one, then you can return to your respective work and duties with a balanced state of mind. You will have to struggle and for that you need endurance. You would also have to sacrifice many comforts in life, face hardships, and let go of many things. In fact, even after going through all of these challenges, the lack of common sense can make people unsuccessful. I don't know if you will be successful, but I wish well for all of you. But you must remember to do all that I mentioned and put in your level best.

I have been repeating the term 'borolok' so many times, but does everyone understand what I mean? There was once a man talking about the expenses he had to incur for his son's wedding.

'I spent lakhs for my boy's marriage.'

Someone asked him, 'When you mention lakhs, can you tell me the exact figure?'

'Why? That's easy,' the man replied immediately. A lakh rupees means two twenty and one ten.'

The man's lowly behaviour and incompetence in understanding the value of money was a perfect example of what we call a 'rogue'. Hear my advice. If you cannot be wealthy, that's fine. But do not become a rogue.

If you are very good at something, that's when you become a rich man, a real borolok. Let's take the examples of Vidyasagar, Maharshi Debendranath Thakur, Dr Mahendralal Sarkar, and Lord Ripon. They are not known for the same reasons, but if you look carefully, they are revered for their work. We think of them as wealthy men. But if you come across an infamous thief or a dacoit, you wouldn't call them wealthy no matter how well-known they are!

Now here's another thing to think about. We do not refer to Vidyasagar as a borolok simply for his sea of knowledge. Nor do we refer to Mahendra Babu as one because he sits all day, engrossed in his science experiments. No, that is not the case. In fact, we do not even know if Debendranath Thakur or Lord Ripon were well-versed in a particular subject. Surendra Babu has a school and he teaches there, but he is not known as wealthy simply for that. One earns respect and love from the people for the work that they do for others. To be a borolok, one has to be a bhadrolok, a good man. While it can be rather difficult to be a borolok it is quite easy to be good. That is the first thing one should aspire for. Even if one possesses a crore of rupees, he cannot be called wealthy simply because of that. But if he has earned all his money through hard work and honest means, that is when he becomes a truly wealthy man. If we see him help his country prosper by judiciously utilizing his riches, then of course, he is both a wealthy man and a good man. Being borolok is good, and being a good man is important, but it is indeed very respectable to be a good borolok.

THE MONKEY PRINCE

BANOR RAJPUTRA

There was once a king, the raja, who had seven queens, the ranis, but no heir to the royal throne. It would cause him great sadness, and he would sulk all day, visit the court, but hardly speak a word.

One day, a sage came to visit the raja in his court. The sage saw his forlorn face and asked, 'Raja, I can see that there is something deeply troubling you. What is the matter?'

'How do I explain it to you, O great sage?' he answered. 'I have everything in the world—a kingdom, money, and loving subjects—but there is no heir to take my place. Who will look after all of this after I am gone?'

'Oh! So that's what's bothering you. Do not worry. Tomorrow, you must wake up early and immediately set to travel to the north. After a while, you will reach a forest. There, at the border of the jungle, you will find a mango tree. Pluck seven mangoes, and bring them home. Pound them to a paste, feed it to your seven wives, and very soon, you will be blessed with seven sons. However, I must warn you. While returning with the mangoes, do not look back at all.' The sage left with these words of caution.

The rest of the day went well; shortly it was nighttime, and soon dawn arrived. The raja got up quickly, got dressed, and started off for the forest in the north. After travelling for a while, the raja saw the mango tree and seven ripe mangoes on its branches. He was amazed. He had visited the forest numerous times before during his hunts, but had never noticed this tree. Remembering the sage's directives, he fetched seven fruits and headed home. Just as he started off, the raja heard a voice calling out from behind.

O Raja, return for a few more
mangoes to take with you for sure.

The raja had completely forgotten the sage's warning. Hearing the sudden voice, he turned around to see who was speaking. Immediately, the mangoes jumped out of his hand. They flew off and once again latched themselves to the branches of the mango tree. One more time, the raja climbed the tree and plucked them. This time, he remembered the sage's wise words and he refrained from looking back. However, the voices continued and having failed to illicit a response from him, they had begun to hurl accusations: 'Stop, thief!' But nothing could stop the raja. He sped off on his horse, straight for his palace.

Upon his return, the raja called for one of his ranis and handed over all the mangoes. She pounded all of them into a paste and called out to all the other ranis. Everyone came, except the youngest, Chhoto Rani. In her absence, the mango paste was distributed amongst all the six ranis and they finished every bit of it. After they were done eating, Chhoto Rani's maid quietly collected the scattered pieces of mango peels, cleaned and washed them, and then mashed them into a paste. Then she took it to her mistress and said, 'Dear, do have this medicine. It will do you good.' Chhoto Rani was an obedient woman and consumed the paste without any further questions.

Soon, all the six queens were blessed with bonny babies—six beautiful boys. The king was ecstatic. Celebrations were organized with several musicians and a lot of merrymaking across the kingdom. Even Chhoto Rani was blessed with a boy. Alas, he was a banor—a monkey! Furious, the raja banished the unfortunate Chhoto Rani from his kingdom. But his subjects took pity on the poor queen and built her a thatched hut on the outskirts. They requested her to stay there with her son, Banor Rajputra, the monkey prince.

The Monkey Prince

Time passed.

Chhoto Rani continued to live in the thatched hut and Banor Rajputra began to grow. He would speak like a human and was extremely bright. He never needed to be taught or trained. He spent his time galloping from one tree to another in search of fruits. If he liked any particular fruit, he would bring them home for his mother. No one did mind Banor Rajputra visiting their orchard. On the other hand, they would often be glad to show him the juiciest fruits in the tree. His sharp intelligence left everyone amused.

In the meanwhile, the king's six other sons grew envious of Banor Rajputra. If ever he wanted to join them in a game, they would immediately beat and shoo him away.

One day, Banor Rajputra saw a tutor arriving at the palace to teach his stepbrothers. They opened various books to learn from. Banor Rajputra too wanted to learn. He went straight to his mother and said, 'Ma, I want to study. Do get me a few books.'

'Dear, how will you read?' Chhoto Rani answered with tears

in her eyes. 'You are just a monkey.'

'I promise you, Ma. I will learn to read and write. Get me a few books, and you will see it for yourself.'

Now, because the monkey was very intelligent, he would finish every book in a matter of days. In two years, he had grown to be quite a scholar. During the same time, the six other children in the palace had merely finished a few. They would often be scolded by their teacher.

Upon hearing the scholarly achievements of his banished son, the raja wondered, 'Is it so? Is the monkey truly that clever? I have to see that by myself. Do fetch him.'

Banor Rajputra feared nobody, not even the raja. Upon hearing he had been summoned, he immediately arrived at the court. The raja was so impressed upon conversing with Banor Rajputra that he repented his cruel decision of banishing his youngest wife. Chhoto Rani was called back by the king, who built her a new palace where she could stay with their son. Soon, people began to call the new palace the 'House of the Banor'. But these developments did not go down well with the other princes. Their jealousy grew by leaps and bounds with each passing day.

Over time, the young princes grew up to become handsome lads. Everyone instructed the raja, 'They are fine young men now. You should get them married.'

'Let them travel and see the world. Then they should find a suitable girl on their own,' was the Raja's answer.

'Well! That sounds fine,' everyone agreed

Regally dressed, riding the finest steeds, and provided with adequate money, the six princes set off to see the world.

Banor Rajputra too desired to travel. He went and told his mother, 'Ma, I too would like to go.'

'Dear, why would you want to travel? Which rajkanya or princess would marry you? And to tell you the truth, I cannot stay away from you for so long.'

'I promise to return very soon,' Banor Rajputra pleaded. 'I beg of you, please let me go.'

What more could Chhoto Rani do or say? She permitted her son to travel and go see the world.

In the meantime, the six princes had travelled far and reached a dense forest. They decided to rest a while and sat talking when all of a sudden, Banor Rajputra sprang out of a bush and exclaimed, 'Brothers, I too have come. Take me along with you all.'

The group was furious. 'Is it so! How dare you think such a thing? Each one of us is on our way to marrying a rajkanya and you think that you too can do the same? Wait, we will teach you a lesson,' and they ganged up to beat the poor Banor Rajputra and then left the forest after tying him to the trunk of a tree.

Now in that forest, lived a band of dacoits. They spotted the regally dressed princes, carrying treasure and money along with them, and immediately surrounded the group. Scared to death, the princes forgot to reach out for their scabbards to attack the men with their swords. The dacoits looted everything: money, horses, even clothes. Then they tied up the princes and took them along with them.

Just as the dacoits were returning, they spotted a monkey, half-beaten and tied up to a tree. Thinking he was someone's pet, they untied him and took him along with them. Pretending to be very happy at being rescued, Banor Rajputra began to prance around and waited for an opportune moment to help the rest.

The dacoits' den was in the same forest. Exhausted after returning home, they had a quick dinner, loosely tied up the monkey and went off to bed, leaving the six princes in a corner, tied up tightly. When everyone was fast asleep and snoring in their beds, Banor Rajputra undid the loose knots of his rope, slowly crept, and set his stepbrothers free. This time, the six boys were too ashamed to leave Banor Rajputra behind. They gathered their belongings and quietly escaped the den. The slumbering dacoits got to know nothing.

The princes rode off as fast as they could. Soon, it was dawn and they realized they had arrived in a wonderful kingdom ruled by a powerful monarch. One could see his palace in the distance, standing like a white mountain.

The six princes went strutting through the palace's main gate. Upon sighting their regal attires and the majestic accessories adorning their horses, the guards stood aside in admiration, saluting rather demurely. Banor Rajputra however did not go through the gates. He knew that if he even tried to pass by the guards, he would be arrested. But he had thought of a plan. He went close to the banks of the pond behind the palace and lay down to rest.

Coincidently, the raja of that kingdom had seven ranis too. Six of them were self-centred and egotistic. But the youngest, the kingdom's Chhoto Rani, was a kind-hearted woman. She was as beautiful as a fairy, and it was rather unfortunate that the six older ranis ganged up against her and were so successful in mongering lies that the ruler had banished his youngest queen from the palace. Just like Banor Rajputra's mother, she too resided in a mud hut next to the pond behind the palace and he sat resting next to this very same pond. The raja never enquired after his wife who lived away from the palace. Many years ago, a daughter was born to each queen and the princesses grew up to resemble their respective mothers, both in manner and in nature. So Chhoto Rani's daughter grew up to be exactly like her mother: benevolent, humble, and beautiful. As expected, the other ranis were envious and even spread malicious thoughts in the mind of the raja about his youngest daughter, telling him she was unintelligent, ugly, hunchbacked, and walked with a pronounced limp.

Now, when Banor Rajputra was resting next to Chhoto Rani's hut, the six older rajkanyas arrived with their small metal water-pots to have a bath in the pond. So did the youngest daughter with her little pot. But while walking back with the pot full of water, some accidentally spilled out and fell on Banor Rajputra. The six vicious half-sisters wasted no time in making a mockery out of the situation. They immediately began to shout:

'Oh my! Oh my! Do come and see,

The daughter of Chhoto Rani just married a monkey.'

Their malicious mothers came running too and joined in the fun. They chimed in the same nasty manner: 'Oh indeed, it is true. The youngest princess has married a monkey.'

No time was lost in conveying the false news to the raja, who heard it along with all his attendants, while they were at court. The youngest princess is now married to a monkey? Everyone was shocked.

Poor Chhoto Rani was heartbroken. She hugged her dear daughter, slumped down on the floor of her little mud hut, and cried her heart out. Banor Rajputra saw this and came to the door of the hut. He stood there with folded hands and said, 'Dear mother, do not cry thus. Whatever happens, happens for the good. Believe me, this too, will turn out well for you.'

Chhoto Rani was amazed to see the monkey speak like a human. She wiped her tears and felt better. So Banor Rajputra took residence at a tree near Chhoto Rani's hut and began tending to all the queen's needs all day long. When Chhoto Rani heard that the monkey was a prince, her admiration for the animal grew several folds. She felt there couldn't be a human who was more kind-hearted and cleverer than Banor Rajputra.

In the meantime, the six princes had met the king in his court. Upon hearing their father's name and getting to know that the six princes were in search of suitable brides, the raja was delighted. He remarked happily:

'Bah! You all are my dear friend's sons. I am happy to know you are out searching for suitable brides. I will marry my six daughters to the six of you.'

It was at that moment that news arrived in the Raja's court about the youngest daughter marrying a monkey. The princes immediately understood that it was their brother. Jealousy returned. How did Banor Rajputra manage to marry a princess even before they did, and to top it all, everyone said that she looked like a fairy and was more beautiful than the Raja's six elder daughters. Their envy knew no bounds.

But soon, the six princes were married to the Raja's daughters. With much aplomb and accompanied by many musicians, they boarded a specially constructed ship known as a Mayurpankhi, its mast elaborately built to resemble the head of a peacock. And then they set sail for their home. Banor Rajputra and his beautiful wife followed the ship in a small boat of their own. At once, the scheming princes began to hatch a plan that would prevent both of them from reaching the kingdom. Nasty as they were, they continued their usual interactions with their stepbrother throughout the day, but were careful that he received no inkling of his impending doom. At night, when the boat was nearing its destination and Banor Rajputra was asleep, they tied his hands and legs and threw him off his little boat. Fortunately, his wife had seen all of this happen and had thrown a pillow for him to float with. Somehow, he swam ashore and got saved.

Next morning, the ship reached the bank near the palace. The king came out happily to welcome his sons and daughters-in-law into his palace.

'But where is Banor Rajputra?' he asked his sons.

'He is no more. He has drowned,' they said.

Unknown to the princes, Banor Rajputra had followed them all the way from the banks. As they were speaking to the prince, he was hiding behind a nearby tree. And the second he heard his brothers declare him dead, he leapt out from behind the tree and came in front of the king.

Performing the most gracious namaskar, he said, 'Father, I haven't drowned. They had tied my hands and feet and had thrown me off my boat. I swam ashore with much difficulty.'

As the six princes stood in guilty silence, the king thundered, 'Is that so? This is unbelievable. I don't want to see your faces henceforth. You all must leave my kingdom at once. All of you are banished.'

So, the king drove out his cruel sons and brought home the youngest and his wife with much affection. Chhoto Rani, who was long awaiting the return of her dear son, was overwhelmed when she saw Banor Rajputra and his bonny bride.

Thus, they started living happily ever after. Soon, the young bride noticed that her husband remained a monkey only during the daytime. Every night, he would shed his skin and would step out as a handsome prince. The young bride informed her mother-in-law, who in turn went and told the king.

Amused at the discovery, he summoned the prince's wife

and instructed, 'Dear daughter-in-law, do one thing. Tonight, when he takes off his monkey skin and sets it aside, I want you to burn it.'

A massive fire was lit in the room beside Banor Rajputra's bedchamber. He knew nothing of the plan. But once he had gone to bed, keeping his monkey skin aside, his wife immediately threw it in the fire. The next morning, the handsome prince went in search of his skin, but couldn't find it anywhere. It was an uneasy feeling to be noticed without his usual garb of a monkey. But that was it—he could never become a monkey again.

Word spread throughout the kingdom about the handsome prince soon. People from all over came dancing in joy to meet him. Oh! How thrilled they were, it was such a wonderful time for merriment. Everyone was happy.

THE ELABORATE MEAL

PAKA PHAWLAR

In a certain village lived a Brahmin priest, Bamun Pandit, who was very fond of the delicious phawlar. A typical phawlar spread is quite uncomplicated and consists mainly of fruits and other simple items, but a more elaborate phawlar consists of luchi fried in ghee, sweetmeats, fruits, flattened rice, curd, and many other delectable items. Because it is an expensive spread, this is referred to as 'paka phawlar', denoting something which is 'ripe' or bountiful and well-made. Because Bamun Pandit was always on the lookout to enjoy a lavish spread, everyone called him Phawlarey Bamun. Unfortunately, he was always disappointed at the many invitations that would come his way as most were from very poor people who could offer nothing more than a simple meal of curd and dry, flattened rice. Bamun Pandit was never happy with these simple meals and always craved for more. Thus, one day, when he heard about a paka phawlar, he realized that it is far more delicious than the plain meals which he is generally served. So when the next invitation came his way, he stated 'You have to serve me a paka phawlar.'

The man who came to invite was rather poor. How would he arrange an elaborate and expensive paka phawlar?

'O Bamun, only the emperor and the rich can serve a paka phawlar. How can a simple person like me even think about such a luxury?' he beseeched.

'Well then,' Phawlarey Bamun replied. 'I will have my paka phawlar at the king's palace then.'

He then set off for the palace, asking for directions every step of the way. Finally, a stranger pointed to a large house in the distance and said, 'You see that? That is a paka bari, a house made of bricks. That is the raja's palace.'

Now Bamun knew as much about a paka bari as he did about a paka phawlar. He had seen neither in his life. In his village, everyone resided in mud huts with thatched roofs of dry grass. Nobody had a paka bari made of bricks, except the raja.

Misunderstanding the whole thing Bamun felt great pangs of hunger the moment his eyes fell on the palace, 'Aha! A paka bari indeed! And why not? He is the raja; he can definitely make one. God knows, how much rice, kheer, cottage cheese, and sugar went into its construction.' Foolishly, Bamun rushed to bite off a corner of the Raja's palace. Immediately, he withdrew his teeth with a loud, 'Yak thuuuu!'

Then he sat down thinking, 'Goodness, that's why everyone speaks of a paka phawlar. It must be something truly mighty. Oh ho! Now I understand. It must be like a coconut; the soft flesh is hidden inside.'

Happy with his epiphany, he began to bite harder. Instantly, the brick caused his teeth to break. Even then, Bamun remained determined. He refused to give in, biting harder until pieces of the cement and brick began to break off. All this while, he was thinking, 'I'm almost there. Anytime now I'll taste the juicy interior of the paka phawlar.'

Suddenly, a guard with a large turban came rushing out. 'Oh my, Bamun Moshai. What are you doing? You are eating Our Majesty's edifice. Come with me,' and the guard took him to the raja.

Upon hearing the guard's account, the raja asked 'What happened Bamun Moshai? What were you doing there?'

'Your Majesty!' Bamun complained, quite irritated at being disturbed in his endeavour. 'I was about to enjoy a paka phawlar and had just about broken the tough outer layer, when this guard ruined it all and brought me here.'

The king burst out laughing. He well understood how 'clever' the priest really was, but couldn't help but like the simplicity of his thoughts. He instructed his attendants to provide Phawlarey Bamun with an ample amount of flour, ghee, and sweetmeats. Bamun gladly blessed the Raja, took all the ingredients, and returned home. While leaving, he left with a note saying he would return to bless the king once again after he had consumed the paka phawlar in his home.

Early next morning, just as the Raja had arrived in his court, he saw Phawlarey Bamun. 'So Bamun Moshai how was your meal yesterday? Did you enjoy the paka phawlar?' he asked.

'It was wonderful, Your Majesty,' Bamun replied. 'I had a great meal. How can a paka phawlar be bad? At first, the powder was difficult to swallow and was choking me. So, I mixed it with some water. Even then I could finish only half of it and puked it all up.'

Now, the poor Bamun did not know what to do with all the ingredients given by the raja. From the flour, one needs to prepare luchi and then deep fry them in the ghee. Poor Bamun had mixed all the dry ingredients and tried to swallow it as a whole. When he realized that the mixture was too hard to consume, he added water to it. He did enjoy the strange concoction, but his stomach could not take it any more and he puked it out.

The raja figured that the only way the poor Bamun could enjoy a paka phawlar was if he was served readymade luchi as he seemed to have never eaten any. So, he summoned a cook from the royal kitchen and instructed him, 'Take flour and ghee from my larder and prepare luchi at your residence and serve the Bamun. Make sure he enjoys a hearty meal.'

Showing him the direction of his house, the chef told Phawlarey Bamun, 'I will finish cooking by evening. You then come and have your paka phawlar. I will not be at home, my son will be there. He will serve you.'

Bamun happily agreed and returned home and patiently waited for evening.

Preparations were in full swing at the cook's house. He cooked lots of luchi, curries, and sweetmeats. Before returning to his duty at the royal kitchen, he left instructions for his son on how to host Phawlarey Bamun: 'When the man arrives in the evening, do feed him well and see that he has a hearty meal.'

'You don't worry Father,' his son said, 'I will feed him with utmost care.'

Now, in reality, the cook's son was a nasty fellow who had a terrible group of friends, including one who was a thief! He called this thief home and cunningly, left only four pieces of luchi and a little curry for Phawlarey Bamun's meal in the evening. Then he put away the rest of the food, including all the sweetmeats.

When Phawlarey Bamun arrived he was served the little food that the shrewd boy had kept aside. Phawlarey Bamun, who had never eaten a luchi in his life, that too one cooked by a royal chef, was in awe of the delicious meal. However, his hunger persisted and he left the cook's home, grumbling to himself: 'Aha! I wish he had served me a little more.'

On the way, he met Bhandari, who was in charge of the royal larder. That same morning, Bhandari had measured copious amounts of ingredients for the Bamun's meal and handed them over to the cook. When he heard Phawlarey Bamun mumbling, he asked, 'What happened, Bamun Moshai? What is it that you are mumbling to yourself?'

Bamun replied, 'I am disappointed with the paka phawlar. May God grant the raja a long life. May he live forever since he blessed me with such a delectable meal. If only they had just served me a little more....'

'How many pieces of luchi did they serve you?' Bhandari questioned a little amazed.

The Elaborate Meal   157

'They had served me four paka phawlar,' by which he meant four pieces of luchi.

Bhandari understood everything. He knew the cook's son well. 'What? How can that be? I had packed two seers of flour. How could the cook make only four pieces of luchi with so much flour?'

Phawlarey Bamun replied 'Yes, it was only four, but they were excellent.'

'You don't understand, a lot more than that four can be prepared from so much flour I know the cook's son. He's quite the character, and I feel that he has hidden the rest of the food for himself in the attic of their hut. Phawlarey Bamun, you must follow my instructions. Return immediately, and this time, go directly to the attic. You will find the rest of the food hidden there.'

'Is that so? God bless you,' the simpleton Phawlarey Bamun replied and left for the cook's place, abusing the boy the whole way, 'that shameless, monkey, devil, rogue....'

In the meantime, the cook's son had gone to his friend's house, the thief, to invite him, 'Brother, I have prepared a delicious meal and kept it in the attic. You head to my home, and I will join you there shortly. First, I have to pick up something from the market.' The thief reached the cook's hut and climbed into the attic. But just as he was about to open the lid of the vessel where his friend had stored the food, Phawlarey Bamun arrived. As instructed by Bhandari, he went straight to the attic in search of the food.

The thief was in trouble. Where would he hide as there was no way he could escape? He saw a wooden pillar in the attic and tried to conceal himself behind it as much as possible. Phawlarey Bamun was engrossed in finding the vessel of luchi and curry and did not sense the presence of a second person in the attic. He sat down to finish his sumptuous meal of luchi, curries and sweetmeats. He ate to his heart's content, so much so that there was no space even for a digestive pill.

Now, what followed was a hilarious turn of events. The cook's wicked boy had just returned home, and at the same time, so did his father! The cook had returned to fetch his skimmer ladle.

'Father, why you are home now?' the boy asked, surprised to see his father home at that time. On most days, he would only return late into the night.

'I came back for the skimmer ladle.'

Right then, Phawlarey Bamun had finished his meal and was so full that he was unable to move. Thirsty and immobile, he sat in one spot and croaked for water, barely able to form sentences: 'Water, water.'

Upon hearing the faint croaking, the cook was perplexed. 'What was that?' he asked his son.

The boy knew he was in grave trouble. He thought the strange sound was this friend, choking on a dry sweet. But he knew far too well, his father would beat him black and blue if he discovered what he had done and how he had invited a thief to eat the food prepared for Phawlarey Bamun. Thus, he lied,

'Father, I think it is a ghost. What else will make such horrid sounds in the attic?'

His son's answer frightened the chef. What was even more troubling was that the ghost in their attic was asking for water. The cook was in two minds: whether or not to serve water to the ghost. Though it is indeed dangerous to offer water to a ghost, there were also chances of him getting angry if he remained thirsty for long. But the cook saw his son was more than eager to take water to the ghost in the attic.

'No! Don't go. He might break your neck,' the cook said. He stopped his son from climbing into the attic but then remembered that he had left a few coconuts up there. He called out to the ghost, 'There are coconuts in the attic. Crack them open against the wooden pillar inside the attic and drink its water.'

Phawlarey Bamun located the coconuts. One was lying right next to where he was squatting. He picked it up and threw it, aiming for the wooden pillar. Alas, he missed it badly and it went straight and hit the thief's forehead. Oh, what a shot that was! The thief jumped out from his spot behind the pillar, screaming in pain and clutching his burning forehead.

A commotion ensued. At the sight of the wailing thief, Phawlarey Bamun began to yell as well. All that screaming alerted the neighbours and they came rushing to see what the matter was. After that, it did not take others long to understand what had happened. The thief was arrested, and the royal cook beat his mischievous son black and blue, with the skimmer ladle.

DUKHIRAM, A SAD MAN

DUKHIRAM

Dukhiram belonged to a very poor family, and had a far better name than this. Unfortunately, I have forgotten that.

Dukhiram lost his parents when he was around two years old. Unfortunately, apart from his parents, Dukhiram had no one else to call his own in the whole world other than Keshto, who was his maternal uncle. However, Dukhiram knew nothing about him and neither did Keshto ever think of enquiring about his nephew. So, poor Dukhiram was brought up by the people in his village. And thus, this unfortunate name.

Life is hard when you are poor. Forget about receiving a formal education, it is often difficult to procure two square meals a day. Dukhiram too faced a similar fate. He grew up flipping through old and torn pages of discarded textbooks and doing odd jobs for the villagers. And then one day, he discovered that he had an uncle named Keshto. He decided to go in search of him.

Dukhiram managed to locate Keshto's house with much difficulty, but Keshto did not seem very happy upon seeing him. He begrudgingly welcomed him, 'So you are Dukhiram. But dear, you do not know how many difficulties you will face here? We can barely manage to eat once in two months. We ate yesterday, and the next meal will be after two months.'

'That's fine, uncle,' Dukhiram answered. 'Do not worry. I will eat whenever you eat.'

That was it. Keshto could not say anything further.

At his uncle's house, apart from Keshto, lived his cousin, Hori. Dukhiram decided to stay back and began addressing Hori as 'dada' or elder brother.

Dukhiram, a Sad Man

That day, both Keshto and Hori did not eat the whole day. So, Dukhiram too remained hungry; it did not bother him much as he was accustomed to going hungry for days at a stretch. Towards the evening, Dukhiram told Keshto, 'Uncle, I am very sleepy. I would like to sleep now.' Upon hearing these words, Keshto rather happily spread out a mat for his nephew. Dukhiram lay there, feigning sleep. Shortly, Keshto and Hori joined him on the mat and pretended to snore. In reality, none of the three were sleeping. Keshto kept waiting for Dukhiram to drift off, while Dukhiram kept thinking about his uncle's next move.

Soon, Dukhiram heard Hori snoring—dada was finally asleep. Right then, Dukhiram began to hear a series of peculiar sounds. First, he heard a *khhawchhmawchh* from a corner of the room. He understood his uncle was up. Then came the sound of a pot being washed in the kitchen, followed by the *phuu phuu* of someone igniting the clay oven. He got up silently, went outside the kitchen, and peeped in through a small hole in the wall. He saw his uncle was preparing rice pudding, payesh!

Dukhiram went back to bed and soon got up again to peep through the opening in the wall. This continued for a while until Keshto had finished cooking. Finally, when Dukhiram realized that the payesh was done, he went back inside, laid down on the mat, and then pretended to wake up in fright. Keshto heard the loud noise and came rushing from the kitchen to ask, 'What was it, Dukhiram? What happened?'

'Mama, you were doing something in the other room and I saw a man peeping through a hole in the wall,' Dukhiram answered.

Of course, Dhukhiram was referring to himself, but Keshto thought there actually was a thief. So he picked up a stick and ran out to the small jungle behind the house to drive away the thief.

As his uncle rushed out, Dukhiram woke up Hori and said,

'Dada, wake up. Quick. Mama has rushed out with a stick.'

Hori thought that if his father had stepped out with a walking stick, he must be travelling quite a distance, probably to his sister's home, three miles way. Probably his sister was sick and his father had thus gone to enquire about her. So even Hori left in a hurry. Soon Keshto returned, unable to trace the thief, but badly bruised by poison ivy. His body was itching all over.

When he couldn't find his son, Keshto enquired, 'Where did Hori go?'

'Uncle, right after you left, the thief who was peeping through the hole, woke up Dada, spoke to him, and Dada rushed out with him.'

Now Keshto thought Hori had left to play cards with one of the rotten kids in the neighbourhood. He left in a frenzy with the stick still in his hand, aching and itching all over from the bruises of the ivy. He looked for the boys all over the neighbourhood, adamant to punish them severely.

This was the time Dukhiram was waiting for. He knew both his uncle and cousin would be away for a while. He tiptoed to the kitchen, brought down the pot of payesh from the oven, and sat down to eat. His uncle was a good cook and Dukhiram was very hungry. He finished every last drop. What a meal that was! Then Dukhiram tiptoed back to his mat and went back to sleep.

In the meanwhile, Hori had reached his sister's home. He was surprised to find her in fine health, but his sister forbade him from returning at night. In the time being, Keshto had spent hours searching for his son. Not being able to trace him anywhere in the village he was furious and his anger was exacerbated by the increasing pain inflicted by the poison ivy. It was early morning when Hori returned to find his father livid with anger and ache. He received a few good whacks of the stick.

Later, when Keshto entered his kitchen and saw the empty pot and missing payesh, he understood what had transpired.

That day, when Dukhiram woke up, he said nothing but kept smiling to himself, looking slyly at his uncle.

The very next day, Keshto left with Hori to complain to the king, who summoned Dukhiram and asked, 'Tell me why did you do all this? Why did you steal their food and cause trouble by lying?'

Dukhiram pleaded with folded palms, 'Spare me, Your Majesty. My uncle and cousin had told me that they eat only once in two months and that they had eaten the day before yesterday. Then why did he decide to prepare payesh last night? I think they should answer my question. And you speak about "troubling" them? I did not lie and said nothing but the truth. I said a thief was peeping into the kitchen because I was indeed peeping. I just did not mention my name. I did not lie. Now, if they are troubled with that, what can I do? It is not my fault.'

The raja had a hearty laugh at this and dismissed the case.

Realizing that Dukhiram was a smart young man, the raja appointed him to his court. Within a short span, he received many promotions and finally became a junior minister. All because of his diligence and hard work. Observing Dukhiram's fame and assiduous nature everyone assumed that as soon as there would be a vacancy for the post of a senior minister, Dukhiram would be promoted immediately. However, trouble had already started brewing. Dukhiram's rising popularity did not go down well with the senior minister who was not a nice person. He grew extremely envious of Dukhiram and mostly began spending his time planning to put him in trouble.

Now, the senior minister had a friend who was a merchant. The merchant owned a beautiful, winged horse, a Pokkhiraj, that could speak like a human, foretell the future, and fly across large distances which would otherwise take a month to cover. The greedy minister had his eyes set on the creature, but the merchant refused to part with it.

Once, the merchant travelled to a faraway land from where he had brought a unique and magical mango seed. If one would take it out of its box and bury it in soil, the seed would immediately germinate and grow into a fruit-bearing tree. The mangoes from the magical tree would be ripe enough to be consumed right away, and when one was done eating, then one could dig out the seed and put it back into its box.

'I don't believe this,' the minister contested.

'Fine, let us bet. What happens if I am right?'

'Then tomorrow you come to my house and whatever you touch first, will be yours to take. Now, what if I am correct?'

'Well then, you come to my house tomorrow and whatever you touch first, will be yours to take,' the merchant repeated.

As decided, the minister was invited over for lunch to test the merchant's magical mango seed. Unfortunately, the seed had been boiled before that and nothing happened. You can understand how the merchant must have felt. It was almost like the sky had fallen on his head. He realized that now it would be impossible to protect his Pokkhiraj; the minister was sure to take it away.

After a long deliberation, the merchant approached Dukhiram and narrated everything with tears in his eyes.

Upon hearing his predicament, the junior minister gave a piece of sound advice. The merchant listened carefully, went home, tightly shut the gates of his stable with a rope, and went off to sleep rather peacefully.

Early next morning, the senior minister arrived early at the merchant's house and called out to him, 'My dear friend, where are you?'

Hearing the senior minister's loud voice, the merchant hurriedly came downstairs and welcomed him in.

'Friend, what about your promise?' the senior minister went straight to the point.

'I am ready,' the merchant said. 'You may take whatever you touch first.'

The scheming minister immediately left for the stable. The door was tied up with a thick rope. He pulled hard and untied the knot in no time at all.

Immediately, the merchant arrived and remarked, 'What is this, brother? A distinguished person such as yourself wants a mere length of rope? I would have been happier if you would have taken something more worthwhile.'

The senior minister stood with a gaping mouth. Goodness! He never imagined that he would be fooled so easily. He could barely utter a word, stammered for a while, and ultimately started for home, completely shocked.

On his way back, the senior minister realized that the merchant must have been helped by the junior minister. Later, when he heard that the merchant had visited Dukhiram the night before, he became doubly sure. 'All of this was the work of that clever junior minister,' thought the senior minister.

The next afternoon, as the raja slept, the senior minister went and stood right before the king's bed, his palms folded. When the raja awoke, he was very surprised to see him in his room. 'What happened senior minister?' the raja asked.

The senior minister started off in a forlorn tone, 'With due respect, Your Highness, the merchant Sulakshan has a Pokkhiraaj horse, but you have none.'

'Is that so? Well, I want that horse then.'

The minister, pretending to be on the verge of tears, answered in a rather nasal voice, 'I always want the best for you, but the junior minister always seems to create trouble and get in the way.'

'How is that?' the raja asked. He was now curious.

'When I had gone to fetch the horse for you, I discovered that Sulakshan had been advised by the junior minister to not part with it.'

You see, in those days, rajas were rather whimsical in temperament. They would turn joyous but could also become furious over something rather inconsequential. If they would be happy with someone, the person would be rewarded with half of the land in the kingdom. But if they would be upset with a subject, the poor man or woman would be immediately sentenced to the gallows.

So far, since the raja had been happy with Dukhiram, he had been appointed as his junior minister. But after listening to the account of the senior minister, the raja grew furious. He issued orders for Dukhiram's arrest.

Poor Dukhiram. He was sleeping peacefully, when suddenly, the raja's men arrived, tied up his hands and feet, and took him to the court.

Dukhiram was served a severe sentence. He was instructed to be put inside a large cloth sack, which would be tightly tied with a rope that had a large stone tied at its loose end, and then thrown off a cliff and into the sea. The king personally ensured that the mouth was firmly secured and ordered four of the royal executioners to fling the cloth sack containing Dukhiram into the water.

Now everyone adored Dukhiram; they were devastated when he was subjected to such a harsh sentence. So, on the way to the cliff, the executioners decided to disobey the king's orders and leave the sack somewhere in the depths of the jungle.

'Dear sir, what else can we give you?' one of the executioner's told Dukhiram as they prepared to leave him behind in the jungle. 'Here, take this axe and a piece of cloth. You can chop wood and sell timber to survive. But never return to the kingdom or the king will not spare your life.'

Time passed, and Dukhiram began a life as a woodcutter.

He would cut and sell wood, living off whatever money

he made from that. He had discarded his royal robes and only wore the cloth which was given to him by the executioner. He barely bathed, and his skin had turned brown with grime and dust. Unable to arrange for enough food, he had lost so much weight that he resembled a bag of bones. It was difficult for anyone to recognize him. Dukhiram was scarcely able to live a half-decent life.

One day, while Dukhiram was on his way to chop wood, he noticed an old woman asleep under a tree near a waterfall. Suddenly, he spotted a poisonous snake slowly and silently creeping towards the sleeping figure. Dukhiram jumped up and killed the snake in one stroke of his axe, hacked it into many pieces and threw those into the waterfall. The minute the pieces of flesh touched the water, it began to boil. This woke the old woman up. She kept looking at the boiling water for some time and then asked Dukhiram, 'Who are you dear?'

'I am Dukhiram.'

'Son, what do you want?'

'I want nothing. But you are an elderly person. What are you doing inside such a dense jungle? There are several wild animals all around. You must leave immediately.'

'Child, you have saved my life. I will not leave without rewarding you.'

But Dukhiram refused to take anything and resumed his journey. The old lady too walked away, but she whispered something that Dukhiram couldn't hear as he was well out of earshot already. She said, 'You did not ask for anything, but I will nevertheless reward you. Whatever you wish, will come true.'

Meanwhile, Dukhiram had other thoughts. He was quite troubled. It was getting late, and he had yet to chop wood, after which he had to sell that in the market, earn a little money, buy things, go home, cook a meal, and then finally get to eat. Occupied with thoughts of all that needed to be done, he didn't notice a stub of a tree trunk on his way. He stumbled and fell on a small tree nearby.

Exhausted and angry, Dukhiram shouted, 'Go to hell. I wish there were no trees in this region.'

In an instant, the jungle vanished and all that remained was a wide, bare, open field. Goodness! Now from where will Dukhiram get wood and how will he eat?

The poor man stood flummoxed and could not understand what had just happened. Perplexed, he decided to keep walking but soon felt extremely hungry and thirsty. The heat was bearing down on him. Adding to his woes was Dukhiram's heavy axe, which was given to him by the executioners. On that particular sweltering and tiring day, the single axe seemed to weigh like ten. Dukhiram simply could not carry it any more.

'I wish this axe had legs and would have followed me easily,' he said.

Just as Dukhiram had uttered those words, the axe sprouted two thin, spidery legs and began walking ahead of Dukhiram. By then, Dukhiram thought he was going insane. He kept following the axe, all the while, still trying to make sense of the strange incidents.

After a short while, Dukhiram arrived at a kingdom's bazaar. Dukhiram knew the place well. This was the same kingdom where he once lived and served as a junior minister in the court. The loyal axe was still walking ahead of him, strutting with a confidence that made it look like there was nothing unusual about a walking axe and that he had been walking forever.

Now, imagine the scene: an axe, walking with great strides, in front of your eyes. What will you do? And then imagine such an axe entering a busy bazaar. How would the people react?

At the very entrance of the bazaar, there was the milkman's shop where the gatekeeper of a rich house had come to fetch some ghee. He had just handed over the bowl to the shopkeeper and had sat down to relax and have a puff of his tobacco when he saw the axe walking up. It came and stood right in front of the guard. And what did he do?

He shrieked, 'Hai Baap!', jumped up high and landed right in the milkman's lap. The milkman, who was also surprised, immediately pushed off the guard from his lap, ran indoors leaving his shop, and shut the door of his house with a bang.

The poor guard meanwhile, had fallen right into a large pot of butter kept in front of the milkman's shut door. After a while, when both the guard and the milkman realized that the axe was quite harmless and was not causing any harm, they came out of their hiding and began to follow the axe, which, by then was headed towards other shops.

That day, the bazaar was nearly shut down as everyone lined up behind the axe. People followed him in amazement, including servants who had come to buy things for their masters, the shopkeepers selling their wares, the police, and the royal guards. Everyone followed the axe. Slowly, the crowd grew so large that it looked like the entire kingdom had gathered behind the strange object. And in that swarm of people was Keshto and Hori, Dukhiram's uncle and cousin.

Keshto and Hori, engrossed in the axe's antics, had failed to notice Dukhiram. But the moment they saw him, they were petrified. They rushed to the scheming senior minister and complained, 'Sir, Dukhey has returned.'

Now the minister rushed to the raja and said, 'Your Majesty, an axe can never walk. I believe Dukhiram must have performed some kind of black magic and has returned to the kingdom with evil intentions.'

'Right you are,' the king agreed. 'I will send ten sepoys right away. Arrest him, and bring him here.'

Ten sepoys as massive as monsters, went off to fetch Dukhiram.

Meanwhile, the crowd in the bazaar had tied a rope around Dukhiram's axe and wanted to drag it to show the raja. But that was not meant to be. The axe was so strong that even though the entire bazaar pulled at the rope, the tool didn't budge. Instead, the axe dragged everyone for about half a mile in the other direction.

When all this was underway at the bazaar, the raja's sepoys came to arrest Dukhiram. They were accompanied by the senior minister who stood instructing, 'Tie him up tightly.'

Unfortunate Dukhiram. What else can he do? He stood there and surrendered to fate. Then he addressed the senior minister, 'It is easy to torture others. I would like to see you suffer this way, and I hope you are tied up just as I am. Then you will understand the pain.'

The moment he said those words, the sepoys left Dukhiram, grabbed the senior minister, flung him on the road and began tying him up vigorously. The minister was completely taken by surprise, then grew livid at the sepoys, but did the muscular sepoys listen to him? No! In fact, they did not even bother to listen to what he was saying. The helpless minister turned red in the face; he didn't know what else to say but kept wailing and shouting in vain. His eyes grew large and wide, as if ready to pop out of their sockets. The veins around his neck began to throb, and he started to fume at the mouth but the sepoys did not stop. When they had finished, they inspected closely the minister to ensure that the punishment meted out to him was exactly what Dukhiram had suffered. Finally, when the sepoys were satisfied, they flung both arrested men across their shoulders and started off for the royal court. All the while, an amused crowd was watching all that transpired before their eyes and as the sepoys left, they too followed them to the palace. There at the palace, Dukhiram lay on the floor, all tied up, surrounded by many royal sepoys and the senior minister too lay next to him.

Poor Dukhiram! How do I even begin to describe how sad he felt.

He had forgotten all his pains; only hunger and thirst remained. The raja and his men were at lunch. So Dukhiram lay there in the room, imagining all the scrumptious food they would be eating. 'Aha,' he sighed, 'I wish I could enjoy such a royal feast.'

Right then, the raja had sat down to eat. Utensils made of gold had been placed in front of him, with several dishes neatly arranged all around. The delectable aroma was pure bliss. But just as the raja had washed his hands, the elaborate arrangement disappeared. *Poof!* The senior minister, now released from the bondage of the ropes, had also sat down to eat. All his food disappeared too.

On the other hand, as Dukhiram lay lamenting, several plates of the most delectable food appeared in front of him. By then, he was quite used to the unusual situations occurring around him that day. So instead of being surprised, all he said was, 'Oh no! I am all tied up. I wish I was free,' and immediately the ropes fell apart. Dukhiram jumped up and sat down to gorge on the large selection of luchi, pulao, payesh, goatmeat curry, many sweetmeats made from cottage cheese, and many other wonderful items of food. He gobbled all of it at once.

The guards who stood surrounding Dukhiram were the first to be alert. 'Arey! Catch him or else he will run away,' they said. But soon, they too calmed down. One of them remarked, 'Where will he run? There are so many of us surrounding him. The poor man has finally found some food. Let him eat.' Even the sepoys agreed.

Mighty pleased at the kindness of the sepoys, Dukhiram blessed them, 'Good men, I wish you all to be a raja.'

In an instant, thousands of grand thrones appeared out of thin air. The sepoys' uniforms got replaced with regal robes, and they took their place on a throne each. Each sepoy had become a king, just as Dukhiram had wished.

The raja returned to his court to see thousands of kings sitting next to his throne. He was terrified. When the sepoy-kings ordered the release of Dukhiram, what else could he have done? It is not simple to deny the requests of so many rulers. Dukhiram was released without further ado.

In the meantime, the senior minister had arrived. Stupefied at the presence of so many kings, he pleaded to each one of them, pointing to Dukhiram, 'Sirs, please reconsider. This is a cunning man. If he is released, he may cause great harm to others.'

At his request, one of the rajas proclaimed aloud, 'We cannot understand what kind of harm this man is capable of causing. He has been very kind to us all. I was your sweeper once. But he has made me a ruler. Today, because of him, you are bowing before me.'

The minister looked closer and realized that yes indeed, the man who was talking to him was a sweeper once. He looked around and saw each new king had once been an ordinary man in the kingdom—perhaps a guard, a shopkeeper, a stableboy, a police constable, and even a beggar.

Troubled at the tense turn of events, the king and the minister instructed that the court be summoned and the culprit captured. But who would do it? Everyone was a king now. Finally, the minister decided to take up the task himself.

Upon hearing the minister's decision, Dukhiram said, 'Sir, why take all the trouble? You want to arrest me? Here I am. But if you serve me a death sentence, who will execute me? You see, the executioner is a raja now. For now, only you or the king can be an executioner.'

In the blink of an eye, their royal robes disappeared, and the king and the minister stood wearing loincloths, holding an axe each. Their palms were folded in anticipation of further orders.

But who was to give the orders?

By now, Dukhiram had realized the trick. Whatever he was wishing for was being granted. He could have wished something nice for himself, but instead, he said, 'Your Majesty, I have worked for you. I will not betray you. You look after your kingdom, and allow me to leave.'

The king was ashamed. He had no words to say. Finally, he said, 'You could have taken away my kingdom and gotten me killed. But you did none of that. You are indeed a generous soul. I would like to gift you half of my kingdom and get you married to my daughter. You stay here and rule like a Raja.'

So Dukhiram got married to the princess and peacefully ruled his kingdom.

And the rest of them?

Well, since Dukhiram did not say anything about the evil minister, he remained an executioner. And the other thousand kings? They began to run into several problems since there were so many of them and no kingdom to rule. Moreover, blinded by their newfound position as kings, they refused to work. All of them started to demand, 'I am a king now, why will I work?' This created further problems.

Ultimately, Dukhiram had to intervene. He said, 'My good men, all of you need not be a raja. You must return to your respective professions and do your work honestly. I wish for all of you to live in peace and happiness.'

THE STORY OF GRANDFATHER

THAKURDA

Once in a village somewhere, there lived an elderly Brahmin scholar. His name was Bhabanicharan Bhattacharya. He had struck up a great friendship with all the youngsters of his village. They would refer to him as grandfather, Thakurda. So the rest of the villagers also used to refer to him as Thakurda too.

Thakurda had a strange relationship with the village youngsters. He would spoil them silly, and they, in turn, adored him, but also loved to play pranks on him. Though Thakurda was quite a scholar, he had a deep-rooted fear of the police who were known as the Peyada. The very mention of one would send him into a frenzy. The children were well aware of his fear and would often use it to their advantage. At times, in the hopes of scaring Thakurda, they would dress like a Peyada in a red turban and a dhoti, carry a stick, and hide in the Chandimandap of Thakurda's house, where he would conduct religious ceremonies The children would then emulate the typical regional accent of a Peyada and call out loudly 'Bhawani Bhatchaj kaun hai (Who is Bhawani Bhatchaj)?'

This would put Thakurda in a frenzy. He would fumble at his desk, look around, and if he would catch a mere glimpse of the red turban, he would not stop to think whose head the turban sat on. He would dash indoors and only stop when he had reached the innermost chamber, where Didima, his wife, would be working. The kids would also joke that Thakurda had an obsessive disorder of taking a bath when he sighted a Peyada and ran inside, but I think that is exaggerated and that never really happened.

The Story of Grandfather

Thakurda had no inkling that these pranks were the actions of mischievous young minds. He had great affection for all of them. In his house, there was a berry tree. Every year, when its fruits would ripen, Thakurda would call each and every child of the village, make them stand in a line, and give a berry each. Not one child would be deprived of the treat. However, it was always one berry for each child, and nothing more than that. This calculation was very specific and everyone knew about it, but as Thakurda's berry tree bore the sweetest fruit in the region, the kids would desire more and they would always be saddened when he stopped at one. In fact, nobody could remember ever having tasted a second berry from his tree in one year. From where Thakurda sat in the Chandimandap, he could clearly see the tree. If he sensed anyone creeping slowly towards it, he would holler, 'Who goes there?' This shout was stern enough to make anyone flee immediately. In fact, it would be so loud that even two miles away, people could hear and remark, 'There he goes. That's Thakurda guarding his berry tree again.'

Once, the kids managed to make Thakurda part with some of his money for a quarter of a kilogram of sandesh, a sweetmeat made from cottage cheese. This happened because of a particular incident. One day, while Thakurda sat writing in his Sanskrit book, a large monkey kept as a pet at the neighbouring Bose residence, came romping in, picked up his thirty-five-year-old ornate hookah and went off skipping and hopping. Finally, the animal perched himself on the topmost branches of a tall tree. Thakurda realized what had happened only when he reached out to have a puff and saw the monkey on the tree with his hookah. Thakurda grew livid, threw a few pebbles, and hurled some abuses in Sanskrit. Nevertheless, the monkey refused to part with it. Instead, he made a few faces at Thakurda and jumped across the wall, disappearing into his neighbour's mango orchard.

If not for the children, it would have been difficult for Thakurda to ever retrieve that hookah. They had agreed to work only if they were rewarded with sweets. Soon they had managed to get the hookah, and the very next day, Thakurda fetched a quarter of a kilogram of sandesh from Bechu Moira's sweetshop. But the kids were not happy, screwed their noses, and complained, 'This is way too sweet', to which Thakurda had replied sarcastically, 'Oh is it? I did not know that all of you preferred bitter sandesh instead. I brought sandesh which is sweet to taste as I know that's how they are.'

In spite of all the affection the villagers had for Thakurda, he was known as quite a miser. Apart from the time when he bought sandesh for the kids, he had never bought anything for anyone. It was rumoured that he was so selfish that all his money was securely stored inside three large clay pitchers buried under his house somewhere. But from what Thakurda portrayed about himself, one would think that he struggled to afford even one square meal a day. One day, Didima had poured an extra dollop of ghee while cooking dal, and it was rumoured that Thakurda grew so angry at this wastefulness that he did not speak to her for two months straight.

Ever since Thakurda fed them the terribly sweet sandesh from Bechu Moira's shop, the children were furious. And why wouldn't they be? What an exhausting time they had while rescuing the hookah from the naughty monkey. Twenty kids toiled for three hours straight, climbing several trees, running across orchards, splashing through mud, getting stung at several places by nettles of poison ivy shrubs, and what did they get in return? A sandesh like that?

So the angry boys decided to hold a meeting to teach Thakurda a lesson. This was held in the potters' neighbourhood, where all the potters were hard at work preparing clay idols for the upcoming Durga Puja festival. Frequently, the kids would go over to see the potters at work. At the meeting, it was unanimously decided that the best punishment would be to make Thakurda part with a good portion of his wealth. But how does one do that? It is not easy to make a miser part with his money.

The boys thought hard and soon various ideas started to trickle in. One said, 'Let's cut down that berry tree', another quipped in, 'Let's hide the hookah'. But none of them seemed appealing enough. To top it all, they realized that they wouldn't result in Thakurda spending money. In fact, even if they did hide the hookah, sooner or later, they would have to return it. You see, in reality, the kids did adore him and although they sat scheming, they meant no real harm. They agreed that they needed to make Thakurda spend his wealth in such a manner that it should not cause him trouble.

The boys thought hard; the job was not easy at all. Finally, an old potter came up with an answer. The boys agreed readily and returned with a smile on their faces. They decided to execute the plan the very next day.

Early the next morning, like every day, Thakurda woke up before dawn. Following his daily schedule, he spent some time in bed, reciting shlokas in Sanskrit in his usual rhythmic manner. Then he left to bathe and finished his morning puja. Finally, as was the norm every day, he sat at the Chandimandap to begin writing at his books. It was still dark, and not even the early morning magpie had started chirping. Thakurda opened his books, and began reciting his customary verses in Sanskrit before beginning: 'Brahmamurarisgachhpurantakari'. Just then, he heard a voice from somewhere in the Chandimandap: 'Bhawani Bhatchaj gharmey hai (Is Bhawani Bhatchaj home)?'

That was it. Thakurda couldn't proceed any further. He left his desk for the day, finished his morning bath and other rituals in the small pond behind the house, and then spent the entire day enquiring after Didima's cooking in the kitchen. This went on till the afternoon. By then, Thakurda had come to notice that no Peyada had come calling for him after the morning's incident. He realized it was important to go and look into the matter, so he left for the Chandimandap and what a shock he had when he arrived.

Standing right in the centre of the Chandimandap was a marvellous idol of Goddess Durga. It was a beautiful statue whose presence illuminated the entire space. But despite its stunning appearance, Thakurda stood frozen in fear. He then slumped to the floor and sat with his head held in his hands.

Goodness, who can do such a thing? Having an idol of the goddess in the Chandimandap meant that one had to duly perform all religious ceremonies with great accuracy or else be cursed. And all the arrangements would mean spending at least three hundred rupees. 'Oh, what will I do now?' Thakurda lamented.

But while Thakurda may have been a miser, he was nevertheless a spiritual man and a great scholar. He was quick to realize that what needs to be done, has to be done. He had a sudden change of heart. The true worth of money would be in performing the rituals properly. Perhaps the gods wanted to teach him a lesson, and so the idol had landed at his doorstep. Finally, he decided to perform a Durga Puja every year.

While Thakurda sat squatting and thinking, the kids began to arrive at the spot, barely able to control their chuckles. The sequence of events had been their doing that had sent Thakurda dashing indoors early in the morning. Later, they had placed the idol in the Chandimandap. Seeing the chortling kids, Thakurda instantly understood who was behind the prank. But this time, instead of getting angry, he yielded to his young friends: 'Bless you all for teaching this old sinner a rightful lesson. However, what bothers me is that Durga Puja is a grand event, and I do not have anyone to help me. I don't know how to go about it.'

Thakurda's answer surprised the children who had come expecting him to chase them off in sheer annoyance. But this was a welcome change.

'Don't worry Thakurda,' they reassured him. 'We will organize everything. All you need to do is instruct and direct us.'

Thakurda smiled warmly. He was overwhelmed, and his eyes brimmed with tears. He patted the kids and pinched their cheeks. And this time, the sandesh which Thakurda gave them as a reward were quite good. No one scrunched their faces.

A PURANIC STORY FROM NORWAY

NORWAY DESHER PURAN

Just like the tales of many Gods and demons in the Puranas of our country, there are several stories in Norway and Sweden.

The Purana from Norway speaks about a time in the hoary past when there was no earth, sea, or air. There was only the 'All-Father'. Nobody created him and nobody could see him, yet everything took place according to his wishes. Before creation took place, it was empty and dark all around and within this existed a massive void called Ginnunga. Towards the north of this void stood the land of mists and in the middle of this, there was Hvergelmir, a fountain of boiling water. South of this deep, black void lay Muspelheim—the land of fire. A massive giant called Surtr stood guard at the entrance of this land with his flaming sword.

The void Ginnunga had a deep, cold centre. The boiling waters of Hvergelmir poured into this space, cooled down immediately, and then froze. But it could melt at the touch of Surtr's flaming sword. The tussle between fire and ice continued for long and from this was born a ferocious giant named Ymir and a gentle calf named Audumbla, who began to lick the salt from the dense, surrounding snow right after it was born. Audumble's licking cleared the snow and gradually revealed the god, Buri.

In due course, the demons were born from Ymir and the gods were born from Buri and they remained in a constant state of war from the moment they were born. The war continued through several thousands of years till one day when the gods slayed Ymir. Ymir's flowing blood created a colossal ocean and a great flood took place, drowning all the demons. Everyone perished, except Bergelmir and his wife. They rode a boat to the very end of the universe and built a house for themselves. The place came to be known as Jotunheim, in other words, Daityapuri, the land of giants. Gradually, within Jotunheim, the demon race started to grow once again. Soon, the war between the gods and the demons resumed.

On the other end, the gods were enjoying a sense of relief after slaying Ymir. They felt the need to change the morbid surroundings of the void including the mist, fire, and ice, and they decided to use Ymir's body to create shrubs and trees, rivers and lakes, mountains and hills. So they threw Ymir's massive body into the great big void and filled it up. Not only was the void filled up, but Ymir's body became the base for the creation of life. The sea had been created from Ymir's flowing blood, and now the gods created the earth out of Ymir's flesh. Thereafter, they created hills and mountains from Ymir's bones and teeth, shrubs and trees from the hairs of his body, the great sky from his skull, and clouds from his brains. Then several flickers of fire were brought in from the land of fire, where the giant Surtr lived, to create the sun, moon, and stars.

Soon, the gods discovered that Ymir's rotting flesh had started to house worms and insects. They wondered, 'What do we do with these?' and decided to make fairies, ghosts, and dwarfs. The fairies looked beautiful and resided in the space between the sky and the earth. They played around in the moonlight and rode on the backs of several butterflies. They made the flowers bloom and would help humans in various ways. The dwarves and the ghosts looked scary and were extremely mischievous. They stayed underground and knew the whereabouts of prized treasures, including gold and precious and semi-precious stones. They would creep out of their underground lairs at night, only to harm humans. They could never come out of their homes during the daytime, and if they even dared to venture out, they would be immediately turned to stone.

In the middle of all of these, the gods had arranged for their residence, known as Asgard, in other words, Swarg or heaven. The king of Asgard was the 'Father of All'—Odin, also known as Woden. It is assumed that the word 'Wednesday' comes from this word, Woden. From Odin was born all of mankind, and thus, he was referred to as the 'All-Father'.

Odin would sit in heaven along with his wife Frigga, and he looked after everything happening across heaven, earth, and hell. Nothing escaped his attention. He had only one eye, having donated the other to an elderly man, Mimir. This old man had a magical waterfall which had the power to grant all of the knowledge of the past, present, and future to anyone who drank from it. When Odin went to drink from the waterfall, Mimir stopped him and demanded, 'You will only be allowed to drink from the waterfall when you give me one of your eyes.' Odin had to pay the price. The old man took Odin's eye and kept it submerged in the waters of the waterfall. As the eye shone within the waters, Odin drank the water and acquired the famed all-powerful knowledge about everything. To commemorate the event, Odin took a branch from the banks of the waterfall and sculpted a special weapon out of it—a spear. It was a magical spear that stopped for none, and no one could defeat it.

Odin had a son named Tiu, and it is believed that the word 'Tuesday' is derived from this. He grew up to become the god of bravery and valour. Just like Odin's spear, Tiu had a magnificent weapon too—a sword. Everyone respected this sword, and it was placed with great reverence within the precincts of a temple. It was believed that those who possessed this mighty sword would be unbeatable at war. Alas, one day, this sword was stolen. It is often heard that many wars were fought with this sword and many battles were won, but it never returned to Tiu.

Odin had another son named Thor. It is believed that 'Thursday' is named after him. He was the greatest and the mightiest of all. He carried a hammer and even the mightiest of mountains crashed at the slightest touch of this sacrosanct weapon. There was a massive burning bridge—Bifrost (for all mortals, this is known as the rainbow.) The gods had to cross Bifrost to traverse between Midgard (earth) and Asgard. Every god could walk across Bifrost, except Thor, for it would crumble under his massive strength.

It is said that the name 'Friday', comes from the God of Beauty: Freya. Some say that this was Odin's queen, Frigga. She resided in Folkvangr, where she would receive half the souls who died in battle. Freya would visit the battlefields herself, along with her companions, the Valkyries. The souls would be overjoyed upon reaching Freya's court. There, in the court, there was a goat named Heidrun who could give endless quantities of sweet milk. Finally, there was the brilliant cook of the gods, Andhrimnir. He would slay and cook the sweet meat of the heavenly pig called Saehrimnir, every day. So, the supply of meat was endless too. You can imagine how the hungry brave hearts would eat to their heart's content. After every meal, Saehrimnir would be alive once again and romp around in his usual manner, snorting to glory.

THE GRANDMOTHER'S BRAVERY

THANDIDI'S BIKRAM

There was once a Thandidi, and of course, there was also a Thakurda, or how would we get a Thandidi? But people did not know Thakurda well. They only knew Thandidi. Thakurda's name was Ramkanai and people called him Kanai Ray. Some even said Ray Moshai.

Let me tell you about an episode that further goes to show how little people knew about Thakurda. Thandidi owned a dense bamboo forest, which had a cluster of excellent Burmese bamboo. Also known as polymorpha bamboo, these are thin and soft and can be easily fashioned into durable fishing rods. One day, some naughty boys stole a bamboo stem to make their own fishing equipment. They had just dragged it out on the road and were about to escape when Ray Moshai appeared before them. Immediately, they put their palms together and pleaded, 'We beg of you, please do not inform Thandidi.'

Thakurda was more than amazed. 'What is this? You are running away with my bamboo and telling me "Do not inform"?'

'We beg of you, please do not inform,' the boys begged to Thakurda.

Now Ray Moshai was really in a quandary. He asked the boys, 'What will you do with it?'

'We will make fishing rods out of the bamboo.'

'Very well then! Take it and be off.'

The boys ran off, still shouting, 'Do remember not to inform Thandidi.'

So, you see, most people had no idea about who Ray Moshai was; they didn't know that he was, in fact, Thakurda and related to Thandidi. Everyone thought the house belonged to Thandidi alone along with the adjoining bamboo thickets and the nearby jackfruit free, berry tree, and guava tree.

Thandidi did not have a son but had three daughters. The elder two were already married and the youngest was just about nine or ten. Thandidi was over forty, and she was quite brave. Though there was no other person in the house, she never needed an assistant. Whenever Thakurda would be away for a couple of days, she never asked for a guard or an old woman to keep her company or to spend the night with her. Thandidi never feared staying alone; she could easily manage everything on her own.

On one such night, when Thakurda was away and Thandidi was home alone with her youngest daughter something happened. Suddenly, the little girl said, 'Mother, I felt a hand.'

'Hush child. Don't utter a word,' Thandidi said for she had already realized that a thief had entered the house, and he was in the room. When she was sure that the man had left their room and proceeded to other parts of the house she slowly crept out of bed, fetched the pestle from the kitchen, and placed that at the sheendh, a gaping hole on the mud wall which the thief had dug to enter the house. Now most of you living in big cities wouldn't understand this. But in villages, most huts are made of mud. So a thief had to dig a hole with a thin, iron instrument that looked like a ladle or a crowbar. They call it a 'sheendh kathi'.

There is a popular rural saying, 'A thief and a blacksmith never meet each other.' Now, since the sheendh kathi is made of iron, so of course, it is the work of a blacksmith. But it sounds impossible that a thief would approach a blacksmith and say, 'Brother, would you make a sheendh kathi for me?' I don't think something like this can ever happen or else one would instantly find out about the thief's identity. Even if the blacksmith and the thief turned out to be dear friends, he would at some point speak about it to another friend, and if need be, even inform the police.

Then, how does a thief make a sheendh kathi? There's a story we often heard as kids. It seems, whenever a thief needs a sheendh kathi, he would take a piece of iron and fifty paisa and silently keep both at the doorstep of the blacksmith's workshop. It was placed in such a manner that when the blacksmith would open his shop the next morning, he would know what to do. The fifty paisa was the blacksmith's payment. He would take the articles, keep all other work on hold, mould the sheendh kathi and put it back in the same place outside his workshop before shutting it for the day. The thief would visit at night and collect his sheendh kathi.

Now, back to the story. Thandidi sat silently after placing the heavy pestle against the sheendh. Soon, the thief arrived, dragging a box, and immediately, Thandidi pounced on him and grabbed him tightly. The thief began to yell in a nasal voice, 'Do let me go please.'

'Tell me who you are or I will call the neighbours and they will drag you to the police station right away,' Thandidi demanded.

The thief knew Thandidi would never release him if he didn't reveal his name. 'It's me, Sheetol,' he confessed.

'You wretched person,' Thandidi fumed. 'Of all the places, you thought you would steal from my house. Go outside, you'll find a pitcher there. Take it and fetch water from the pond, come back, and then fill this sheendh you've made in the wall with a mixture of mud and cowdung. There's cow dung kept in the cow shed. Mix it with water, and after you are done closing the sheendh, apply another plaster of cow dung all over the spot to secure the area. If you don't do this, I will have to do all of this and it is too much work which I most certainly am not willing to do.'

Spring had arrived, but it was still very cold in the village, especially the water in the pond. But poor Sheetol had no respite. As instructed by Thandidi, he fetched the water, mixed it with cow dung and mud, and sat down to repair the hole he had made. It was only when he had finished the task that was he permitted to leave.

Now, all you clever kids must be thinking that Sheetol is indeed a foolish thief, for he could have easily escaped, along with the pitcher, when he was sent to the pond. But what would have happened then to him? I will surely tell you, but some other time.

GHYANGHASHUR, HALF-BIRD, HALF-BEAST

GHYANGHASHUR

Somewhere long ago there lived a king, and his daughter. Unfortunately, she had always been emaciated from her very childhood and the raja's efforts to employ the best of physicians had proved to be in vain. Nobody could find a solution that would improve the princess's health. She seemed to be getting thinner by the day. This made the king very unhappy, for all the wealth in the world couldn't make the princess well.

Time passed by. One day a sage came to meet the raja and said, 'Your Highness, the princess will recover if she eats a lemon.' But he left without telling the king where he would find the said fruit or whose garden should he take it from.

The sage's words put the king in a predicament. He sent his messengers throughout his kingdom and announced, 'I will give my daughter's hand in marriage to the person who gets that suitable lemon that will cure her. He will also inherit my kingdom.'

Now, there was a problem. No one in the entire kingdom had a lemon tree, except a poor farmer. He had procured it with much difficulty from Srihatta, the old name for the city of Sylhet in Bangladesh, and it so happened that year itself, the tree bore fruits for the very first time.

Goodness, what large lemons they were, each as smooth and round as a rasogolla and as large as a stone apple. Dear reader, this lemon was very different, and I am certain that you too have neither seen nor eaten such a fantastic fruit in your life. I too have never seen anything like that and would love to taste it.

Ghyanghashur, Half-bird, Half-beast

That poor farmer had three sons: Jodu, Goshtho, and Manik. When he heard the raja's announcement, he instructed his eldest Jodu to take twenty lemons to the raja, 'Quickly take these to the palace. If the princess gets well from eating any one of these, you'll have a princess as a bride.'

Jodu started off for the raja's home. On the way, he met a man, who was only one foot tall. 'What do you have in your wicker basket?' he asked.

'Frogs,' Jodu lied. 'Fine! So be it,' the one-foot-tall man answered.

The palace guards were elated to hear that Jodu had arrived with lemons. They welcomed him with great care and took him to the raja, who was equally delighted. He rushed to open the lid of the wicker basket. Alas, four frogs jumped out and landed on the raja's turban. All the lemons had morphed into frogs. And that was it. The ill-fated Jodu couldn't cure the princess or inherit the kingdom. In fact, he barely managed to escape the palace without too much thrashing from the guards.

After that, the farmer sent his second son Goshtho with another wicker basket of lemons. This time too, the one-foot-tall man appeared out of nowhere and asked Goshtho what was inside. Goshtho replied, 'The seeds of ribbed gourd.'

'Fine! So be it.'

At the palace gates, they retorted sceptically, 'Someone just like you had come the other day. He dirtied the raja's turban. We are not sure what you will do,' and refused to allow Goshtho inside. However, after much pleading, he was finally allowed to enter the premises. But dear readers, I believe you can imagine what happened inside and how many lemons Goshtho fed the princess. He too received a justified punishment.

Now, the youngest of the brothers, Manik, was considered a halfwit by all. So nobody thought about sending him to the palace with another wicker basket of lemons. But Manik kept nagging. He too wanted to go just like his elder brothers. Finally, the old farmer had to relent. So Manik set off for the palace with a wicker basket of lemons.

On the way, he too met the one-foot-tall man. Once again, he asked, 'What do you carry inside that basket?'

Manik replied, 'I have lemons inside my wicker basket. The princess will eat these and be cured of her illness.'

'Fine! So be it,' came the man's answer.

As you might have guessed, Manik had a tough time trying to enter the palace. Finally, after pleading and begging for long, the guards agreed, but with a note of caution: 'Be warned. You better not be carrying either frogs or ribbed gourd seeds or else, you will lose your life.'

But when Manik's wicker basket was inspected, they indeed found lemons. The raja was delighted and immediately took them to his daughter who was resting in the inner chamber. The raja left, but with a note for the attendant: 'Do come and inform me immediately if the medicine worked.'

The raja sat restless in his court waiting for an update. But instead of the attendant, the girl herself arrived. She had recovered from her illness the minute she put one lemon in her mouth.

The raja was ecstatic, but immediately remembered the promise he had made so publicly. Then it struck him, 'Goodness, what have I done? Now I have to get my beloved daughter married to a poor farmer's son. I have to think of a way to trick him.'

Poor Manik was feeling rather happy about the whole affair and was eagerly waiting for his bride to arrive. Suddenly, the raja arrived instead and told him, 'Son, you have indeed done a great job. But you see, it is not easy to marry a princess. You need to complete another job for me, then we will see what can be done. I want you to build me a vehicle which runs equally on land and water. You must do this, or there's really no hope for you.'

Manik left with an enthusiastic 'Yes Sir!' and reached home, where he narrated everything.

Everyone at home, who had always thought Manik to be quite a simpleton, was surprised to see that he had helped cure the princess's ailment. So they assumed that since the primary task was successfully completed, the boat could be prepared by anybody else and not necessarily by Manik.

So Jodu, the eldest son, was chosen for the task. He took an axe and set off for the forest. He found the finest timber that he could find and began the construction of the boat there itself. He was hard at work when suddenly the one-foot-tall man appeared again and enquired 'So Jodunath, what are you building? A tub? So be it,' and with these words, he disappeared.

After that, no matter how hard Jodu tried, each time the wooden planks would curve themselves to only create a cylindrical shape. None of them stood straight enough to be moulded into a boat. Furious, Jodu discarded the planks and started all over again, but every time, the wood would assume the shape of a tub. This continued until finally, he gave up by the evening and started for home. The four tubs he had built were quite sturdy and good-looking, and Jodu didn't have the heart to leave them in the forest. So he took them along with him.

When Jodu returned home unsuccessful, the middle brother Goshtho was called to prepare the boat. Once again, the one-foot-tall man appeared in the forest, asked Gostho what he was making and by evening the poor chap returned without a boat but with five fine-looking crowbars of excellent quality. You see, both brothers got what they told the petite man and thus however much they tried, they remained unsuccessful.

Finally, Manik went to try his luck. Because the elder brothers could not complete the task, no one stopped Manik. Once again, the one-foot-tall man appeared and asked Manik what he was doing, but instead of a lie, he got a rather innocent reply, 'I have to prepare a boat which runs equally well on land and water. I have to present this to the raja and only then he will give his daughter's hand in marriage.'

'Fine! So be it.'

Now Manik had just begun to chop the wood when he decided to rest for a while. And all of a sudden, the wood started to run. It had transformed into a sturdy boat, but one without a sail, oars, or a rope. Yet it didn't matter. Because this magnificent vehicle understood everything, knew where it had to go, and when to stop—all on its own. The inside was lined with a soft mattress that stretched from one corner to another and was wrapped in the finest fabric. There were cushions for a comfortable seating. The boat's exterior was wonderfully decorated with such gorgeous fixtures and accessories that I cannot even bring myself to describe them. I don't even know the names of such objects; perhaps they could only be found in the world of that one-foot-tall man.

When Manik's boat reached the raja, he was attending his court. The arrival surprised all, and they praised the bedecked boat. The amazed king, trying to conceal his surprise, said, 'No! This will not do, you have to pass another test. I need a handful of feathers from the tail of Ghyanghashur. I want to decorate my crown with those plumes. Now, if you can get those, I can assure you that I will allow you to marry my daughter.'

Manik left with a 'Yes Sir!' to fetch feathers from Ghyanghashur's tail.

Ghyanghashur looked odd and was half bird and half beast. He had a haughty temper, was extremely knowledgeable, and very wealthy. Everyone thought he was a demon. Ghyanghashur lived near the banks of a river called Ojana Nodi, in an unknown city made of gold, at a distance which took a month to traverse. However, such a journey was always dangerous as Ghyanghashur would gobble any man who dared to come his way.

So our guileless Manik started on his journey to meet Ghyanghashur and get a handful of feathers from his tail for the raja's crown. On the way, Manik asked directions from innumerable strangers. They instructed him and Manik followed them blindly. He would rest for the night at someone's house and resume his expedition in the morning again.

Everyone who provided Manik shelter for the night felt pity at the thought of him visiting Ghyanghashur and thus, would always treat him well. One night, he was welcomed by a rich man at his residence. After chatting for a while, the rich man asked, 'Son, you're going to Ghyanghashur's kingdom. I know he has a lot of knowledge about many things. I've lost the keys to my iron chest. It would be wonderful if Ghyangha could tell me its whereabouts. Do please ask him.'

'Okay sir, I will ask him,' Manik answered.

Another time, Manik was given shelter at the residence of another rich person whose daughter was terribly ill. Her parents were worried sick. She was growing thinner by the day, so after a warm welcome, the head of the family asked Manik, 'It would be immensely helpful if you could ask Ghyangha for a cure for her illness.' Manik assented.

A month passed, and finally, Manik reached the banks of Ojana Nodi. From there, he could see Ghyanghashur's golden palace on the other side of the river. Ojana Nodi did not have any boats. There was an old man who carried people to and fro on his shoulder. As the old man carried Manik across, he asked, 'Son, do ask Ghyangha when will I be freed from this pathetic condition? I am tired of ferrying people on my shoulders. This is all I have been doing since I was a child, and I have grown old doing the same job day in and day out.'

'Do not worry,' Manik said, 'I will definitely ask him about you.'

Manik soon reached Ghyanghashur's residence. He was not

at home, but his wife, Ghyenghi, was there. The minute she saw him, Ghyenghi cried out, 'Leave! Run immediately. Ghyangha will surely gobble you the minute he sees you.'

'But I just want a handful of Ghyanghashur's tail feathers. I cannot leave without those. I also need to know where the key to one man's iron chest is, how to cure the daughter's illness of another man, and how can the old man who helped me to cross the river, return home?'

'Instead of running to save your life, you're asking me for feathers from his tail and the answers to so many questions? Who are you?' Ghyenghi questioned.

'I am Manik. And if I do not take these feathers, the raja will not allow me to marry his daughter. I simply must take a handful of them.'

Ghyenghi took pity on Manik. 'Fine,' she agreed, 'do crouch and hide under this bed. If you're destined to have the feathers, you will definitely get them.' So he hid under Ghyanghashur's bed, who returned in the evening.

Ghyenghi fetched water to clean his feet and then served him food on a golden plate. Ghyanghashur was a hot-tempered creature. He sat down to eat and began to sniff all around, 'How come I smell a human? Give me one, I want to eat.'

Manik froze with fear. Even Ghyenghi was terribly scared. Her heart beat wildly. She quickly concocted a plan.

'Yes, a human did come to visit,' she explained. 'But the minute he heard about you, he fled.'

Her words momentarily calmed Ghyanghashur, and he continued with his meal.

Soon after, Ghyanghashur lay on the bed for his afternoon siesta. As he rested, his long tail rolled out from under his blanket and hung from one corner of the bed. It almost reached the floor; its tip had beautiful feathers. This was the opportune moment Manik had been waiting for. He grabbed a feather and snapped it off within seconds. But the slight pull awoke Ghyanghashur. He sat up and asked Ghyenghi, 'Who was it? Who pulled my tail? Uh ho, I smell a human again.'

'No, you're mistaken,' she intervened in order to pacify him. 'You've such beautiful long feathers and some of it must have gotten stuck at the corner of the bed. I did tell you that a human had come to visit. You're smelling the scent of the same man. He had a great many things to say. Some man had lost the keys to his iron chest....'

Even before Ghyenghi could finish, Ghyanghashur replied, 'Yes, yes that iron chest? I know where that key is. Their little toddler has pushed it through a small hole in their mattress.'

'And someone's daughter is terribly ill...' Ghyenghi continued.

'A kona byang (Asian common toad) which lives in a corner, kona, of her room, has taken her hair with it. This toad lives in a burrow in the corner of her room. One needs to fetch that toad and bring the hair back. That's how she will be cured,' Ghyanghashur revealed

Finally, Ghyenghi asked: 'What about the man who helps people across Ojana Nodi?'

Ghyanghashur replied irately, 'He's a fool. He needs to drop a man midstream. That's it. He will be free to return home. The person he would drop will continue to ferry people across the river, till the day he drops another individual in the same manner.'

Manik had heard everything. His job was done. Now all he had to do was wait till dawn when Ghyanghashur would leave his home. At daybreak, Ghyanghashur had his breakfast and set off. Manik too had a hearty meal served by Ghyenghi, who then bid him farewell.

While returning, Manik met that same old man near the river. 'Did you ask about me?' he asked Manik.

'Yes, and I will tell you all about it, but first, you must help me cross the river. I am in a hurry.'

The old man carried Manik to the other side after which he said, 'After this, when you carry someone, just drop the person mid-stream. That's it. You will be free forever.' The old man was overjoyed, 'I can't express how happy you have made me today. I feel like carrying you across a couple of times more.'

'No, that's not needed. You've done enough for me already. Anyways, I don't like riding on the shoulders of elderly people. I must hurry now to reach my home.' and Manik set off.

Within four days, Manik reached the house of the sick girl. Upon carefully listening to Manik, the master of the house immediately retrieved the hair from the kona byang's burrow, and within a moment, the girl was up and about. Everyone was delighted as she had been suffering for more than two years and had been completely confined to her bed. The family was so happy that they rewarded Manik with such copious amounts of wealth that it was difficult for ten horses to carry. Then came the man who had lost his key. When Manik explained what he had heard from Ghyanghashur, the delighted man gifted Manik more riches.

By the time, Manik reached the palace, he had accumulated a mound of treasure. He entered the palace and handed over the tail feathers of Ghyanghashur to the raja. The people of the kingdom were overwhelmed and praised Manik's perseverance. They felt that it was time for the raja to fulfil his promise to the boy. With no excuse left, the raja agreed to have his daughter marry Manik.

It was a brilliant celebration, and Manik had achieved such prosperity that it was enough to lead a luxurious and comfortable life. His meteoric success made the raja jealous. He thought, 'If one can acquire so much wealth just by visiting the kingdom of Ghyanghashur, I too will go there.'

And so the envious Raja left for Ghyanghashur's kingdom.

However, he never reached his destination. Midway through Ojana Nodi, the old man who ferried people on his shoulders dropped the raja into the water. At first, the raja found the old man's behaviour rather amusing. Slowly he turned livid and began to hurl abuses. Finally, he pleaded, but nothing helped. The old man had skipped over to the bank and headed straight for his home at top speed. In fact, he was in such a hurry that he forgot to inform the raja of how he could free himself from this eternal bondage. To date, it is believed that the king continues to ferry people on his shoulders across Ojana Nodi.

If any of my young reader friends here ever visits the kingdom of Ghyanghashur, do tell our king the trick to free himself. But a word of caution. You must tell him only when you have returned to the bank safely. Or you'll find yourself in deep, deep trouble.

THE 'INTELLIGENT' SERVANTS

BUDDHIMAN CHAKOR

A certain Babu had a very intelligent chakor, his servant. His name was Bhawjohari. One day Bhawjohari, while walking down the road, saw his master, whom he used to refer to as Babu hurrying towards him. He looked worried and said, 'Bhawjohari, we are in great trouble. Come quickly. Our house is on fire.' Bhawjohari replied calmly, 'Don't worry Babu, that's all a lie. How will our house catch fire? For I have the key to our house!'

Bhawjohari once went to the Kolu's shop to get one seer of oil. Kolu measured the amount and filled the can that Bhawjohari had brought along. All of a sudden, Bhawjohari remembered and asked Kolu, 'Wouldn't you give me a little extra?

'Of course,' Kolu said, 'but where will I give it?

Bhawjohari began to think, 'True, where can I carry the extra oil? And if I don't take it, Babu will think that I am a fool.' What to do? Then Bhawjohari had an idea. The base of the oil can that Bhawjohari was carrying had a smaller cup attached, which faced downwards. He immediately upturned his oilcan and held out the small cup. Kolu laughed and finally poured a little oil into the tiny cup, and Bhawjohari returned home happily.

Once, Bhawjohari and his Babu were crossing a river in a boat. It was a crowded one, and Bhawjohari thought it would be wise to reduce the burden on the boat, lest it upturns suddenly. They were carrying their belongings in a small bundle. Bhawjohari took the bundle and put it on his head.

'Bhawjohari, why are you unnecessarily carrying it like that? Sit comfortably. Put that down,' Babu said.

'Na Babu, the boat is full. If I put down the bundle, it will become overcrowded.'

One night, Bhawjohari realized that a thief had entered their home. Bhawjohari decided to nab him. So he disguised himself as a goat, put on a set of horns and a tail, went out into the open courtyard in the middle of the house, and stood hidden in one corner. He assumed that thief was bound to come in there and mistaking him for a real goat, would want to take him along. Then Bhawjohari would nab him. As the thief entered the various rooms of the house, Bhawjohari bleated... *myaaaa!* Finally, the thief entered the courtyard where he was hiding dressed as a goat. The man had brought out all the items he had stolen, spread out a rug, placed them, and tied everything neatly into a sack. Once again, Bhawjohari said, '*Myaaa!*' He grabbed the stolen goods, crossed the garbage dump at the back of the house, and ran as fast as he could. He was soon out of sight. Bhawjohari stood smiling though and felt he had had the last laugh as he thought 'What a stupid bloke that was indeed. He stepped over the garbage dump. Now, he has to have a bath after reaching home.'

Another person, Ramdhan was a simple man but was hot-headed. Once, he took up a job in a house owned by a band of thieves. One night, when all the thieves left to rob a home, they took Ramdhan along with them. Upon reaching, the thieves made Ramdhan sit inside a taro thicket and whispered, 'Sit here silently. We will rob the place and bring all the things here. You will help us in carrying them.'

'Okay,' Ramdhan assented.

So the thieves began to dig a sheendh in the wall. Now a sheendh is a hole dug by thieves on mud walls of houses for them to rob the place. As the thieves entered the house, Ramdhan waited in the taro thicket. The place was infested with mosquitoes that bit Ramdhan furiously. Initially, Ramdhan tried to bear the assault. Then he could no longer take it and started to slap here and there to kill the insects. Finally, when he had just had enough, he took a stick and began swaying it wildly, trampling the taro thicket all over. This created a din and awoke the members of the family who came rushing out. They caught hold of Ramdhun and asked, 'Who are you? Why are you creating such a ruckus at this time of the night?'

'It's me, Ramdhan.'

'What are you doing inside our taro thicket?' they enquired.

'Some people are trying to dig a sheendh on your wall even as we speak,' Ramdhun snapped at them.

You can imagine the commotion that ensued. That night, the thieves barely managed to escape. When they reached home and confronted Ramdhun, the servant replied rather calmly, 'What can I do? Those terrible mosquitoes made me furious.' The band of thieves let him off with a warning.

The next day too, when the thieves left to rob another house, they took Ramdhan along. This time he had decided that even if the mosquitoes killed him, he would not utter a word. But after the last incident, the thieves wanted to avoid all kinds of trouble. They decided to stay outside and send Ramdhan into the house. When they reached, the thieves managed to unlock the latch of the main door from the outside. Then instructed Ramdhan in a whisper, 'Now you enter and quietly bring all their belongings. Be careful. You should not make a single sound.' However, the hinges of the door were already rusty and when Ramdhan tried opening the door, they creaked...*kyanch*.

Startled, Ramdhan stopped.

He paused a while and tried again. *Kyanch!* It was heard again. Ramdhan couldn't stifle his groan. Within seconds, his temper rose. He became wild, took hold of the wooden door, and shouted at the top of his voice, '*Kyanch, kyanch, kyanch*!' You can guess what must have happened after that.

The 'Intelligent' Servants

All of these narratives are merely stories. Now, let me tell you a true incident about another servant. Let us call him Kenaram. Kenaram and his Babu were once inside a spacious boat, which had a small cottage built in its centre. One day, Kenaram sat atop the cottage on the boat, all dressed up and waiting for his Babu to arrive. They were about to leave to see a village play. Suddenly, Kenaram heard footsteps from inside the cottage. He thought his master must be ready to leave and that he should hurry. So Kenaram jumped from the top of the cottage, and can you guess where he landed? Right on his Babu's head.

When Babu had first employed Kenaram, his old servant had instructed him: 'When Babu returns from the office, serve him a nicely arranged betel leaf. Do this every day. Never forget. Never delay.' One day, it so happened that immediately after having returned from work, Babu urgently had to visit the bathroom. Not to miss out on his work and lest it gets delayed, Kenaram took the paan, went inside the lavatory, and said, 'Babu, here's your paan.'

BYACHARAM'S SERVANT KENARAM

BYACHARAM KENARAM

FIRST SCENE
(*Enter* Kenaram, *the servant, while repairing a torn garment.*)

Kena: There again, it tore off a little more. How can I repair a garment which tears at the slightest touch? A grand master, a monib I have. He has only given me this one garment all these years. It's been three years now; let's see how many more years I have to see this. I would have still understood if he had provided me with a square meal every day. And how does that go? In the morning, when monib has rice for his breakfast, I merely get to drink the rice water, and at night, he licks the clay pitcher clean, in which rice is prepared, while I only get to sniff it. And then he is hard of hearing. Just the other day, the landlord came asking for rent. He had said, 'Give me the rent; it is due for many months now.' My monib had replied, 'Oh really, we are invited to your house today? That's great.' The landlord had replied, 'This will simply not do; you haven't paid rent in months.' My monib retorted, 'Fine, I will bring my servant along with me as well.' The landlord finally gave up and left in a huff. If one wants to become a wealthy person, one has to behave like my monib. But I guess, from such a person, one will only learn the process of becoming rich, but will never get any help to become one. When he agreed to employ me, he had promised so many things. However, in the past three years, I have not been paid even once. Let me see if today I am paid my salary. If today he doesn't pay me, I will stop working here.

(*Exits*)
(*Enter* Kenaram's *master*, Byacharam Monib.)

Monib: That servant said so many things about his shirt. I heard everything. The scoundrel thought I was deaf. If he had ears like me, he would never have been able to stay in a job. He gets to eat from the work I do. I can hear everything: how many people are there inside a room, of which how many are sleeping, and how many are awake. I can hear every word from merely sitting and listening on the porch. I can distinctly hear how many cockroaches are scuttling within a chest. Bapu hey! I can hear it all. I can hear everything. It is important to hear, but it is even better to pretend not to hear. Now see, just the other day, that rogue landlord, was about to make me part with my money. There are so many advantages of pretending not to hear or see what happens. You don't need to pay the loan sharks, neither do you need to pay the rent, or pay the servant's salary.

(*Enter* Kenaram)

Kenaram (*in a high pitch tone*): Sir, you haven't paid me in three years. Pay my salary today, or else I will leave this job.

Monib: The postman? Letters? Show me.

Kenaram (*to himself*): Very difficult. But this time, I have written down everything. (Loudly, for all to hear.) A letter indeed. Here it is.

Monib (*reads the letter*): Monib Mahashay, you can't hear, but you can definitely read. Please pay me my three year's salary, and let me go. Regards, your servant, Shree Kenaram. True, I have to pay your salary. You see, when I had appointed you, we did not decide upon anything. Moreover, you have not been doing your work properly. So for the past three years, your salary only comes to three paisa. So, here it is. (*Gives three paisa and shoves him out of the room.*)

SECOND SCENE
(*Enter* Kenaram, *also referred to here as* Kena.)

Kena: I am indeed a rich man now. My earnings from the past three years will be lots of money, lots of money. One, two, three, four, five, six, seven, eight, nine, ten, eleven, twelve. (*Keeps the paisa in the pocket.*)

(*Doot, a messenger from heaven, appears in disguise.*)

Heavenly Doot: Oh brother, you're in a great mood.

Kena: Who is it? A small human? Let me take out my glasses to see him clearly.

Heavenly Doot: Why? Do you have poor eyesight?

Kena: Not at all, but I am a rich man now. I can no longer easily locate small people.

Heavenly Doot: Is that so? And how did you become such a rich man?

Kena (*patting his pocket*): My salary of three years (*takes out each paisa and counts them carefully, with a serious face*). One, two, three (*upturns his pocket and sits down*).

Heavenly Doot: So Brother, what will you do with so much money? I am poor, please do spare me some.

Kena: You want some? Here, take these. God has given me enough strength to work and earn. I'll work and earn more. You take these (*hands over all three paisa*).

Heavenly Doot: Kenaram, you are a good person with a great heart. I am a Doot from the heavens. My work is to reward good people when I meet them. Tell me what you want. I will grant you whatever you wish for.

Kena: Oh! Sir, you are truly a Heavenly Doot? I have misbehaved in front of you.

Heavenly Doot: Don't fear. You may or may not refer to me as sir. I will not count it as misbehaving. Now, tell me, what do you want?

Kena: Sir, if you indeed want to give me something, I desire a violin that plays such divine music that whoever listens to it, starts dancing immediately.

Heavenly Doot (*takes out a violin*): Take this.

Kena: Bah! Wonderful! But I hope I will not be dancing with the rest.

Heavenly Doot: No, don't worry. Go and enjoy now.

(*The* Heavenly Doot *prepares to leave.* Kenaram *starts playing his violin.*)

Heavenly Doot: Oy! Don't go experimenting with your violin when I am around.

Kena: But you just told me to enjoy myself.

Heavenly Doot: Arey! But you must let me leave, and then you may play the violin.

Kena: Okay, as you say.

THIRD SCENE

(*Enter* Byacharam, *also referred to here as Byacha.*)

Byacha: I had left it in that bush here. The police were after me. It was a wild chase. In fact, they had nearly gotten hold of me, and just in the nick of time, I managed to dump my little bundle of money here in this shrub. Now let me find it. (*Enters the bush to find the bundle of money*) Goodness, what dangerous thorns. Oh! Here it is.

(*Enter* Kenaram)

Kena (*to himself*): There goes Bechu Babu, entering that shrub full of thorns. Let me play a verse now. You see, after all, he's my old master (*plays violin*).

Byacha (*starts dancing and says*): Arey, arey. What is this? Uuh, aah, arey, you will? Arey, uhuu, no more, please. There goes my shirt. God, my skin feels like it is tearing...uhuu.

Kena: Sir, I am your servant in arrears. Just because you've paid me little money, doesn't mean I will forget such a fantastic master. My violin is blessed from being played in front of you (*and continues to play the violin with double the enthusiasm*).

Byacha (*continues dancing*): How troublesome is this? Kenaram, save me. What kind of music is this that whoever listens to it starts dancing? Save me, I don't want to dance any more. I am handing over this bundle of money to you. Consider this to be your salary, but relieve me first. Don't make me dance any more (hands over the bundle of coins to Kenaram).

Kena (*doing courteous salutations*): Why not Sir? One has to be a Monib like yourself to understand the true worth of a person. I can see that my violin has perfectly cured you from being 'hard of hearing'. Well, well. But if you do find that disease flaring up again, let me know, and I will arrive with my violin and will treat you to its enchanting music (exits, still performing grand salutations).

Byacha: Scoundrel, rascal, rogue, robber, dacoit. I will teach you a lesson. Police! Police! Thief, thief! Catch that thief!

FOURTH SCENE
(*At the courthouse*. Byacharam *enters, looking busy*.)

Byacha: Save me, Your Honour. He's robbed me of my money and soul. Oh, ho, ho, ho (*bursts into tears*).

Judge: Arey, what is this? Tell me what is the matter with you.

Byacha (*showing the numerous bruises and scratches he received from the thorns in the shrub*): See how he's robbed me of my money and my soul. Just next to the road, Kenaram thrashed me and robbed me of my money...e e e e e (*continues crying*). That scoundrel! I kept him in my house for three years and looked after him. Yet this is what I get in return. That scoundrel just roams around with a violin day in and day out. Do send your men to catch him. You will not have any trouble recognizing him at all.

Judge: Four of you go and bring Kenaram here.

(*Four men enter with* Kenaram.)

Byacha: There, there, there. Lord, that's the rogue. He's robbed me, please do punish him....

Judge: Quiet! (*looking at* Kenaram): Did you beat him and take away all his money?

Kena: What? My Lord, he had rewarded me with all this money after listening to my violin recital. I am telling the truth.

Judge: Looking at his condition, I can't believe that he rewarded you with all his money. I can also see bruises all over his body. Thus, I believe that you attacked him and then robbed him of his money, and the only punishment for such a crime is death. You will be hanged. What is your last wish?

Kena: My Lord, I don't have any other wish, but I would like to play my violin for one last time.

Byacha: Careful, My Lord. Don't allow that.

Sweeper: (*poking* Byacharam *with a long ruler*): Quiet now.

Judge: You don't desire anything else? Well, then you may play.

(Kenaram *starts playing enthusiastically. From the judge to the sweeper, everyone starts to dance.*)

Judge (*panting*): Arey! Stop, stop, stop immediately I'm pronouncing you as not guilty. This is killing me. Stop this music at once. Goodness, what kind of a violin recital is this?

Kena (*bowing to the judge*): My Lord, you should immediately ask Bechu Babu to tell the truth or I will once again start playing my violin.

Judge (*to* Bechyaram *in an irritated tone*): You rascal, tell me exactly what happened tell me the truth. NOW!

Kena: Here I go again with my violin!

Byacha: No, no, My Lord, not again. I—last night I—had robbed—save me My Lord, forgive me.

Kena: You get your karmas worth. Did you see that Bechu Babu?

Judge: Give him a punishment of twenty-five lashings.

CHANU THE ADEPT THIEF

JHHANU CHOR CHANU

Ever since he was a little boy, Chanu had always been a very naughty fellow, and this would often leave others in great trouble. His father was a poor man, and so one day, Chanu thought of venturing to a foreign land to earn some money. So he set off, and after travelling a distance, came across a narrow path in the middle of a forest. He took the road and kept walking. Soon, it started to rain, and Chanu got completely drenched. As dusk fell and having walked in the rain for a long time, he thought of resting a while and reached a mud hut.

Inside this mud hut, an old woman sat near a fire. 'What do you want, lad?' she asked.

'What else can I ask for? Give me something to eat and a place to rest.'

'You leave this hut at once,' the old woman snapped. 'You wouldn't get anything from here. I have six sons. After a long day's work, they will be home soon. They are all thieves, chors and famous ones at that. If they see you here, they will beat you black and blue.'

'That's okay,' he said. 'I would rather be beaten up black and blue than stand outside in the cold rain and get wet.'

The old woman realized Chanu was a hard nut to crack. What else could she do? So she served him some food, and he ate to his heart's content. As he was about to go to bed, Chanu told the old woman, 'If any of your sons come and wake me up, there will be great trouble. I am warning you.'

The next morning, Chanu woke up to find six rogues standing in a circle around his bed. Chanu pretended he was not bothered by their presence.

'Who are you and what do you want?' the leader amongst the six questioned Chanu.

'My name is Sardar Chor, the leader of thieves,' Chanu answered. 'I am searching for suitable members for my gang. If you are clever enough, I can teach you many ingenious things.'

'That's fine,' the leader replied. 'You get off the bed, freshen up and eat, and then we will see who is the true sardar.'

Soon, Chanu sat down to eat with the rest of the men. After finishing their food, they saw a farmer walking past their hut with a beautiful goat in tow. Pointing to the farmer, Chanu remarked, 'Will it be possible for any of you to get that goat from the farmer by simply tricking him and not using any force?'

One by one, each of the six nodded their heads, 'No, none of us can do that.'

'There we go!' Chanu exclaimed. 'See that's why I am the Sardar of all of you. I will immediately go and get that goat,' and saying so, he ran off to reach the main road via the jungle. First, he left his right shoe at the turn of the road. Then he walked a little and placed his left shoe at the second turn of another road. Finally, he sat between the bushes and waited patiently. Soon, the farmer came along with his goat. He saw one shoe and thought, 'That is an excellent shoe, but what good is it? I need the other pair too. Then down the road, he saw the second one and immediately thought, 'I am such a silly man. I wish I had taken the other pair I saw before. Let me go and fetch it.' The farmer left the pair he was holding on the road, tied his goat to a tree, and went off in search of the first pair of shoes. Immediately, Chanu came out of his hiding place, gathered the goat and both pairs of shoes and took a detour through the forest to reach the old woman's hut in no time.

Oh, the poor farmer. He couldn't find the first pair nor the second pair, and above all, when he returned, he was deeply troubled to see that his goat was missing too. He stood there, deep in worry, 'What do I do now? What will I tell my wife? I had thought of selling the goat to buy a shawl for my wife. Let me go and buy another animal, or I'll be caught. My wife will think I am a real fool.'

All the six thieves stood with gaping mouths as Chanu entered the old woman's hut with the goat. Despite being asked several times, Chanu refused to reveal his tactics. A while later, the farmer was back again, but this time, he had a fat sheep walking alongside. Chanu told the others, 'Let's see which of you can get that sheep without using force.' Immediately, all the six refused. 'Let me try again,' Chanu said. 'Hand me a rope', and he entered the jungle.

Meanwhile, the farmer was on his way with the sheep, all the while thinking about his stolen goat. In a short while, he discovered a corpse hanging from a tree near the turn of the road. He shivered. 'God save me. Even a short while ago, there was no corpse here.' As he proceeded, he found a second corpse hanging from another tree. 'Ram, Ram, Ram. What is this? Am I seeing things?' The farmer quickened his pace. But again within a short distance, a horrible sight awaited him—he found a third corpse hanging at the next turn. Now, having seen three corpses hanging in such close proximity, the farmer started to question his sanity. 'Nah! This cannot be. I believe I am going crazy. Let me go and see if the previous two corpses are still there,' and just as he left, the corpse came down from the tree, untied the sheep, and took it along with him.

At the other end, the farmer retuned to find nothing hanging and once again, his animal gone. You can imagine how he felt then.

His head started to reel, 'Hai, hai. I wonder whose jinxed face I saw before starting from home today. Now what will my wife say? I've spent the entire morning thus and lost both my goat and my sheep. What will I do? I simply must buy something and sell it in the market to buy the shawl for my wife. Earlier, I had seen a grazing buffalo. Let me go and fetch it. My wife will never get to know.'

Meanwhile, as Chanu reached with the sheep, all the six thieves stood stupefied. Their Sardar Chor challenged Chanu again, 'If you can display such a shrewd act one more time, we will unanimously declare you to be our sardar.'

By then, the farmer had returned with the buffalo. Chanu said, 'Let me see which one of you can fetch that animal without force?'

No one replied. Once again, Chanu set off to complete the task.

From the depths of the jungle, the farmer heard the bleating of a goat and a sheep. That was it. He tied the buffalo to a tree and ran to retrieve his animals. The deeper he went, the bleating seemed to be moving further away. The farmer chased the sound for half a mile. Suddenly, the sound stopped. The search had exhausted him, and there was still no sign of his goat and sheep. Upset, the farmer returned only to find the buffalo gone. He combed the jungle, but his three animals were still missing.

When Chanu arrived with the buffalo, no one uttered a word, and the six chors unanimously declared Chanu to be their sardar. What a happy moment that was for Chanu. They celebrated the entire day. The thieves stored their loot in a special room. After dinner, they showed Chanu that specific room. Since Chanu was their sardar now, he must know about everything.

A week passed and one day, the six thieves left for a loot, leaving behind their mother and Sardar Chanu. After they were gone, Chanu asked the old woman, 'Achha, you look after the band of thieves so well. Do they pay you or give you any kind of reward?'

'Reward, my foot,' the old woman spat at Chanu. 'They give me nothing.'

'Oh, is that so? Well, come with me, and I will pay you handsomely.'

Chanu took the old woman to the room where the six thieves stored their wealth. She had never seen such treasures in all her life. She stood staring at all the money and then squatted on the floor, beaming from ear to ear and sifting through the pile of gold coins, mohurs. In the meantime, Chanu filled up his pockets as well as a large bag, came out of the room, and locked it firmly from outside. The old woman stayed locked inside.

After coming out of the room of treasure, Chanu changed into a fresh set of clothes, took the goat, sheep, and buffalo, and went straight to the farmer's house. He was sitting at the very doorstep of his home, along with his wife, and was ecstatic at seeing all of his lost animals.

'Would you know to whom these belong?' Chanu asked.

'Of course! They belong to us. But where did you find them?'

'Well, they were grazing in the jungle. And there was a small sack tied to the neck of the goat, which had ten mohurs in it. Is that yours as well?'

'No sir, we are poor souls. How can we possibly have ten mohurs?'

'You may keep them too. I don't need the money.'

The farmer happily took the mohurs and blessed Chanu. He then left the village and headed home. In the evening, when he reached his house, he entered to find his parents sitting. He asked them in jest, 'God bless you all. Can I spend the night here?'

'Can a distinguished gentleman like yourself spend the night at this poor man's house? We truly have nothing.'

Chanu couldn't take it any more and blurted out, 'Father, can't you even recognize your son?'

Chanu's parents stared at him for a while and then embraced him tightly, 'From where did you find these wonderful clothes, dear?'

'If you are so surprised at my clothes, then let me show you the money I have,' and Chanu emptied his pockets and poured out the mohurs that he was carrying with him. At first, his father was terrified at the sight of so much money. But when Chanu told them the remarkable story of how he had acquired it, he was overjoyed by his son's quick thinking and intelligence.

The zamindar of that village lived in a large house and had a daughter of marriageable age. The next morning, Chanu told his father, 'Go to the zamindar's house, and ask for his daughter's hand in marriage.'

Chanu's father's eyes widened with wonder, 'What are you saying? He will release his dogs after me.'

'No, he wouldn't. Tell the zamindar that I am the Sardar Chor. There exists no such seasoned thief, a jhhanu chor, in the whole wide world as myself. I am an amazing, masterful thief who has cheated some of the cleverest people of millions. Remember to say all of this when you see the daughter of the zamindar present there.'

'Okay! I'll go if you so insist, but I have my doubts. I believe it is a futile attempt.'

Chanu's father returned after two hours. 'Well! It was not bad,' he said. 'I don't think the daughter was disinterested, and I believe, dear son, you have already proposed to her, isn't it so? In any case, zamindar moshai said that next Sunday, they will feast upon an entire fried duck. If you successfully steal the bird from the frying pan, then he said he will consider your proposal.'

'Well, that doesn't sound too difficult. I'll think about it.'

On Sunday, the zamindar's entire household gathered in their kitchen. Suddenly, its door opened and an odd-looking old man entered the room. He was dressed in tattered clothes, looked like a beggar and carried a large sack on his back. He remarked loudly, 'Jai ho! If you're done with your food, then will you be kind enough to spare some leftovers for this old beggar?'

'Of course, you will get some. Please have a seat next to the door and wait for a while,' the zamindar replied.

Now in reality, the old man was Chanu in disguise. He sat near the doorway. Shortly, a servant said loudly, 'Arey! Look, there goes a large rabbit in the garden. We can catch it. It will make a nice meal'

The zamindar scolded the man, 'We will have plenty of time later to catch a rabbit. Now you sit quietly.'

The rabbit entered and disappeared into the garden. Now Chanu, dressed as the old beggar, took out another rabbit from his large bag and released it. Immediately the servant shouted again, 'Sir, sir, the rabbit is still there. We can still catch it.'

'Sit quietly I said,' the zamindar landlord rebuked.

Within seconds, Chanu released a third rabbit from his bag. Once again the servant shouted out, and that was it. One by one, the servants rushed out of the kitchen and into the garden. The landlord followed them. In a while, everyone returned with a rabbit only to find no sign of either the old beggar or the duck in the frying pan.

'That Chanu tricked me,' the zamindar remarked incredulously.

Very soon, a servant arrived from Chanu's house and informed the zamindar, 'Sir, my master has requested your presence at our home for lunch. Please do come.'

The zamindar was a simple man with a good heart. He left for Chanu's house at once, along with his wife and daughter. There, he sat down with Chanu's family and enjoyed a hearty meal, including the fried duck. He had a good laugh about being tricked that morning. His daughter was mighty thrilled as well. She had always been fond of Chanu, and now after observing his grand clothes, behaviour, and mannerisms, she was quite pleased.

After lunch, the zamindar said, 'Chanu, I will try to consider your proposal if you can successfully steal six horses from my stable tomorrow night. Remember there will be six stable boys, one atop each horse. You will have to prove yourself worthy again. I cannot agree to give you my daughter in marriage just because you were successful once in stealing the duck.'

'Okay, I will try,' Chanu agreed.

On Sunday night, six stable boys sat atop six horses in the zamindar's stable. It was such a cold night that it felt that the blood in their veins would freeze. So each stable boy had a small bottle of liquor in his pocket. They took a sip from time to time to keep themselves warm. But they were also careful about not falling asleep and engaged each other in conversation to keep themselves awake. The door of the stable was kept open for Chanu. As the night progressed, the cold became more severe. The little sips of liquor were insufficient to keep any of them warm. The stable boys sat shivering.

Suddenly, a poor old lady appeared at the door of the stable and said, 'Young men, I am freezing in the cold. Can you give me a handful of hay? I would take that and lie down in a corner of this stable. I am quite old and cannot take this cold any longer. I fear I will die.' The old lady carried six bags on her shoulder and strangely, had a two-finger-long beard on her chin. She looked very odd.

The old woman pointed to a corner of the stable and said, 'Good men, I'm almost dying from the severe cold. Can you please make some space for me in that corner? I will lie there with a handful of hay.'

The stable boys agreed to help her. 'She is too old to create any nuisance; she will be no trouble at all,' they thought. Soon she sat in one corner of the stable amidst a small pile of hay. Then they saw her take a swig of liquor from a black bottle from her bag. Thereafter, smiling contentedly, she asked the stable boys, 'Good men, I believe you all have finished yours.

I have plenty, but I was afraid to offer you any as I was a little sceptical about what you would think of me.'

You see, the cold was very severe indeed and by then, the liquor bottles the men had brought with them were already empty. So they were tempted by the old woman's offer, and said, 'O old lady, if you offer some of yours, it will be a lifesaver. We too are dying from the cold.'

The old woman offered her bottle and within minutes, it was over. Then she offered a second flask and that too was quickly finished off by the stable boys. Unknown to them, the liquor was spiked. Within minutes of drinking from the old woman's bottles, they had fallen into a deep slumber, all the while sitting atop their respective horses. Then the old woman carefully got up, brought down the men, laid them on the bed of hay, and put socks on the hooves of the horses. Slowly, she tiptoed out of the stable and reached an outhouse connected to Chanu's house.

And what did the zamindar moshai see early the next morning? He saw Chanu passing by his house, sitting atop a horse and holding onto five more which were following him.

The zamindar was indeed very surprised and quite irritated too. He muttered to himself, 'Go to hell, you Chanu and all the silly people you have tricked.' Later that day, he had to work very hard to wake up all of his stable boys lying in the stable.

That morning, while having his breakfast, the zamindar called for Chanu to join him. As they sat eating, he said, 'You have successfully tricked a few fools. I don't consider that to be something great. I will roam around on my horse in front of my house today, between one and three in the afternoon. See, if you can then steal my horse. If you can manage to trick me, I will consider you to be worthy of becoming my son-in-law.'

Chanu bowed and said, 'I will try. Let me see.'

Later that day, the zamindar was pacing up and down the

road on his horse. When it was past three, he felt tired and also thought that Chanu had given up. Right at that moment, a servant came running pensively, 'Lord, come quick. You simply must go to your house this instant. The lady of the house, your wife, has had a serious fall from the steps. She's probably broken all her bones. She's lying unconscious. I'm off to fetch the doctor.'

The zamindar was shocked. 'What are you saying?' he exclaimed in horror. 'Oh my goodness! But the doctor's place is very far away. Here, you take my horse and be off quickly.' Immediately, the servant was on his way to fetch the doctor.

The zamindar soon reached his house, exhausted and worried, only to find everything quiet. He entered the inner chambers but found his wife and daughter sitting and chatting. At once, the landlord realized this was all Chanu's doing, and yet again, the thief had taken him for a jolly good ride.

Very soon, the zamindar saw Chanu, riding his horse in front of the house. However, the servant couldn't be found anywhere. Well, his job at the landlord's house didn't matter to him any more. The ten mohurs which Chanu had paid him would take care of him for years to come.

The following day, Chanu visited the zamindar's house but was greeted with an angry welcome.

'You tricked me rather badly this time,' the zamindar complained. 'I am very upset with you. But if you can steal my shawl from my bed tonight, then tomorrow, I will arrange for the wedding first thing in the morning.'

'Fine,' Chanu said, 'but if this time too, you go back on your word, I will steal your daughter from right in front of your eyes.'

That night, the full moon shone brilliantly. As the zamindar and his wife lay on their bed, the room was flooded with the moonlight, shining through the glass panels of the window. Suddenly, he saw something which looked like a head, and it disappeared outside the window.

'Did you see that? That has to be the rascal Chanu,' the zamindar told his wife. He then lifted his rifle and said aloud, 'Now I will teach him a lesson.'

The rifle shocked his wife. 'What are you doing?' she said. 'Do you want to shoot Chanu?'

'Of course not! Are you crazy? There are no real cartridges in this rifle, only duds.'

Soon enough, when the head peeped once again at the window, the zamindar fired a shot, 'Boom!' Immediately, a loud thud was heard, as if something had fallen to the ground, followed by the noise of a person rolling on the ground and struggling in pain.

The zamindar's wife shrieked, 'My God! You must have killed him. Either he is dead by now or blinded or will remain physically challenged for life.'

Frightened by what he had done, the zamindar ran to see what the matter was. The door of the room was left ajar. In the meanwhile, as he was still on his way to the outside windows, where he had seen the peeping head, his wife noticed someone exactly like him standing at the very door of the room.

'Quick, give me the shawl from our bed,' the figure said. 'He's not dead yet but is bleeding profusely. I will clean the wound, tie it tightly, and bring him along with me.'

The zamindar's wife pulled out her shawl and threw it at the door. The man caught it and ran. However, almost instantaneously, the zamindar was back. It would have been impossible for him to reach the garden window and return to the bedchamber within such a short span.

'Chanu, you rascal,' the zamindar fumed as he entered the room. 'You need to be hanged.'

Hearing her husband, the zamindar's wife replied, 'He is hurt so and here you are abusing him?'

'He should have truly been hurt. Can't you see how cunning

he is? He made an effigy of hay, dressed it in real clothes, and held it at the window.'

'What gibberish are you talking? I cannot understand any of it. If it was an effigy made from hay, why would you ask for a shawl to wipe its blood?'

'The shawl from our bed? What are you saying? I never came back to ask for any shawl.'

'I don't know whether you returned or not, but you did stand at the door and asked for the shawl. Then I threw it at you.'

Hearing his wife, the zamindar slumped down to the floor, holding his head with both hands. 'What a cunning man Chanu is. I can't deal with him any more. I have to arrange for the wedding tomorrow itself.'

After that, the zamindar's daughter married Chanu, who turned over a new leaf. In fact, he became such a good fellow that it is hard to find such a son-in-law anywhere. The zamindar and his wife would go around, proudly calling him, 'Our Jhhanu Chor Chanu.'

THE YOUNGEST BROTHER

CHHOTO BHAI

There once lived seven brothers, and the youngest of them was Ruru. All seven brothers were quite handsome in comparison to the other men in the kingdom in which they lived, and amongst them all, Ruru was surely the most good-looking. This made his six brothers very envious of him. They would wear all the good clothes, and Ruru would be left with mere rags. They would make Ruru do the menial jobs and loiter around themselves, spending their days behaving rather high-handedly. People loved Ruru the most and could hardly tolerate any of his brothers. This often angered them and would frequently lead to Ruru being severely beaten up by his six elder brothers. The poor boy hardly had a moment of peace.

Far away from Ruru's village, there lived a girl named Rawronga, the most beautiful maiden in the whole wide world. The minute Ruru's elder brothers heard about Rawronga, they said, 'Let's go to meet her. We are the most handsome men around. If she meets us, she will definitely marry one of us.'

Thrilled at the prospect, each of the six brothers thought, 'Rawronga will marry me,' and they gathered a wide variety of jewellery and tied them inside their bundles. A panshi was prepared for the voyage, a small boat which could travel very fast. The six elder brothers dressed regally, combed their hair, and climbed into the panshi to bring home their wife.

When they were ready to depart, their mother asked, 'Will you not take Ruru along?' At once, all six brothers replied in unison, 'Of course, we will. Or who will cook for us? We will make him stay home when we will go to meet Rawronga. We will be greatly ashamed to introduce him as our brother with the kind of tattered clothes he is always wearing.'

Ruru heard everything and didn't say a word. He silently boarded the panshi along with his brothers. Soon, they reached Rawronga's kingdom. It so happened that the people of that kingdom had already gotten to know that a group of handsome men were coming there to look for suitable brides. So the minute the panshi arrived, they gathered to fetch the brothers and take them to their village. A residence had been prepared to welcome them, alongside a splendid feast.

Before the six brothers left to attend the welcome celebrations with the villagers, they instructed Ruru, 'Prepare the home and fetch all our belongings from the panshi,' and with these words, they left. There were several fair village maidens at the feast and none of the brothers could understand who was Rawronga. Each bhai asked the girl sitting next to him, 'Who is Rawronga?' and each girl replied, 'I am Rawronga. But don't tell anyone.' The brothers were ecstatic. They had never imagined that they could meet Rawronga so easily. Within a couple of days, all the six brothers were married and each one was under the impression that he had married Rawronga. Not for a second did they think they had been cheated.

Ruru did not know any of this. To be honest, there was no need for him to find out what had transpired as he was busy looking after the house. On the very first day, after he finished setting up the residence, he left to fetch water with a pitcher. Unaware of where to find drinking water in an unknown land, he asked a young girl for directions. The child replied, 'Can you see that house? It belongs to Rawronga. Just next to is a waterfall. You will not miss it.'

Ruru went to fetch water from the waterfall and suddenly he thought to himself, 'I know that Rawronga is away at the feast. Why don't I peep in to see what her house looks like?' So he silently crept up to the door of Rawronga's house. Now the second he looked inside, Ruru forgot where he was. For he had caught a glimpse of the most beautiful woman in the world. It must be Rawronga for no one could be as exquisite as the person before him.

Rawronga was happy to meet Ruru. She called out to him, 'Come, come in and have a seat.'

Ruru entered with trepidation in his heart.

'Who are you?' she asked.

'You must have heard of the six brothers who have come in search of wives? Well, actually there are seven of them. I am their youngest brother.'

'Then why aren't you at the feast?' she asked.

'They did not want me to accompany them. They left me at home to finish all the chores. I don't have a second piece of clothing. Because I work all the time, these garments have become soiled and are torn in places.'

Rawronga had liked Ruru the minute she met him and was deeply saddened to listen to his painful story, about how his elder brothers always harassed and ill-treated him. Such sympathetic thoughts made Rawronga love Ruru even more, and within a couple of days, they were married.

The next day, Ruru's brothers prepared to depart for home. Ruru had already concealed Rawronga inside the bottom of the panshi. None of the elder brothers found out, and they returned home amidst much pomp and splendour. Upon reaching, the eldest of the six called out to their mother and said, 'See Mother, I have married Rawronga.' Immediately, the next brother retorted, 'No Mother, he is lying. I have married Rawronga and brought her home.'

An amusing situation unfolded as each brother contested the other, claiming that he was the one who had married the true Rawronga. A furious fight was just about to erupt, with all the six wives standing in one corner. They had never thought that they would be caught so early on.

Finally, their mother intervened and said, 'All six girls cannot be Rawronga, and to be honest, none of these girls are beautiful. It looks like you've all been cheated.'

Ruru, who till then had been standing silently, decided to speak up, 'You are right, mother. They have gotten cheated. You come with me, and I will show you Rawronga.'

The brothers erupted into laughter, but their mother insisted, 'Let me go and see what Ruru is talking about.'

She reached the panshi with Ruru, and the minute she met Rawronga, she hugged the beautiful girl, took her in her arms, and danced in joy. News spread fast, and people from all over the village rushed to see the bonny bride. Celebrations and dancing ensued. All this merrymaking angered the elder brothers, and they frowned, bared their teeth, and screamed at their wives, 'You thought you could cheat me?' It was a hilarious sight, and everyone had a good laugh.

Their mother interrupted and concluded wisely, 'What is this now? You have all gotten what you deserved.'

THE VERDICT OF THE JUDGE

KAZIR BICHAR

Raamkanai was rather innocent a person; in fact, he was a simpleton, while Jhhutaram was equally shrewd. When they met each other for the first time, Jhhutaram said, 'Brother, why do we both need to suffer thus, carrying a bundle with us? Here take my bundle. You carry it, along with yours, and while returning, I will carry both our bundles.'

Raamkanai, like the typical simpleton that he was, carried both bundles on his shoulders. `

Upon nearing the village, they realized that they were both hungry. Raamkanai said, 'Come, let's eat. What do you think?'

'Fair enough,' Jhhutaram agreed. 'Let's do one thing. Let's not eat from both pots of food that we are carrying. It will lead to wastage. For now, we will eat from yours. And on our way back, we will feast from mine.'

As they began eating from Raamkanai's pot, he began to talk about his home, the members of his family, his parents, siblings, children, and many other things. He spoke about how big his daughter has gotten and what work his son does—everything. As Raamkanai continued, Jhhutaram asked more and more questions, keeping him busy with the answers while he continued to devour the food. Engrossed in his stories, much later Raamkanai realised that all the food was over.

Jhhutaram rinsed his mouth, and said in a rather serious voice, 'Raamkanai, the food you just fed me was pathetic. I never imagined you to be such a nasty person. What else can I say? But after such a meal, I cannot remain your friend any more. I am leaving,' and he lifted his pot full of food and walked away briskly. Raamkanai, poor chap. He was still hungry, and now

Jhhutaram had left, so there was no possibility of finding any food. It was already dusk, and his stomach grumbled. Worried about walking home in the dark and with such hunger in his stomach, Raamkanai began to cry.

At that moment, the guards of the kazi, the judge, were passing by. He saw Raamkanai sitting and weeping and enquired about what happened. Raamkanai told him everything. 'Oh! I see,' the guard said. 'Come with me, we will go to Kazi sahib. He will pass a verdict on this.'

When Raamkanai told the kazi what had happened, he burst into laughter: '*Ha ha ha, ho ho ho*! I have never heard something so hilarious. A man made you carry his luggage and then went away after eating your food? Where had your senses gone off to? Alright then, call Jhhutaram.' The guard immediately left and within three minutes returned, dragging Jhhutaram by his hair.

'Now call the head of the village panchayat, the merchant, the chief police officer, the physician, and the erudite schoolteacher,' instructed Kazi. 'They too should have the opportunity to listen to such an amusing story.'

Soon the court was full of people.

Upon being asked what had happened between him and Raamkanai, Jhhutaram lied to the judge, 'Forgive me, my Lord, but I don't know anything. This scoundrel forced to eat a small portion of his meal. My head has been reeling ever since, and I feel unwell.'

The judge was furious and hollered, 'You rascal Jhhutaram, you completely ruined my funny story. You ate the food, and then your head started to reel—is this even true? Guard, search him and find out what is he carrying with him. Take away everything. The rogue's story has absolutely no sense of comedy. Take away everything, and give them to Raamkanai. Whatever he is saying, whether it's the truth or not, at least his story is humourous.'

SAATMAAR PALOWAN

THE MIGHTY WRESTLER WHO COULD SLAY SEVEN AT A GO

Once, in the kingdom of a certain Raja, there lived a potter called Kanai. Unfortunately, he was very bad at his work. Every time he would attempt to mould something out of clay, it became disfigured. However, Kanai's wife was an excellent artist. She would make beautiful pots, pitchers, and a variety of utensils from clay. Now ideally, his wife's hardwork and creations should have been of help to Kanai. He should have been roaming around, a freeman without having to do any work at all, but this was not meant to be as Kanai's wife was a very angry woman. She would chase him with a broom the moment she spotted Kanai idling around. As you can see, the man lived a rather troublesome life.

One day, Kanai's wife had placed some clay pitchers to dry under the sun. She left Kanai with instructions: 'Keep an eye on these. Be careful. No one should trample upon the pitchers.'

Kanai sat just next to the pitchers with a stick, keeping a close eye on the wares as he gulped down handfuls of flattened rice and nolen gur, the delicious liquid jaggery.

Now a few drops of Kanai's nolen gur had spilt over one of the pots. It attracted flies, and when Kanai saw them buzzing around, he thought they were out to trample the pots. Keen to teach them a lesson, Kanai picked up his stick and brought it down with such force that all the gathered flies died, but alas the beautiful pitchers broke into pieces.

Kanai counted that he had killed seven flies. Finally, he tucked the stick under his arms and sat with a rather serious expression on his face. Hearing the sound of the crash, Kanai's wife came running with a broom in her hand. 'What happened?' she asked him in surprise seeing all the broken pitchers. Kanai didn't reply.

The more the wife asked, the more serious Kanai's face became. After a while, courtesy of the continuous nagging and rebukes, Kanai said, 'Be careful of how you treat me. You don't know, but I have slayed seven in one strike.'

Thereafter, Kanai stopped speaking to all. If anyone would pester him, he would simply say, 'Be careful of how you treat me. You don't know, but I have slayed seven in one strike.'

Finally, one day, Kanai bought a great length of markin cloth, wrapped it around his head, and wove a brilliant and massive pagdi, a turban. Then he bought a large branch out of the forest and fashioned a huge walking stick out of that. Then he wore a firan, a long, flowing garment, tied it at his waist, took a shield in one hand, wore his shoes, and set off for the raja's palace in search of a job as a wrestler, a palowan. As he was leaving, he told his wife, 'I will not stay here any more. You know, I can slay seven at a time.'

On the way, many asked Kanai where he was off to, but he gave no reply. He had decided hence not to respond to the name of Kanai. Should a mighty person who had slayed seven at go have such a commonplace name? From then on, he should be called 'Saatmaar Palowan', the mighty wrestler who had killed seven at once.

He reached the palace and stood with folded hands in front of the raja, who was amused to see his massive pagdi.

'Who are you?' the raja asked, rather amused.

'Your Majesty, my name is Saatmaar Palowan. I can slay seven at a go.'

At once, Kanai was employed as the raja's security guard, which was a job suitable for a mighty wrestler. His salary was fifty rupees a month, and he was happy and comfortable in his new life, till one day when a tiger appeared in the kingdom. The animal had wreaked havoc in the country and turned into a man-eater, killing several animals and even the king's men who had tried to hunt him down. This worried the raja greatly.

In such a situation, a shrewd man appeared from somewhere and whispered in the raja's ears 'Raja Moshai, why are you so worried? You have kept a palowan for fifty rupees. Why don't you summon him to slay the tiger?'

Immediately, Kanai was summoned and tasked with killing the man-eater. Kanai arrived, bowed deeply and replied, 'Fine, Your Majesty. I will attend to it immediately.'

Upon returning home, Kanai slumped down to the floor, holding his head between his two hands. Not only his cushy job, but his life was at stake too. 'Now what?' Kanai lamented. 'If I go to slay the tiger, it will eat me and if I don't go, the raja will kill me. I'm fed up, I will not stay in this kingdom any more.'

That evening, Kanai put his large pagdi back on his head, wore his robe tied at the waist, took his shield in one hand and his stick in the other, strapped his bundle of belonging, on his back, and wore his nagda shoes. Everyone thought that he was getting dressed to go to slay the tiger but Kanai was plotting his escape. If only he had a horse, he could travel faster and leave the kingdom forever.

Now in the midst of all this, that night, the famous tiger whom Kanai was supposed to go after, was sitting silently outside a house inside which lived an old woman and her granddaughter. The tiger had planned to feast on either of the two, whoever stepped out of the house at any given time. But his plan was not meant to be as the old woman was lying on her bed, cozily wrapped in her warm blanket. It was a very cold night and she had no desire to step out at all and would have dozed off if it wasn't for her overactive granddaughter who refused to sleep. Having a tough time putting the girl to bed, finally the old woman muttered out of exasperation, 'The tiger will come and fetch you.'

'I do not fear any tiger,' the girl replied promptly.

'Well then, tyapa will come and fetch you,' the old lady added without a delay.

Now, there is nothing called a tyapa. The old woman had made it up to frighten the girl so that she immediately goes off to sleep. But the tiger crouching outside their house was not aware of this. When he heard the old woman mention tyapa, he froze in fear. He thought to himself, 'Oh dear! She does not fear me but is scared of a tyapa. How fearsome a beast would this tyapa be? If this tyapa comes this way, I will be in great trouble.'

As the tiger sat thinking and shivering in fear, Kanai came running in that direction. In the darkness of the night, he could faintly make out an animal near the old woman's hut. 'Well, here is a nice horse,' Kanai thought, and he untied his waistcloth and wrapped it around the tiger's throat. Just like Kanai, the tiger too had misunderstood the situation. In the darkness, he mistook Kanai in his robes and the massive pagdi to be tyapa, the terrifying beast he had heard the old lady speaking about, for no human would have the courage to approach a tiger and then act in such a silly manner.

'Goodness, tyapa has got me now,' the tiger grimaced.

'Now that I have a horse, why delay my journey?' Kanai said to himself. 'Let me sleep for a while, and I will start right at daybreak,' and Kanai dragged the tiger to his house. All this while, the poor tiger kept thinking, 'I am helpless now. I simply have to listen to tyapa.'

Upon reaching his home, Kanai put the tiger in one room and locked it from outside. Then he lay on his bed, prepared to rise at daybreak and escape the kingdom. However, Kanai overslept and woke up when it was way past dawn. He hurriedly got off the bed and ran to unlock his horse, only to realize that there was a tiger in the room. Goodness, what would he do now? In a state of panic, Kanai even forgot that the tiger was locked in a room and could neither escape nor harm him. He ran to his room, latched it from inside, and sat quivering with fright.

On the other hand, that morning, all the people, along with the raja, and his subjects had set off for Kanai, the Saatmaar Palowan's, residence. They reached his house and were extremely surprised to see the tiger already locked inside. By now, Kanai had understood everything. He came out promptly stood before the king.

'Saatmaar, why did you not slay this one?' the king asked Kanai.

'Your Majesty, I slay seven at a go, this is merely one.'

After this, Saatmaar Palowan became very famous all over the kingdom. Raja Moshai was ecstatic. He increased Saatmaar's salary by five hundred rupees. So Kanai's days were spent happily, but it was not meant for long. Soon, there was a new trouble in sight. This time, it was not a Tiger, but a ruthless king from another kingdom coming to attack Kanai's Raja and his kingdom with an army of one thousand soldiers. It was heard that the enemy king was so brutal that no one could defeat him.

'Saatmaar, now what to do?' the raja asked in a state of frenzy. 'You must save us or we'll perish. I promise to give you half of my kingdom if you can find a way out of this.'

'Don't worry, Your Majesty. I will look into this; just give me a good horse.'

By the raja's order, the most prized horse used in war was brought over from the royal stable. Once again, Kanai wore his colossal turban of markin cloth, packed his belongings, and all the while, kept thinking of means to escape, along with his horse. Alas! He had forgotten that this was a horse trained for battle. The more Kanai tried to veer the horse towards another direction, it headed for the battlefield. In fact, the horse began to prance about when it heard the gongs and trumpets of the enemy king's battalion. As they galloped towards the battlefield, Kanai tried to grab onto anything that came within his reach, trees, shrubs, and haystacks to stop the horse. But the fierce stallion ran with all that in its tow, with Kanai on his back. With parts of trees, shrubs, and haystacks stuck to Kanai and the horse it almost seemed like a massive thicket was on the move.

On the battlefield, the enemy king had heard rumours of Saatmaar Palowan who could slay seven at a go and had trapped a tiger in his house. These stories sparked a discussion amongst the soldiers. 'Brothers, none of us is a match for that palowan. We are nothing in front of him. Goodness, he will slay seven of us at once.'

Right at that moment, Kanai and the horse came charging at the enemy. The massive pagdi could be seen amidst the moving mass of vegetation as the horse advanced at rapid speed. From a distance, it looked like an entire mountain was running towards the soldiers determinedly. The enemy army did not wait for a second. One of them shouted, 'There he comes. That's Saatmaar Palowan, now he will hurl several trees and stones and mountains at us,' and immediately thousands of soldiers disappeared, shouting at the top of their voices.

Unfortunately, while the soldiers had fled upon seeing Kanai, they had left their poor king behind, who was so perplexed at the turn of events, that he simply stood in the middle of the field with a gaping mouth.

'Oh well, that's pretty convenient,' Kanai thought. 'It was I who wanted to flee, but ended up winning the battle. Now, I just need to arrest this Raja.'

Well, what else? People cheered for Saatmaar Palowan. As promised, he was awarded with half the kingdom and spent his remaining days in great leisure and happiness.

THE HUNCHBACK AND THE GHOSTS

KUNJO AND BHOOT

There was once a man called Kanai. He had an unfortunate large hump, called a kunj, on his back. So he was often called kunjo or the hunchback. He was a rather nice man otherwise and would often help people in times of need, ill health, or sickness by offering them medicines. Unfortunately, nobody liked him because of his hump.

Kanai was an expert cane basket maker. He had a wonderful shop and there was no one in the entire kingdom who could make such beautiful baskets as he did. In fact, he was so good that many were envious and would often speak ill behind his back. This always created a bad impression of Kanai in other's minds, who would think he was quite a nasty person and avoid speaking with him altogether. Thus, poor Kanai was always sad about being secluded, ignored, and ridiculed.

You see, the hump was so large that Kanai constantly suffered, walking with his head bent and the body slouched over. One day, he travelled quite a distance to sell his baskets. But when it was time to return to his village, it was already dark. By the time it was night, Kanai had reached a forest. Exhausted and barely able to take another step, Kanai came across a house in the forest. He knew the house well and knew that it had a bad reputation for being called a haunted house. So he decided to sit down on the road outside instead.

Who knows how long Kanai sat there, but suddenly, he heard sounds coming from the inside of the haunted house. He could hear voices singing a song, and what a wonderful song that was. It was so pleasing to Kanai's ears that he sat engrossed. A pleasant song, but it had only a line of lyrics.

'Lun hai, tail hai, imli hai, heeng hai.'

(We have salt, we have oil, we have tamarind, and we have asafoetida.)

Kanai listened to the song for a while and felt so happy that he too wanted to sing along. He joined in, in a full-throated voice:

'Lun hai, tail hai, imli hai, heeng hai.'

There we go! Just as he finished that one line, he felt himself becoming wiser. Excited, he raised his voice even higher and continued by adding his own lyrics:

'Lasoon hai, marich hai, chyang byang shutki hai.'

(We have garlic, we have chillies, and we have some tasty sun-dried fish.)

So loudly did Kanai sing that it reached the ears of the singers inside the haunted house. They were all ghosts! Ecstatic at having found a new singer, they ventured out. When they found Kanai, they picked him up. and went back inside, frolicking and dancing in great excitement. They took great care of him, fed him all kinds of sweetmeats, and then encircling Kanai, started to sing happily:

*'Lun hai, tail hai, imli hai, heeng hai,
Lasoon hai, marich hai, chyang byang shutki hai.'*

Kanai joined the ghosts in their dance but suddenly realized something odd. All his life, he could not even walk properly because of his hump but was now dancing to his heart's content. Kanai reached out to touch his back, and to his amazement, the hump had vanished! Kanai was not only dancing but he was standing straight.

'Hey, what are you searching for?' one of the ghosts asked.

'The hump is not there any more. See, it is lying next to you on the floor.'

Truly, the hump was not on Kanai's back, but was lying next to him, on the floor. Oh! How happy Kanai was. In fact, such relief flooded over him that he immediately lay down on the floor and went off to a deep sleep. When he awoke, it was morning and he found himself sleeping on the road, next to the haunted house. The band of ghosts had changed his clothes; he was now wearing a rather grand set of garments. He started for his home, and upon reaching his village, was unrecognizable by the people. No hump, new clothes... Kanai looked very different and quite distinguished. It took him a lot of effort to convince the villagers about what had happened.

As the unusual news of Kanai's encounter with the ghosts and the disappearance of his hump spread, people stopped disliking him. They cordially invited him to their homes, introduced him to their families, and asked him to narrate his unusual tale. Many people would turn up to buy his cane baskets just so they could hear him recount the incident. Soon, he had become a wealthy man by selling his beautiful baskets.

One day, as Kanai sat weaving a cane basket at his doorstep, an old woman appeared and asked, 'I want to reach Kebolhaati. Which road do I take?'

'This is Kebolhaati. What do you want?'

'I have heard that there is a man in your village called Kanai, whose hump was cured by the ghosts. If I can learn the mantra for that cure, I too would help to cure my son Manik's hump.'

'I am that Kanai, and yes, the ghosts cured my hump. But there is no mantra as such,' and then he went on to tell her everything that had happened—the beautiful song, him joining in their singing, being taken inside the haunted house, and the celebration that followed when he realized that his hump has fallen off. The old woman heard every detail, blessed Kanai with all her heart, and left for her village.

The old woman's son Manik, had a hump on his back, which was even larger than what Kanai's had been. But the difference was that he was a rather nasty and selfish person. No one liked him. To cure his hump, one night members of his family brought him to the road outside the haunted house and left him there with instructions. Manik sat wondering when the ghosts would start singing and if he could join them. Then he would be cured of his disfigurement. Suddenly, he heard the voices:

'Lun hai, tail hai, imli hai...'

The ghosts hadn't even finished their song, when Manik shouted:

'Gurcharan Moirar dokaner kanchagolla hai.'

(We have tasty kanchagolla from Gurcharan Moira's sweet shop.)

Well, not only did the singing inside the house stop immediately, but after hearing Manik sing about the kanchagolla from the sweet shop of Gurcharan Moira, a few of the ghosts started to puke. You see, ghosts do not like such sweet treats from sweetshops, so much so that they cannot even bear to hear their names. They only sang about the things they liked like salt, oil, tamarind, and asafoetida. They had liked Kanai's lyrics as he sang about things which they liked too like, garlic, chillies, and sun-dried fish. But listening to Manik, they grew furious.

'Who are you?' they roared angrily. 'You offbeat rascal. You completely ruined our song. Wait, we will teach you a lesson,' and they took Kanai's old hump and stuck it over Manik's hump in a way that it could never be separated.

The next morning, Manik's family was very sad to see the sorry plight of their son, but the villagers rightly said, 'He was a rather nasty person. Serves him right.'

THE JAPANESE GODS

JAPANESE DEVTA

In Japan, there is a very old manuscript, named 'Kojiki', which speaks about the formation of the earth. According to Kojiki, in the beginning, the earth was like a thin layer of oil, floating like a bubble on the sea.

At that time, there were only three gods. When they died, two more were created, who were succeeded by two more, and when they too passed away, two more were created. Finally, from the penultimate duo, ten gods were created, and amongst these were Izanagi and his wife, Izanami.

The rest of the gods, handed a long and sharp instrument with a very broad base, resembling a spear, to Izanagi and Izanami and asked them to create earth from the oil.

Izanagi and Izanami agreed, took the instrument, and started to churn the sea. When they withdrew it, the drop of water that dripped from its tip created an island. This was named Ongoro. On this island, Izanagi and Izanami built a beautiful home for themselves, and it is from here that they gradually built the rest of Japan. We may call the country Japan, but the Japanese call it 'Nippon' or 'Dai-Nippon'.

Izanagi and Izanami had many children, and one of them was the God of Fire. Unfortunately, Izanami passed away while giving birth to this son. Struck with great grief, Izanagi began to sob and from his tears was born the Goddess of Tears. Unable to control his anger at his wife's death, Izanagi decapitated the God of Fire in one stroke, and from his blood, sixteen more deities were created. However, Izanagi continued to grieve and then went out searching for his wife. Thus, he reached the netherworld, what we call Pataal lok.

Izanagi met his beloved wife Izanami at the very gates of Pataal. Upon seeing her husband, Izanami said, 'Just wait for a while. I have to go in and get permission.' So Izanami disappeared and Izanagi stood waiting. Time passed and Izanami grew curious and impatient. He wanted to go inside to see what was taking his wife so long. Impatient, Izanagi entered the netherworld and was shocked to find himself in the middle of terrible, gross surroundings. A horrifying and pungent stench filled the air. He had never encountered an odour so powerful and to his dismay, when he finally located his wife, he saw that she too was covered in such filth that it was difficult for him to even approach her. So Izanagi covered his nose and fled from Paatal lok, the guards of the netherworld in hot pursuit.

After returning to his kingdom, Izanagi wanted to cleanse himself from the stench of the netherworld. He took off his robes and went to bathe in the river. At that time, several gods were created from his robe and his body and amongst them were the deities of the sun, the moon, and the sea. The Goddess of Light was the deity of the sun. Born from Izanagi's left eye, she was the most beautiful woman anyone had seen. And from Izanagi's right eye emerged the God of Sea, Tejveer.

Izanagi took off his necklace, put it around the Goddess of Light, and said, 'Dear, you will be the queen of the heavens.' He told the deity of the moon, Chandrapati, 'You will be the king of the night.' And finally, Izanagi proclaimed Tejveer as the god of the oceans. But Tejveer was not happy. He cried all day and night long, so much so that his beard grew right up to his tummy. Finally, Izanagi asked him, 'Son, what has happened to you? I gave you a kingdom to rule but you never went there and you only sit and weep. What is the matter with you?'

'I do not want a kingdom,' Tejveer wept. 'I just want to go to my mother in the netherworld.'

'Then get out of my sight,' Izanagi thundered, and thus

The Japanese Gods

Tejveer was driven away by his father. From there, he headed out to heaven to meet his sister, the Goddess of Light, who had always known that Tejveer was unhappy.

'Why are you here to see me, Tejveer?' she asked.

'Our father has driven me out. I am on my way to meet Mother and thought of meeting you on the way.'

'If that is so, do give me your sword,' the Goddess of Light demanded.

She chewed the sword and turned it into powder. From that powder, three more gods were created.

Now it was Tejveer's turn. He took his sister's jewels and chewed them into another powder from which five more gods emerged.

But who did these gods belong to? It was decided that the ones created from Tejveer's sword belonged to him while those which emerged from the powdered jewels belonged to the Goddess of Light. Well, you see, it was a good decision, but since the number of gods created from jewels was more, Tejveer did not like the proposal. Angry at the injustice, he trampled all over his sister's agricultural fields, filled her narrow canals, and destroyed her garden. As the destruction was underway, the Goddess of Light was sitting and weaving with her women attendants in her home located inside of a cave in a mountain. Suddenly, the roof came crashing down as Tejveer flung a skinned, dead horse at her. Fearing more onslaughts from Tejveer, the Goddess of Light shut the mouth of her cave.

Since the Goddess of Light was the deity of the sun, when she hid inside the cave, the world was plunged into darkness. It struck terror in the hearts of the people. They screamed for help. Finally, they all discussed and decided upon a plan. Accordingly, they created a wonderful, large mirror, beaded together with several precious stones to make a necklace, and gathered many other beautiful objects. Then they worshipped the Goddess of

Light with all gorgeous materials and rejoiced and celebrated by making a lot of noise. They laughed and sang, jumped and screamed with joy, and cuckooed like a rooster. Oh, what a cacophony that was. It had to be heard to be believed. The Goddess of Light heard the noise from her cave, peeped outside, and said, 'What is the matter? What is all this ruckus for?'

'Why not? Why should we not rejoice? Come out and see what a pretty lady we've found. She is much more beautiful than you,' and saying so, the men came rushing with the large mirror and presented it right before the Goddess of Light. When the Goddess saw her lovely face in the mirror, she hurried out to see the other maiden and her subjects immediately ran to shut the mouth of the cave.

The sun rose once again. There was bright light everywhere and happiness spread all over. The people drove Tejveer away, and once again, peace returned to earth.

After being thrown out of the Goddess of Light's kingdom, Tejveer wandered around a little and finally reached the banks of the River Hee. There, he saw an old man and a woman, sitting with a young girl, crying.

'What is the matter?' he asked. 'Why are you crying?'

The forlorn old man replied, 'Dear, what do I tell you of my woes? I had eight daughters. All my eldest seven daughters are dead, gobbled up by a giant snake with eight heads. He comes once a year and gobbles one daughter. It is time for him to return and this time, that demon will eat my youngest and only child. We do not know how to save her.'

'Well, is that so? Don't worry, and do exactly what I tell you to do. Prepare eight cauldrons of the strong alcoholic drink sake and keep them over there. Then wait and see what I do.'

Immediately, the old man did as instructed. When the giant snake appeared, the air was redolent with the strong aroma of the sake. The snake was huffing, hissing and sniffing all around when suddenly, he smelled the liquor. How could he control his greed? He immediately dipped his eight heads into each of the eight cauldrons.

The strong sake had an immediate effect on the snake. The eight heads began to reel and his eyes became droopy. Nevertheless, the snake continued to gulp the sake. Finally, it collapsed and went off to a deep sleep. Tejveer was waiting for that very moment. He flung out his sword and slayed the giant snake with one strike. Then he chopped its body into small pieces. But the tail remained. It was so tough that Tejveer could not slice it, and soon, the tough hide broke the sword into two. Then Tejveer discovered a hidden sword within the tail of the snake. He removed the weapon, and the snake completely perished.

Everyone was incredibly happy. Tejveer married the young girl of the elderly couple and settled down in their kingdom. There, the couple began a new life and continued to live peacefully, along with the elderly couple.

On the other hand, the Goddess of Light had three grandsons: Diptanol, Khiptanol, and Triptanol. Diptanol would fish, while Triptanol would hunt.

One day Triptanol said, 'Brother, let's switch places. Let me do your work and you do mine, and we'll see what happens then.'

Thus, Triptanol gave his bow and arrow to his elder brother and in turn, took his fishing gear. Though Triptanol managed to catch a lot of fish, unfortunately at the end of the day, the line broke and a fish snatched it away, along with the hook. When the time arrived for Triptanol to return all the fishing equipment, all he could do was fumble a guilty reply, 'Brother Diptanol, a fish snatched away the hook and the line. What do I do now?'

Diptanol was furious, 'I do not know anything. I want my gear back.'

What could have Triptanol done? He broke his sword and

fashioned a hook out of that and handed it over to his elder brother. But Diptanol was not an easy one to appease. He remained adamant. 'I do not want this. You had taken my hook and line, and I want that exact equipment back.'

Triptanol attempted to satisfy his brother by fetching thousands of similar hooks, but nothing made Diptanol happy who only wanted the hook and line that the fish had carried away. Every time, Triptanol returned with tears in his eyes. 'The sea is so vast. How can I locate the fish and the line?' he lamented.

Thinking about ways to locate the hook and the line, Triptanol reached the sea and sat down crying. Suddenly, the king of the sea, Labaneshwar, appeared and asked, 'What is the matter? Why are you crying?'

'I had gone fishing with my brother's fishing gear,' Triptanol began. 'Unfortunately, a fish snatched away the hook and the line. Now, he is terribly angry. I tried to conciliate him by gifting many more hooks, but he is adamant about having his original hook back. What will I do now?'

'You do not worry and do as I advise you to do.' Then Labaneshwar prepared a boat, gave it to Triptanol, and instructed, 'Take this boat and keep going straight. After travelling a distance, you will see a house made of fish scales. It is Raja Sindhupati's home, the lord of the sea. Next to the house, there is a garden, and within this garden, there is a well with a tree next to it. You will need to climb to the very top of that tree, sit there and wait, till the princess comes into the garden. Eventually, you must ask her, and she will tell you where to locate your hook and line.'

Following Labaneshwar's orders, Triptanol reached Sindhupati's garden and climbed the tree. Finally, after a short while, the princess arrived in the garden with her attendants. They had all come with pitchers in their hands to fetch water from the well. They noticed Triptanol perched on the highest branch and were very amused to see a very handsome man sitting up there.

He then asked, 'Kindly can you give me some water to drink?'

The maids fetched a golden glass and served Triptanol. He took a few sips from the glass and returned the remaining water but had secretly dropped a precious stone from his necklace into it. It went unnoticed by the maids. They took the glass and placed it in the princess's room. It was her glass, and a while later, when she entered the room for a drink of water, she found a precious stone lying inside her golden glass. She asked her maids who it belonged to, and they told her about the prince sitting on the topmost branches. 'We had served him some water in your golden glass. That stone must belong to him,' the maids added.

The daughter ran to inform her father, Sindhupati. He rushed outside to see Triptanol on the tree. 'Oh my! I believe you are Triptanol. the grandson of the queen of heavens, our Goddess of Light. Why are you sitting here? Please do come inside,' and so the raja welcomed Triptanol inside warmly. The attendants in the court were surprised and happy to see Triptanol, and they greeted him courteously. Within a few days, the raja got Triptanol married to his daughter amidst much pomp and splendour.

Soon after, Triptanol began to live happily in the palace. The kind Raja would enquire after Triptanol's wellbeing every day, and each day, his daughter would reply, 'He's doing well.' Pleased, the raja would return happily. Three years passed, and one day, the princess reported that Triptanol refused to leave his bed and lay sighing miserably. The raja approached his son-in-law and asked, 'Son, why are you sighing? Why are you sad?'

'Father, I had once gone fishing with my brother Diptanol's hook and line, which were then snatched away by a fish. He was very angry and demanded that I somehow find and return his equipment. Where will I find that?'

'Oh, so that is the problem? Do not worry,' the raja replied reassuringly. He called his soldiers and instructed them to gather all the fish from everywhere.

Summoned by Sindhupati, every fish from the whole wide world appeared within no time at all. Then the raja enquired, 'Now tell me, which one of you was bruised by his hook?'

'The Tai fish was hurt by the hook. To date, the bruise hurts,' they replied in unison. The raja called the Tai fish to approach him and told him, 'Now open your mouth wide. Let me see if the hook is still stuck inside.'

As the Tai fish opened his mouth, the raja could immediately see the hook stuck inside. The hook was extracted with a tong and handed over to Triptanol, who was ecstatic.

The raja also gave his son-in-law two precious stones. The first was called the Jowar Manik or high tide precious stone, which when thrown at someone, the sea rushed to drown the enemy. The other precious stone was called Bhata Manik or low tide precious stone, which could make the sea recede.

Finally, Sindhupati summoned the raja of crocodiles and instructed, 'Take Triptanol back to his palace. See that no harm comes to him on the way.'

The massive crocodile took Triptanol, and he reached his kingdom in no time at all. Soon, he returned the hook to his brother, but Diptanol was far from being happy. He took his sword and rushed to behead Triptanol. In a bid to save himself, he flung the Jowar Manik at his brother. In an instant, a massive wave rushed in and swept Diptanol away.

Poor Diptanol could barely stay afloat and screamed, 'Save me, Brother. I have wronged you. Spare me. I will never ever misbehave with you again in my life.'

This time, Triptanol threw the Bhata Manik. The wave

receded and Diptanol was saved. Soon after the incident, he turned a new leaf and left all his kingdom to be looked after by Triptanol.

THE THREE BOONS

TEENTI BOR

There was once a blacksmith, the most unfortunate one in the entire world. If you would give him something to mould, he would create something different altogether. If you would give him something to repair, he would break it even further. On top of it all, he would also cheat people. So, no one liked him, and no one gave him any work. Not being able to afford even two square meals a day, the blacksmith would also often be severely nagged by his wife.

One day, he sat in his shop, deep in thought. It was a very cold day, and he did not have anything to wrap around to keep himself warm. There was no food at home and he was hungry. Suddenly, an old man with an exceptionally long, white, flowing beard, appeared out of nowhere. The old man, shivering in the cold and struggling to keep himself upright with a walking stick, pleaded before the blacksmith, 'God will bless you, son. Do feed this poor man.'

'My dear man, if I had food, I would have eaten it myself,' the blacksmith answered. 'I have not eaten for two days. My family, including my children, are all hungry and no one has eaten. How do you expect me to feed you? But why don't you step out of the cold? Come inside and let me blow at the hot coals and make the fire burn brighter. You can warm yourself and rest before you leave.'

The old man entered his house shivering and said, 'You saved me. I was freezing to death. But now I can see that you are in a sorrier state than myself. I only have myself to tend to, but you need to take care of your wife and children.' The old man sat next to the fire and warmed himself. Before leaving, he told the blacksmith, 'You could not feed me, but you did all that you could. You ask for three wishes, and I will grant them.'

The blacksmith was surprised at his words. He stared at the old man for long, scratched his head, but could think of nothing to ask. The old man grew impatient 'Hurry up, I am in a hurry. I have other work to tend to.'

In a state of panic, the blacksmith blurted out, 'Fine, whoever touches my hammer, will not be able to let go of it without my permission. And if he would start to hammer with that, he cannot stop till I tell him to.'

'Fine. So, be it. What else would you like to wish for?'

'Do you see this comfortable recliner of mine? Anyone who sits on it, should not be able to get up without my permission.'

'Fine. So, be it. What else?'

'And this purse of mine? If I keep any money inside it, then no one should be able to take it out other than myself.'

You see, that old man was a god in disguise. He granted all three of the blacksmith's wishes, but angrily remarked, 'You silly man, you could have travelled to heaven along with your family with the help of these three boons, but look at you. You have no brains at all.'

The old man left, and the blacksmith sat thinking. Suddenly, it struck him that he could earn a little something with the help of his newly granted wishes. So, he went around telling everyone, 'I will work for free for anyone visiting my shop.' This soon spread across the region. Hearing this, several rich, selfish men, started arriving at the workshop. When people would arrive, Kamar would either make him sit on the recliner or make him hold onto his hammer. Kamar would finish his work and would not allow him to leave till he had paid him handsomely. The blacksmith earned quite a lot with this scheme, but soon, people started to understand his tricks. They stopped coming to him.

In a short time, the blacksmith was back to his sorry plight.

Then one day, as he was travelling through a jungle, he spotted a rather plain-looking old man. Going by his attire, the blacksmith thought the old man was a lawyer, but it would be strange to see a lawyer in the jungle. It was then that the blacksmith noticed the old man's feet and saw that it had hooves, resembling a goat's. The blacksmith understood that it was Shaitan and not any ordinary human. When he was a child, he had heard stories about the Shaitan having hooves like a goat's.

If it was anybody else, they would have run away, but the blacksmith did nothing of that sort. He stood there and greeted Shaitan with folded hands, 'Pranam sir.'

Shaitan called out his name and replied immediately, 'So, how have you been?'

'How else will I be? I cannot even afford two square meals a day.'

'Really? If you are suffering so, why don't you work for me?' Shaitan offered. 'I will pay you lots of money.'

Just as he heard the prospect of money, the blacksmith immediately agreed, though he knew very well that whoever would work for Shaitan, could never escape his bondage. Shaitan then gave the blacksmith three bags of gold and said, 'Take this money, eat well, and lead a good life. I will come to you after seven years and will take you with me,' and then Shaitan disappeared. Kamar happily danced home with his bags of, gold coins, mohurs. He decided to spend the next seven years lavishly before Shaitan arrived to take him away.

Everyone witnessed the blacksmith become a wealthy man overnight. He stopped going to his shop or hammering at iron pieces, but lived in a grand house, with a carriage, several horses, and servants to tend to his needs. However, his lavish ways and arrogant attitude began to take a toll on him and much before the end of seven years, the blacksmith had run out of money Shaitan had given him. A day came when there wasn't a penny left, nor a handful of rice. So, he went back to his shop once again or how would he survive?

One day, as he sat hammering in his workshop, an old man slowly approached him. The blacksmith thought it was a customer, but soon realized Shaitan had returned.

'You do remember, don't you?' Shaitan said. 'Your seven years are over. You must come with me now.'

'If I leave, how will my children survive?' the blacksmith pleaded. 'You can take just about anyone else. Please spare me.'

'That cannot be. No one can trick me. You must come with me immediately.'

'Well, since you are adamant, I would kindly request you to allow me to finish this work at hand. It will help my children. They can earn from this. And as I bid farewell to all, please hold onto my hammer and keep hammering at this iron.'

Now Shaitan was a kind man. He immediately took the hammer and began to hammer at a iron. Unknown to him, this was the blessed hammer the blacksmith had received as one of his three wishes. If anyone held it or began hammering with it, he could not stop without the blacksmith's permission. The blacksmith made Shaitan begin the work, went inside his house, and did not come out for a month. After a month, when the blacksmith returned to his shop, he saw Shaitan still hammering away...*thawn thawn thawn.* Oh, what a plight he was in. In fact, if he wasn't Shaitan himself, he would have perished long ago. Upon seeing the blacksmith, Shaitan begged, 'Brother, I have had enough. What will you gain from killing me? Let me give you three more bags of, mohurs and an additional seven years of life. You spare me now.'

The blacksmith was pleased with the bargain. He accepted three bags of mohurs and seven years of life. Once Shaitan had left, the blacksmith resumed his lavish lifestyle, and just like before, the mohurs were over in no time. As per usual, the blacksmith was back at his shop, hammering away. Seven years passed.

This time, when Shaitan came to fetch the blacksmith, he heard a din from inside of his house. He realised that the blacksmith was angry at his wife and was also beating her. His wife, on the other hand, was not a woman who would simply sit and bear. She too was known to be short-tempered. She too was fighting back with a broom, but since the blacksmith held a hammer, it was he who was winning the fight and not the hot-headed wife. Shaitan saw all of this, entered the home, slapped the blacksmith hard and said, 'You rascal, you dare to beat your wife? Come with me immediately.'

Shaitan had assumed that the blacksmith's wife would support him, but surprisingly, she began to scream at him, 'You rogue, how dare you beat my husband?' and she instead, attacked Shaitan with her broom...*shawp shawp shawap.*

Shaitan could barely breathe and sat down on a chair to catch his breath. Now, it was that recliner from which one cannot get up until permitted by the blacksmith. As Shaitan struggled to get out of the seat, the blacksmith fetched a set of hot kitchen pliers, pinched Shaitan's nose, and held it tightly. Then husband and wife both began to pull at Shaitan's nose...*haio haio*. The nose started to stretch like rubber, its length growing one foot at a time. All this while, Shaitan screamed for mercy. When the nose had stretched for about twenty feet, Shaitan broke down and pleaded in his nasal voice, 'Spare me. Do not pull further. I will die.'

'Will you give me three more bags of mohurs and seven more years?' the blacksmith demanded.

'Absolutely, take these,' Shaitan assented and immediately handed over three bright purses full of mohurs to the blacksmith. He put them away in his iron chest and permitted Shaitan to get off the chair and leave. Shaitan ran for his life.

The blacksmith and his wife laughed and laughed, rolling

on the floor. He was a free man for seven more years. However, the same events occurred. Within a short amount of time, he was a pauper again, and back to his workshop.

Then one day, after seven years, Shaitan arrived, but this time, he was doubly careful. Afraid to approach the blacksmith directly, he deduced a plan. He knew that it was impossible to make him leave if anyone welcomed him warmly into their lives. So, he turned himself into a bright and shining mohur and put himself on the street, right outside the blacksmith's shop. He thought that since the blacksmith was so poor and had barely enough money to eat, he would see the mohur and come to pick it up. That was when Shaitan would trick the blacksmith and capture him. True indeed. The minute the blacksmith saw the mohur, he ran and put it inside his bag along with the rest of his mohurs.

Shaitan laughed from inside, 'How will you escape this time? You have welcomed me inside your home. Now you will learn what comes out of this.'

The blacksmith replied, 'Well, is that you? But you shouldn't have done this. Let me teach you a lesson instead.'

Fuming with rage, Shaitan was tempted to beat the blacksmith. But you see, that would be possible only when he could step outside that bag of mohurs. It was that dangerous sack that one could not escape from without the blacksmith's permission. The blacksmith placed the bag on his anvil, lifted his hammer, gave another hammer to his wife, and together, they hit the sack very hard...*dama dam, dama dam, dama dam.*

Shaitan shrieked in horror. Weary of the continuous thrashing he groaned and pleaded to the potter, 'Let me go, spare me. I beg of you. I will give you six colossal bags of mohurs this time, and I promise never ever to return to you.'

At this, the blacksmith's wife said, 'This doesn't sound like a bad deal. Leave him, let him go.'

'But where are the six bags of mohurs?' the blacksmith

enquired, and immediately they appeared, so heavy that neither he nor his wife could lift even one.

Opening the mouth of the blessed purse, the blacksmith ordered Shaitan, 'Now go and never return, for if I catch you here once again, you'll learn the lesson of your life,' but even before the blacksmith could finish his threat, Shaitan had run for his life.

Those six bags of mohurs had so much money that despite spending lavishly, the money did not get over this time. By the time the fourth bag was nearing its end, the blacksmith passed away from old age. After his death, he became a ghost and decided to proceed towards the gates of heaven. At the entrance, he met that same deity, who had granted him the three wishes many, many years ago. The blacksmith thought that the god would be pleased upon seeing him after so many years and immediately would let him enter, but to his surprise, the god bellowed at the blacksmith, 'Why are you here? Get lost, you scoundrel.'

Defeated, he headed towards the netherworld. When he reached the gates of hell, Shaitan's guards asked him his name. The moment the blacksmith answered, around five or six of the guards rushed to inform their king, Shaitan.

Hearing about the blacksmith's arrival, Shaitan was startled and instructed to close the main gates. 'Quickly. Put in the latch and the lock. Be very careful. Don't let that rascal enter. If he enters, no one will be spared.'

In the meanwhile, the blacksmith recognized Shaitan's voice and asked aloud, 'Brother, what's new?'

Shaitan boxed the blacksmith's nose so badly that it caught on fire. The poor ghost ran from pillar to post with a burning nose. That fire is still burning. The blacksmith remains deeply troubled and continues to search for a way to extinguish it. So, he dips his nose in various marshes. Those who see fires in marshlands say, 'There, that's a will-o'-the-wisp, an aleya.'

GUPI AND BAGHA, A SINGER AND AN INSTRUMENTALIST

GUPI GAYEN AND BAGHA BAYEN

Do you know how to sing? Well, today, I will tell you a story of a man named Gupi Kayen, who could sing one song. Gupi was the son of a grocer named Kanu Kayen. Since Gupi could sing and the rest of the villagers could sing nothing at all, they would fondly call him Gupi Gayen, meaning Gupi the singer.

Gupi knew only one song, which he sang all the time. In fact, so fond was he of this one song that he simply could not go without singing it. It would suffocate him if he could not sing it every day. This was his life. Unfortunately, whenever he would sing at home, all the customers in his father's shop would run away. And if he sang in the fields, then all the cows would flee, breaking loose from their yokes. Finally, customers stopped coming to his father's shop altogether, and the cowherd stopped taking his cows out for grazing. Then one day, Kanu chased Gupi away with a big, fat stick. Gupi ran into the fields where the group of cowherds sat. They too chased him away with their sticks. Gupi ran once again and reached the jungle. There, he sat down to practise his song.

Very close to Gupi's village, there was another man named Panchu Payen. His son loved to play the dholak, a type of a drum played with bare hands. But he did so in a strange manner. He would play furiously, nod his head, move his feet and roll his eyes, bare his teeth, and frown all the while. This would make everyone stare in amazement and they would remark, 'Aha, aa! Aw, aw, aw haw, haw, haw!' Finally, when Panchu Payen would shriek, growl, and snarl like a tiger, the frightened onlookers would fall flat on the ground in an attempt to flee. So, they called him Bagha Bayen, Bagha the instrumentalist. It was by this name, which people knew him. Nobody could remember his real name.

Bagha loved to play his dholak. So passionate he was about playing it that he would tear the instrument nearly every day. Panchu, Bagha's father, grew tired of this and finally, there came a day when he could no longer afford more dholaks. But why should that stop Bagha's music? So, the villagers told Panchu, 'If you are unable to afford it, let us all pool in some money and buy him one. We have such a gifted musician in our village. We should encourage him and see to it that the music does not stop.'

So, everyone chipped in to buy a dholak for Bagha, and what a massive one that was. The mouth of the dholak was four and a half feet long, and it had a very sturdy leather covering made from buffalo hide. Bagha was ecstatic. 'I will hence only play on this.' So, he immediately began to play his new dholak, and this continued for one and a half months straight. But this drove his family and neighbours to the brink of insanity. We do not know what would have happened if it had continued like that for a few days more, but one day, the villagers approached Bagha, carrying sticks in their hands, and begged him, 'Bagha, you are a gem, but please go play your dholak elsewhere or it will drive us mad. In return, we will give you ten pots full of mithai.'

What else could Bagha do? He left for another village with his dholak, but even there, he was driven away within a couple of days. This continued for a long time. Wherever Bagha would go, he would be sent away. Finally, he deduced a plan. He would roam around through fields the whole day long, and every time he would feel hungry, he would go to his village and play the dholak. The people would gather and hurriedly give him something to eat so Bagha could satiate his hunger and leave at once. The villagers would heave a sigh of relief, 'Saved.'

This continued until the villagers stopped giving him food. And if Bagha began to play his dholak, a large mob would gather not only from his village but even from the adjoining ones and chase him with sticks. Finally, he decided, 'Enough is enough. I do not need to live amidst such imbeciles. I would rather be eaten by a tiger. At least, I will continue with my music,' and so Bagha flung the strap of the dholak across his shoulder and left for the jungle.

In the jungle, Bagha had a wonderful time. There was no one to chase him. Forget about being eaten by a tiger, there wasn't even a bear in sight. But there was one terrifying animal, but Bagha could never see nor locate it. He could only hear him from a distance and tremble in fear, 'Baba re. If it comes here even once, it will gobble me up along with my dholak.'

In reality, that terrifying animal was none other than our Gupi, and the sound which used to scare Bagha was Gupi singing at the other end of the forest. Gupi, on the other hand, would also tremble at the beating of Bagha's dholak. You see, neither had met each other till then.

Finally one day, Gupi decided, 'I will lose my life if I continue living here in this jungle. Let me escape while there is still time.' So, he tiptoed out of the forest, only to find another man exiting the forest at the same time, carrying a massive dholak on his head.

Gupi was quite amused. 'There! Who are you?'

'I am Bagha Bayen. Who are you?'

'I am Gupi Gayen. Where are you off to?'

'I am off to a place where people will accept me as I am. The people in my village are all imbeciles. They understand nothing about music. So, I decided to come away here, into the jungle with my dholak. But I must leave as I keep hearing some horrific noises of a beast inside the forest. I want to escape before anything happens. So, I am off.'

'I too am running away after hearing the same frightening noises. Do you remember, from which direction the sounds were coming?' Gupi asked Bagha.

'From under a banyan tree from the eastern parts of the jungle.'

'I see! That wasn't an animal. That was me. You had heard me singing. But I know the animal growls under the harad tree in the western part of the jungle.'

'Oh no, that was the sound of my dholak, not a wild animal. I used to live there.'

When the confusion was resolved and they realized that they had been fleeing from each other's music, Gupi and Bagha burst out laughing.

Still in the throes of laughter, Gupi remarked, 'Brother, you are as much a "Gayen" as I am a "Bayen". If we stick together, I am sure we can achieve something in life.'

Bagha loved the idea. Then they sat planning and after much discussion, decided to perform in front of the raja. They were sure that the raja would be elated upon listening to them and would either give them half of his kingdom or get them married to his daughters.

So, the ecstatic duo of Gupi and Bagha started for the royal palace, frolicking, dancing, and humming all the way. Soon, they reached the banks of a very long river which they had to cross to reach the king. Though a large ferry, a kheya, stood on the banks, the boatman asked for money to ferry them across. Now the poor duo, just out of the jungle, didn't have a single paisa with them. They requested the boatman, 'Brother, we don't have any money, but we can entertain you while you take us to the other side.'

This idea appealed to the other travellers on the boat, and they agreed to collect money and pay for Gupi and Bagha's passage provided they played some music along the way.

The boatman, already curious about Bagha's large dholak, agreed quite easily. Gupi and Bagha sat on the boat, and they started on the journey. With plenty of difficulty, the passengers adjusted their seats to make space for Gupi,Bagha and the large dholak to sit right in the middle. By then, the boat had reached midstream. Right then, Gupi cleared his throat, hummed at first, and then broke into a full-throated song. Bagha too joined in, playing his dholak with all his might. What about the other passengers? They received such a sudden scare that in an attempt to flee, many fell from their seats, others hugged each other, and amidst all the commotion, the boat turned over. Oh what a mess that was!

Fortunately, Gupi and Bagha held on to the massive dholak and were saved from drowning. Sadly, their dream of reaching the palace ended there. After floating in the river the whole day, they reached the banks of a great, big jungle. It was so dense and dark that one would be afraid to enter it even during the day.

'Gupida, this looks terrible. What do we do now?'

'What else to do?' Gupi said. 'I will sing and you play. When we are close to being hunted by a tiger, why should we fall short in showing him our talents?'

'Right you are, dada,' Bagha agreed. 'If we have to die, let us end our lives like celebrated musicians and not like foolish rural ghosts.'

So, the duo forgot about their wet clothes and ill fate and once again, started to sing in full swing. Since Bagha's dholak was wet, it emitted a very deep sound, and since Gupi was very sad at the mere thought of meeting death, his voice too sounded grim and serious. You can imagine what a wonderful song that was. As they continued to sing, the day turned into noon, then it became evening, and finally night fell. But the duo kept up their melancholic and beautiful music.

Suddenly, they realized something was happening around them. Hazy, black, tall figures were peeping from behind branches and immediately disappearing. They were ghosts whose eyes burned as bright as furnaces, and their teeth were as large and pointed as radishes. It was enough to make Bagha stop playing. Now Gupi and Bagha were frightened out of their lives. They stood stupefied, their mouths gaping, heads bent, backs slouched, and legs trembling in fear. Every bone rattled in their body, including their teeth. They were frozen to the ground and could not move at all.

Surprisingly, the group of ghosts did not do any harm. In fact, they were so very happy listening to Gupi and Bagha's music that they had come to request them to play their songs at the wedding of their royal prince, the son of Goda, their king.

Seeing that the music had stopped, they said in a nasal voice, 'Why did you stop? Play on, play, play, play.'

Their words gave Gupi and Bagha some courage and they thought, 'Bah, this is good. Let us sing and see what happens,' and they resumed their performance. Gradually, one by one, all the ghosts came down from the tall branches and started to dance, encircling the duo.

What a scene that was! Never in their lives had Gupi and Bagha seen such an appreciative audience. The entire night was spent in song and dance. When it was almost dawn, it was time for the ghosts to leave before daybreak. They called the duo nearer and said, 'Come with us to Goda's son's wedding. We will see that you get handsomely rewarded.'

'But we want to go to the palace,' Gupi replied.

The ghosts were insistent. 'You can go later. You first come with us. Perform for us. We will reward you handsomely.'

Gupi and Bagha set off with the ghosts for their home. Now you can guess the beautiful performance that followed. There's no need to describe that.

While leaving, the ghosts asked, 'What do you want?'

'We want to make people happy with our music.'

'So be it,' they answered. 'If someone begins to listen to your music, they will stand stupefied and cannot move till you are finished. What else do you want?'

'We want to never fall short of food.'

At this, the ghosts produced a cloth bag, handed it over and said, 'At any point in time, you can fetch whatever you want to eat just by putting your hand into this cloth bag. What else do you want?'

By now, Gupi was perplexed. 'Well, I can't understand what else to ask for.'

The ghosts smiled and presented them with a pair of shoes, and said, 'Wear these shoes and they will take you anywhere you want to go.'

Everything was sorted. Gupi and Bagha bid goodbye to the band of ghosts, wore the shoes, and said, 'We want to go to the king's palace.' In an instant, the massive jungle disappeared, and Gupi and Bagha found themselves right in front of a large house with massive gates. They had never seen such a beautiful, large edifice. The shoes had indeed transported them to the palace.

But there was a problem. Muscular sepoys guarded the gates. The moment they saw Gupi and Bagha walk in with the large dholak, they bared all their teeth and rudely shouted, 'Eiyo, where are you going?'

A startled Gupi answered, 'Sir, we are here to perform for the raja.'

At this, the guards became angrier and snarled, 'Get going this instance.'

Gupi screwed his nose and said, 'But we will surely go inside to meet the raja,' and within seconds, the shoes had carried them right before the king.

In the inner chambers, the raja was enjoying a nap, while

the rani sat at his feet, fanning him. Gupi and Bagha reached right at that moment, along with Bagha's remarkable dholak. The magic of the shoes had brought them into the room, despite the windows being shut, and that's when the real trouble began. The rani fainted upon seeing them suddenly appear in the middle of the room. The king woke up in fright and started running hither and tither. Everybody in the palace started to run in all directions. The sepoys and the guards rushed in with their shields and scimitars.

Seeing the commotion, Gupi and Bagha lost their ability to think. Now it would just be sufficient if they had shouted, 'We want to go to such and such place...' and the magical shoes would have taken them away. But they completely forgot to say anything and began to run. The guards caught them within seconds, and the duo received a sound thrashing. Finally, the raja bellowed, 'Put them in jail for a few days. After that, I will decide what to do with them. Either I will chop off their heads or feed them to the dogs.'

Hai Gupi! Hai Bagha! The two had come to earn some money by performing before the raja, and this is what they got in return? After getting a sound beating from all the guards, the duo was arrested and pushed into a dark cell. They could barely move in pain, but what truly bothered them was the loss of Bagha's dholak. Bagha howled uncontrollably, beating his chest, 'O Gupida. O Gupida. I don't care about being thrashed or losing my life, but what about my prized dholak?'

By then, Gupi had composed himself. He calmed Bagha, patted him, and said reassuringly, 'Why do you fear so, dada? We have lost the dholak, but we still have the magical cloth bag and shoes. We were quite foolish to have received such a thrashing. Now what is done is done. Now, let us have some fun while we are still here.'

Feeling slightly more assured, Bagha asked, 'What kind of

fun are you talking about, Gupida?'

'Let us have the fun with food first. Then we can think of other types.'

So, Gupi plunged his hands inside the cloth bag and remarked, 'Let's see if you can serve us one pot of fragrant, flavoured pulao?' Instantly, an aroma filled the cell. Nobody has ever tasted such pulao, not even the king of kings. And the pulao arrived in such a large pot that Gupi managed to pull it out of the bag after much difficulty. Then Gupi said, 'Fritters, curries, chhatni, mithai, doi, rabri, and sharbat, bring them all quick, quick.' Soon, the dark cell was filled with utensils of gold and silver. How could two people finish so much food?

The hearty meal helped ease their aches and pains. Finally, Bagha said, 'Dada, let us escape now, or they will feed us to their dogs.'

'Are you for real?' Gupi asked. 'You believe that we can be fed to the dogs even when we have our magical shoes? Let's just wait and see the fun.'

Once more, Bagha was reassured when he realized Gupi had something up his sleeves. Two days passed. On the day of the verdict, Gupi arose before dawn, dipped his hands inside the cloth bag, and said, 'We want royal garments for the two of us.'

Instantly, the bag yielded such magnificent garments; nothing like you have ever seen. Then they changed into their new clothes, packed their clothes and utensils into a bundle, wore their shoes, and declared, 'Now, let us go gallivanting in the fields.' Immediately, they found themselves in the massive field outside the palace. They hid their belongings in one corner of the field and again approached the palace gates.

The sepoys had seen them coming from a distance and had rushed indoors to inform, 'Your Highness, there are two kings arriving.' The raja was curious. He too reached the main door and stood there eagerly. He cordially welcomed Bagha and Gupi and ushered them inside. They were brought into a guest room and had a battalion of royal staff appointed to look after their needs.

After Gupi and Bagha had freshened up and had a hearty meal, the raja came to see them, all the while thinking, 'They have to be really big and famous personalities.' Finally, when the raja asked Gupi, 'You are the kings of which country?'

'Your Majesty, we are no kings,' Gupi answered demurely. 'We are merely your servants.'

But the king refused to believe Gupi's truth. Instead, he thought, 'What great human beings. Humble and decent. How nicely they talk.'

He did not ask anything more and welcomed the duo into his court. It was the day of the verdict of the two urchins who had been arrested three days ago and put into the cell. As the time of the judgment approached, the guards went to fetch the two men from the cell, but they were nowhere to be found. The cell had been locked up all the while, but in spite of that, there was no one inside.

What a commotion ensued. The chief of police, daroga moshai furiously rebuked all the guards, who begged with folded palms, 'Lord, we know nothing. It is not our fault. We had locked the gates and had carefully guarded the cell.'

'I guess they were not humans but ghosts. Or how else can they just disappear like this?'

Everyone believed this, including the raja, who said, 'Well then they must have been ghosts.' This spared the daroga moshai from the king's wrath.

Everyone agreed with the raja too, 'Yes, yes, true indeed, both were ghosts,' and the fact that the prisoners had been apparitions sent a chill down everyone's spine and left them sweating in fear. They suddenly remembered Bagha's dholak and begged the king to burn it right away. 'It belongs to a ghost,' they said. 'That is a dangerous instrument. Please do not keep it in your home.'

'Dear God! I will never keep a ghost's dholak in my palace. Burn it now.' Now the minute the raja gave the orders, Bagha began howling...*how how how how*.

Bagha was inconsolable, and Gupi had a tough time comforting him. The mere mention of the order had sent him into a frenzy, now imagine what would happen when the dholak would be put up in flames? Would Bagha be able to refrain himself from disclosing that the instrument belongs to him? They could get caught and lose their lives. Gupi was troubled seeing Bagha's behaviour. He thought for a while and even considered running away without his friend, but that seemed impossible as they had taken off their shoes while having a seat in the royal court.

In the meantime, all the ministers too saw Bagha howling suddenly and they sat surprised. They thought that Bagha was probably very ill, maybe even dying. Thus, the physician was called. He arrived, checked Bagha's pulse, and shook his head seriously. He then fed Bagha a small amount of laxative and then applied a thick layer of ointment on his tummy, known as a belestara, generally applied on painful boils.

Then he said, 'If after all these, you still do not feel better, then we have to put in another belestara on your back. And if you still do not recover, then, we have to put two on each side as well.'

Hearing the physician, Bagha's howling stopped at once. The people thought what a fantastic doctor he was. A single dose of the medicine cured everything. But Bagha had stopped because the arrival of the physician meant the discussion about setting his dholak on fire had taken a backseat. He felt slightly relieved, despite the throbbing pain of the belestara's layers. The raja gently escorted Bagha to his room. He lay there, and Gupi sat next to him, fanning his belestara.

When everyone had left, Gupi finally remarked, 'Chhee brother, one should never cry like that in front of all. Now see what you have gotten yourself into.'

'If I had not cried at that time,' Bagha complained, 'they would have burned my dholak by now. I might be uncomfortable and itchy at present, but at least my dear dholak is safe.'

As Gupi and Bagha sat chatting in their room, the raja returned to his court and was approached by the daroga moshai. He whispered in the raja's ears, 'Your Majesty, with your permission, I wanted to inform you about something.'

'What is it?' the raja asked.

'You see that man who was howling and the other person with him, they are the two ghosts. I have recognized them,' daroga moshai said.

'Yes, truly. I too thought so,' the raja agreed. 'This spells great trouble. What do we do now?'

A discussion started about finding the exact solution to the problem. Someone wanted to summon an exorcist. Another suggested setting Gupi and Bagha on fire when they were asleep. Everyone liked the proposal, but there was a problem with its execution. If you try to burn ghosts, there are chances of the entire palace catching fire in the process.

Finally, after much discussion, it was decided that the two ghosts would be made to live in a large house by the garden, and the damage would be far less if that caught fire. The raja added, 'Take that dholak and keep it inside the house as well. When things will go up in flame, good riddance if the dholak goes too.'

Now Gupi and Bagha were extremely happy at the thought of moving to a lovely house. They never suspected anything was amiss and were delighted that they would get to stay in a distant place where they could practice their music in peace and no one would bother them.

The house allotted to them was a beautiful wooden structure. After shifting, Bagha recovered within no time at all. Then Gupi advised, 'Bhai, it is not safe to remain here any longer. Let's move from here.

But Bagha didn't want to leave. He answered, 'Dada, this is such a beautiful place. We will not find another like this. Let's stay for a few days more. Aha, I wish, I had my dholak.'

One day soon after that, as Bagha was roaming on the grounds and Gupi sat humming in one corner of the garden, suddenly there was loud shouting. Bagha was screaming with all his might. Gupi could not understand the head or tail of it, but could only make out his shouts of 'O Gupida, O Gupida'. Gupi came running to see Bagha dancing around the room, holding his dholak high up with both hands. Bagha was so excited at having his instrument back that he could barely compose himself. He was mumbling gibberish, occasionally interjected with shouts of 'Gupida, Gupida'. Bagha was overjoyed.

Half an hour went like that. Bagha finally calmed a bit, but again began in a frenzy, 'Gupida, see, my dholak was in this room. What fun ha, ha, ha,' and he danced for ten more minutes. Finally, he said, 'Dada, I have found my dholak after going through so much trouble. Let's sing a song to celebrate. I would like to play.'

'Not now. I am hungry now. First, let us eat. At night and after dinner, we can sit and relax and sing to our heart's content,' Gupi said.

Meanwhile, the raja had decided to set the house on fire that very night. Daroga moshai was summoned and instructed to organize a massive feast at the house. Daroga moshai was ordered to be present there with at least sixty of his men. After the feast, when Gupi and Bagha would go off to sleep, the men would set fire to the entire wooden house from all sides. This would also seal off the exits.

That night, the feast went very well. Gupi and Bagha waited for the invitees to depart so they could start their music session, while daroga moshai impatiently waited for Gupi and Bagha to go to sleep. Finally, when the duo understood that the inspector would only leave after they had gone off to sleep, Gupi and Bagh went to bed and pretended to snore loudly.

Soon after, when there was silence all around, Gupi and Bagha assumed everybody had left and came out to the veranda. They began singing.

Now daroga moshai had specifically instructed all his men to be on guard: 'You should ensure that every exit is aflame. Double check before leaving.' He had arrived to set fire to the stairs himself. But just as the flames began to burn bright and daroga moshai was preparing to escape the house, Bagha's dholak drummed up a cacophony as Gupi's lyrics joined in. Well, that was it. Neither daroga moshai nor his men could move from their places. They perished with the house. But thanks to their magical shoes, Gupi and Bagha managed to escape unscathed, along with the dholak and the cloth bag.

That night, only a handful of daroga moshai's men managed to escape. When they complained to the raja, he couldn't believe his ears. The next day, he was even more scared when a few men approached him in his court and said that they had heard raucous music coming from the house with the large garden, following which they saw two men fly off into the air. Trembling, the raja left the court and rushed to his bedchamber where he hid under the bed and did not come out for an entire month.

In the meantime, Gupi and Bagha had reached the same jungle where they had met each other many months ago. Feeling quite nostalgic and happy to be back where they had started, the duo thought of returning to their villages to meet their parents.

Finally, Bagha said, 'Gupida, remember, this is where we had first met?'

'Yes, I do.'

'Then we should celebrate that with some music,' Bagha suggested.

'Yes, you are right,' Gupi agreed. 'Then, why delay, let's start,' and so Gupi began singing in his full-throated voice while Bagha began to beat his dholak with all his might.

Now while all this was happening, an incident had taken place at the palace of the king of Halla. A band of dacoits had fled after looting the royal treasury and kidnapping the two young princes. The raja had started along with his men, chasing the dacoits who had entered the same jungle for shelter where Gupi and Bagha were singing. Just as the dacoits entered the forest, they heard Gupi and Bagha. Frozen to their places, they could not move an inch further. As Gupi and Bagha kept up their music all night long, they too stood glued to their places all night long. When morning arrived, the raja of Halla could easily find the dacoits and had them arrested.

The king was extremely happy with Gupi and Bagha, for they made the entire endeavour possible. The princes too chipped in, 'Father, we have never heard such strange music in our lives. We should take them along with us.'

So, the raja of Halla told the duo, 'You should come with us. I will pay you a salary of five hundred rupees per month.'

Gupi was elated, but he had only one request: 'Your Majesty, do give us a holiday for two days. We would like to go and meet our parents and take their blessings before we begin work. Then we will head straight to your capital.'

The raja agreed, 'That's fine. We will rest in this jungle for the next two days. You can meet your parents and then come and find us here We will leave for my palace after that.'

Now ever since he had driven out his son, Gupi's father always remained upset. He was overjoyed to see him return. However, Bagha had no such fate. His parents were no more, and poor Bagha did not know this. When the villagers saw Bagha from a distance, they were not happy and decided to keep him from entering the village.

'Goodness, here comes Bagha again,' they said amongst themselves. 'He will trouble us just like before. Let's beat him and drive him away again.'

Although Bagha implored, 'I am here just for two days to meet my parents. I promise not to play my dholak at all. Please let me meet them,' the people did not listen. They bared their teeth, raised their fists, fetched sticks, and attacked poor Bagha. Then they told him about the death of his parents and drove him away. Injured and devastated, Bagha somehow managed to save himself and ran, in torn clothes and bleeding all over. Poor Bagha could not even grieve his parents. He decided to head over to Gupi's.

Gupi was sitting and chatting with his father at the doorstep of their hut. Suddenly, he saw a dishevelled and injured Bagha limping towards their home.

Gupi rushed to his friend, 'Goodness! What has happened to you? Why are you in such a condition?'

Although he was in great pain, Bagha was unbelievably relieved to see Gupi. He answered with a smile, 'Dada, I got narrowly saved. The foolish villagers almost destroyed my dholak.'

At Gupi's house, Bagha spent a very happy next two days, along with his parents. As they were leaving, Gupi informed his mother and father, 'Please stay prepared. I will soon take some days off and come to fetch you both.'

A few months passed. Gupi and Bagha were happy at the palace of Halla's raja. They also achieved great fame as renowned musicians who performed like no other. The raja of Halla had grown very fond of them. Not a single day went without him listening to Gupi and Bagha's music, and he would also confide in them about the nitty-gritties and practical details of everyday life.

One day, Gupi noticed the raja sitting with a rather sullen face, deep in thought. He looked troubled. Finally, he called him and said, 'Gupi, a problem has cropped up. I do not know what to do about this. You see, there's trouble brewing and there is a tough time ahead for all of us and my kingdom. The raja of Shundi is about to attack us and annex our kingdom.'

Now it so happened that the king of Shundi was the ruler who had tried to kill Gupi and Bagha by burning them in his wooden outhouse. The minute he heard his name, Gupi replied, 'Your Highness, do not worry. I will create such a funny situation that everything will be alright. Trust me. Just permit me.'

The raja of Halla smiled gently and said, 'Gupi, you are a gifted singer, but you know nothing about fights and battles, neither can you understand anything about warfare. Shundi's raja has a massive army. How can I do anything about that?'

'Please do permit me; I can try at least once,' Gupi insisted. 'There's no harm in trying.'

Ultimately, the king assented, and Gupi left to inform Bagha. The duo immediately sat for a long discussion.

Bagha, who was particularly excited, said, 'Dada, this time we must do something. But I'm just anxious about one fact; if we need to run once more, I will probably forget about our shoes and run like a normal person. In the process, I will be beaten up black and blue again. That is what happened when I went back to my village. You remember what they did to me?' Anyways, Gupi's assuring words made Bagha determined to help the raja of Halla, and they both began preparations the next day. According to their plan, they would leave for Shundi at night, roam the kingdom, and be back in Halla by morning. This continued for a few days, and it helped them collect information about everything that was happening at Shundi. What Gupi and

Bagha saw, frightened them deeply. Shundi had a large force that was very well-prepared for battle. Halla was in no position to fight such a mighty army. A massive, ten-day-long puja was being held at Shundi's palace, and the raja was preparing to leave for battle right after receiving blessings from the deity.

Finally, after collecting as much intelligence as they could, Gupi and Bagha locked themselves in a room, dipped their hands into their magical cloth bag, and said, 'Give us a variety of sweetmeats. Great to taste,' and in an instant, all sorts of delectable sweetmeats came pouring out of the bag. Nobody had either seen or tasted anything like those. Gupi and Bagha took all the sweetmeats, arrived right at the top of the temple inside Shundi's palace, and sat down. From there, they could see the many people gathered for the puja inside the temple. The place was buzzing with the chatter and the sounds of conch shells and bells. The air was redolent with the strong smell of incense sticks and frankincense and the thick smoke in the air created a white screen all around. No one could see Gupi and Bagha perched atop the temple.

Suddenly, those gathered for the puja noticed sweets falling from the sky. The chatter stopped. There was silence for a few seconds, and then a commotion ensued. Some fled, some jumped here and there, and a few brave hearts picked up some of the sweetmeats and took them near a light to inspect closely. Finally, a fearless soul broke off a piece, put it in his mouth, and froze. His eyes widened, and he jumped to collect more from the courtyard and stuffed them in his mouth. Watching him devour the sweets that had fallen from the skies, the rest pounced on them, ran helter-skelter, and fought with each other to collect as many treats as possible to stuff them in their mouths.

In the meanwhile, others already rushed to the raja of Shundi to tell what had happened, 'Your Highness, satisfied with our puja, the deity has sent his blessings from heaven. And what a blessing it is...the most delectable sweets ever known to man. Their taste is indescribable.'

The king wasted no time and rushed to the temple to see it for himself, but alas! By then, all the 'prasad' was over. There was not even a speck lying around for him. Enraged, the king of Shundi growled at his subjects, 'This is very unfair. I perform the ceremony, and all of you finish the prasad? You could not spare even a few morsels for me? I will punish you all by impaling everybody.'

At this, all the people trembled and begged with folded palms, 'Spare us. How can we finish your prasad? We had only eaten a few, and magically, all of it was over. Please spare us today. You will be given all the prasad from the puja held tomorrow.'

'Fine. So be it,' the raja said, and then added, 'But be warned. Don't forget your words.'

Early the next morning, Shundi's Raja had already arrived at the temple courtyard and sat waiting for the prasad. The rest gradually gathered and sat at a distance, watching their ruler in trepidation. That day, the puja was the grandest of all days! Everyone thought that the deity would be more than happy with the arrangements and would bless the raja even more with even more scrumptious sweetmeats than the day before. At that moment, Gupi and Bagha, who had taken their seats on the top of the temple once again, sat listening to the activity below. They were regally dressed, with crowns on their head, precious necklaces around their necks, and beautiful earrings adorning their ears. In fact, they resembled gods.

Below, as though the air was thick with smoke once again, rising from the burning frankincense amidst the festivities, the raja sat with his eyes glued to the sky. Suddenly, Gupi and Bagha dropped a few sweetmeats, and they hit the raja's face. At first, he shrieked and jumped up. But then he rushed to pick up the food and stuffed it into his mouth. And then? Well, he started to dance madly, all across the courtyard.

Gupi and Bagha saw this to be an opportune moment, and they climbed down and appeared right before the dancing Raja. Their very appearance flummoxed everyone as they started to shout, 'There are the gods we have been praying to, there, there!' and they shoved and pushed to make some space so they could prostrate before them. The king was already on his knees, ready to seek the blessings of the 'gods'.

Finally, Gupi spoke, 'O Shundi's Raja, we are both very happy to see your dance. Come and embrace us. You deserve it for your devotion.'

Embrace a deity? Shundi's raja couldn't believe his ears. So, the hugs began amidst shouts of 'Jai ho'. And right then, Gupi and Bagha tightly embraced the king and said, 'We would like to return.'

Within seconds, they were standing in their room in Halla, along with Shundi's raja.

In the meanwhile, the crowd in the temple courtyard stood stupefied with gaping mouths. When their Raja did not reappear, they all returned to their homes, nodding their heads and discussing amongst themselves, 'What a miracle we witnessed today. So satisfied they were with our Raja's devotion that the gods returned to heaven with his mortal body.'

In reality, Shundi's raja had fainted as Gupi and Bagha embraced him. He lay unconscious in Halla. Towards dawn, he opened his eyes only to find the two ghosts who had once infiltrated his kingdom and burned his garden house, sitting near his head. Terrified, he fell at their feet and begged, 'Spare me. Please do not eat me. I will offer a sacrifice of two hundred buffalos to both of you.'

'Your Majesty, do not fear,' Gupi comforted the raja. 'We are not ghosts, and we are not going to eat you.'

However, the Shundi's Raja hardly felt assured and began to cry. While Gupi sat with the captured king, Bagha appeared before Halla's ruler and declared to him, 'We have caught and brought the ruler of Shundi. What do we do now?'

'Bring him over here,' the raja of Halla ordered.

When he was brought to the court, the raja of Shundi realized that he was now under arrest. Not only had he failed to annex the kingdom of Halla, he was about to lose his life. But the raja of Halla decided to spare his enemy's life and instead, took over Shundi.

Turning to Gupi and Bagha, the king of Halla said, 'You both have saved my life and kingdom. If it weren't for you, I would have lost everything. How else can I repay you? I gift you half of Shundi and both my daughters in marriage.'

After that, what a merry time it was. Gupi and Bagha became the sons-in-law of the raja of Halla and owned half the kingdom of Shundi. Then they began spending their days practising their music with elan.

How happy were Gupi's parents then!

THE RED THREAD AND BLUE THREAD

LAAL SHUTO AAR NEEL SHUTO

There was once, a weaver, Jola. One day, he told his wife 'I feel like having payesh. Do prepare some for me.'

Jola's wife replied, 'There is no wood at home. Go and fetch some, and I will prepare your payesh.'

So Jola left to fetch some wood. Soon, he came across a massive mango tree. He spotted a dry branch, climbed and sat at its very tip, and started to saw it.

A passerby noticed his antics and remarked, 'You there! Don't cut that branch or else you will fall.'

Jola answered irritably, 'How do you know that I will fall? Can you predict the future to say with such confidence that I will fall if I cut this branch? Will I not have my payesh?'

The passerby walked away in disbelief. Soon, Jola came crashing down, along with the branch.

The minute Jola fell, he thought, 'Goodness! How true indeed. How did the man know that I would fall? He must be someone important,' and Jola ran after that man, fell at his feet, and started howling, 'Lord, who are you? Do tell me the date when I will die.'

Now, the traveller was in trouble. Jola sat clinging to his feet, refusing to let go. The traveller realized that the only way he could carry on with his journey was if he gave Jola an answer. So, he said, 'You will die on the day when red and blue threads, shuto, emerge from your tummy.'

The man's answer satisfied Jola, and he happily went home.

Thereafter, Jola began inspecting his clothes every day to see signs of red and blue shuto emerging from his tummy. Now one day, he did see a few strands of red and blue shuto stuck to the inside of his garments. Immediately, he called out to his wife and said, 'Listen, come quickly, I am dead. The red and blue shuto have come out of my body.'

The wife came running to check, and indeed, it was true. She saw there were red and blue shuto stuck to the inside of the clothes which Jola was wearing. What should she do now? She made Jola lie on a bed, covered him with a shroud, sat down next to him, and sobbed loudly. In reality, nothing had happened to Jola and the threads were part of his garment. Hearing the wife's shrill cries, a few other weavers who were passing by, came in to see what had happened. Hearing everything about the red and blue shuto, they understood that their dear friend had passed away and they decided to arrange for his last rites. It was then that the trouble started.

Upon hearing about his cremation, Jola jumped up. He refused to be cremated. 'Arey, I will burn up then.' So, what else could be done after a person's demise? A burial? Jola objected to that too, 'Arey, how will I breathe then?'

Finally, after plenty of deliberation, it was decided that only Jola's body would be buried and his face would remain above the ground. Jola agreed to this method. He also instructed his wife to feed him some rice whenever he felt hungry. And so this way, his face was kept 'alive', while the rest of him was ceremoniously buried.

An entire day passed, and at night, Jola had a small meal of rice and was just preparing to go to sleep when he heard something. Seven thieves had been creeping towards the raja's palace. Now, a thief does not follow a straight path like the rest of us. They generally travel through small roads, trampling shrubs, trees, and garbage. While walking, they stepped onto something that felt like mud but had a foul stench. They looked around for a place to wipe their feet. This was right where Jola was buried. In the dark, the thief could not make out Jola's presence and went over to clean his feet on his face, who had just dozed off. Immediately Jola woke up from the ferocious rubbing on his face.

'Uh, hu, hu hu. Can't you see?' he screamed at the thief.

'And who are you?' the thief asked in amazement.

'I am Jola.'

'What are you doing here?' the thief questioned, still amazed.

'I am dead, you see. The red and blue shuto have come out of me, so they have buried me here.'

The thieves broke out into a loud laughter. Finally, one of them said, 'Let's take him with us.' They explained to Jola that he wasn't dead, and if he accompanied them, he would be fed very well. Jola asked, 'What will you feed me? Payesh?'

'Yes, payesh. Now, let's move on.'

Upon hearing about payesh, Jola did not utter a single word and agreed to follow the band of thieves. They dug him up and carried him along.

At the palace, the thief dug a very large sheendh, a hole in the wall through which one could enter the premises. Then they took Jola, put him through it, and instructed him, 'Take the raja's crown, and bring it to us.'

The raja was in deep sleep, surrounded by a large mosquito net. Having never seen a mosquito net in his life, Jola was very surprised and mistook it for a contraption. He roamed all around the net but could not locate an entrance. So he returned to the thieves and said, 'No, couldn't do it. There's another room inside that room, and it does not have any door to it.'

'You are a fool indeed. That's not a room, it is a mosquito net. All you have to do is lift it.'

Jola entered the raja's room once again.

This time, he tried his best to lift the net, but it didn't budge even an inch. You see, what Jola was trying to do was lift the raja's heavy bed along with the net. He returned once again and said, 'No, can't do it. It is too heavy.'

'Never in my life have I seen such an imbecile,' said one of the thieves. 'You must have tried to lift the entire bed. You just need to pull at the cloth.'

This time, there was no mistake. With just a mild pull, one side of the large mosquito net became undone. Inside, the raja was sleeping on thick mattresses, covered up with an equally thick blanket bordered with lace. This blanket was pulled up to his chest and only his face was visible. Seeing the raja in such a position, Jola thought that the king too had been buried just like him and must have died when red and blue shuto came out of his stomach. The more Jola likened the king's death to his own, the more intrigued he became. Finally, he couldn't control himself any longer, awoke the king, and asked with bubbling curiosity, 'Did you find the red and blue shuto coming out of yourself?'

Well, a pandemonium broke out all around. Everyone in the palace woke up, and the seven thieves were caught in an instant, including Jola.

The next day in court, Jola narrated everything right from the very beginning. He told the raja and his ministers about the red and blue shuto, being buried with his face above the ground, the thief wiping his feet on his face, the band of robbers offering to feed him payesh...every little detail was recounted. He didn't leave a single detail out of his account.

In the end, a verdict was passed. The thieves were punished, and Jola was allowed to go home a free man. But before that, he was fed the most scrumptious payesh from the royal kitchen.

THE NAUGHTY DEMON

DUSHTU DANAV

Once, a giant and a farmer were busy playing a game of pasha, a kind of dice game. The farmer lost and began to lament loudly. You see, just before the game, the farmer had made a bet to pawn his son if he lost the game. It was decided that the giant would then take away the farmer's son. So, now what to do? The giant refused to give up. 'I will come tomorrow and take your boy away. If you want to keep him safe, hide him in such a place that I am unable to locate him. But if I can, I am warning you, I will definitely take him away with me.'

My goodness, what a tragedy. Where could he hide his son now? The giant was sure to find him in any place that the farmer chose. Finally, unable to find a solution by himself, the farmer summoned the Raja of the Gods.

The king took pity on the farmer and said, 'Do not worry.

The Naughty Demon

I will hide your son in such a place that not only the giant, someone even mightier than him, will not be able to find the boy,' and saying so, the king took the young boy into a field of wheat and hid him inside a minuscule kernel of the grain.

The very next day, the giant visited the farmer's home and searched for the son. He looked everywhere—the house, garden, pond, and inside boxes, ovens, pots, and the farmer's hookah— but the boy was nowhere to be found. However, this was an extremely naughty and shrewd giant. He realized that the boy must have been hidden in the field of wheat. He took a sickle and sliced through the tall blades of wheat. In no time, he had destroyed the crop and was sifting through each kernel of wheat. Soon enough, he found the one in which the farmer's son had been hidden. He was just about to grab the farmer's son when the Raja of Gods arrived, snatched it from the giant's hands, handed the kernel over to the farmer and said, 'Here, I have done all that I could do. I cannot help any further.'

Furious at being tricked, the giant vowed to return the next day.

When the farmer saw that the Raja of the Gods failed to help him, he approached the God of Light who metamorphosed the son into a feather and stuck it to the neck of a beautiful swan. But this time too, the giant could not be fooled. He arrived, slayed the swan, ripped apart the feathers from his neck, and was just about to pop the farmer's son into his mouth when the feather got stuck on his lips and he was unable to swallow it. The minute the God of Light saw the feather stuck to the giant's mouth, he blew it away with a gust of wind. It landed on the farmer's hand, and the God of Light said, 'Here is your son. I have done all that I could do. I cannot help any further.' Cheated for the second time, the giant promised to return the following day.

As both the gods failed to protect the farmer's son, this

time, the farmer decided to approach the God of Fire to save his child. The God of Fire took the child to the deep ocean. He then transformed the boy into a small egg and hid him inside a giant fish.

Once again, the cunning giant discovered the boy's location. He managed to find the fish amongst hundreds and thousands of them in the water and inside it, he weeded through millions of fish eggs to find the one in which the farmer's son was hiding.

Luckily, the God of Fire snatched the egg from the hands of the giant and whispered into the boy's ears, 'Run for your life, and hide inside your home. Bolt the door securely.'

The giant hadn't heard what the God of Fire had whispered. The giant chased the boy but finally lost him when he went straight into his home and hid there, tightly shutting the door behind him. The giant approached the gate in suspicion, but the clever God of Fire had already planted a sharp, three-foot-long iron rod in front of the door. The giant hit the sharp pole and fell with a loud shriek.

Immediately, the God of Fire came rushing and cut off one of his legs. But it was not easy to cut his limbs. You see, the giant practised all sorts of magic. So when the God of Fire cut off the leg, it immediately flew back and latched itself again to the giant's body. In an instant, the leg was as good as new.

Nonetheless, the God of Fire was an even more powerful sorcerer. He knew that to outsmart the giant, one needed to pour massive chunks of stones and iron into the wound when the limbs would be dismembered. So when the other leg was cut off by the God of Fire, he immediately poured massive stones and iron into the cut. The giant's powers waned, and the dismembered leg could not reattach itself to the body. The giant perished.

The farmer was immensely relieved. He thanked the God of Fire and bowed before him several times. Then he went around telling everyone about the greatest god of all, the God of Fire.

A TRUE INCIDENT, NOT A STORY

GOLPO NOI SHOTTO GHOTONA

Translator's Note: This is a story from a long time ago, from a foreign country. For long, wildlife has been used for recreational and entertainment purposes in public spaces, including circuses in India as well as in other countries. However, owning wildlife or using them for recreational purposes is illegal now. In this story, the trainer and owner of the wild animals is referred to as the jontuwallah, with the word 'jontu' meaning animal in Bengali.

The jontuwallah had rented a place in the city to reside with his many animals. The day this incident took place was the day of the local farmer's market, and a massive crowd had gathered at the venue. The jontuwallah had imagined the day to be a good one to earn quite a lot of money for his many animals. But something seemed to be bothering the animals that day; they appeared to be quite out of sorts. This was reflected in their performances too. Soon the few people who had gathered inside to watch the animals, began to mock their antics. Right at that moment, the tiger rose from his corner, came closer to the front of the cage where the people were gathered, and growled loudly. What a thunderous growl that was. The people who stood mocking jumped up with fright and retreated a few steps.

Now what was the matter? Why this angry behaviour? Did the tiger react so ferociously upon seeing the sailor who had just entered the performance arena? He was a fat man with a red moustache and wore a blue coat and a blunt hat. Was the tiger angry at his sight?

The sailor slowly approached the tiger, making the creature growl even louder. The gathered crowd looked on fearfully. Suddenly, he put his hand through the bar of the cage and began stroking the tiger's forehead as if it were a mere cat.

'So my little Billi, how are you, brother?' the sailor asked the tiger.

By now, the crowd was petrified. Goodness! What large teeth the tiger had. One massive bite and the sailor's entire hand would be gone. But the tiger did nothing of that sort. The name of the young sailor was Jack and he kept referring to the tiger as Billi, meaning cat. Jack cradled the large head of the tiger on his palm and started to rub it gently. The tiger purred like a pet cat.

The news spread throughout the market. People started pouring into the performance room. Soon, there was quite a crowd, and no space remained to accommodate even a single person more. The spectators were ready to pay almost anything. It began with one paisa, some paid twenty-five paise or even two annas, and the rest dropped anything they could gather. People were desperate to enter the room. Slowly, the jontuwallah's collection box was full, and it made him immensely happy.

Suddenly, Jack asked one of the guards surrounding the cage, 'Please open the gate. I have known Billi for long. I would like to go in and say a proper hello.'

The guard was confused, and why should he not be? After all, it's a wild animal. How does one trust a tiger? No one desired to witness a live demonstration of a tiger gobbling up an entire human. On top of it, what was the guarantee that the tiger would remain within the cage once the gate was opened? He just might slip out—what would happen then?

'But are you sure?' the perplexed guard fumbled.

The guard's hesitation upset Jack. 'Do you think I am lying? You are indeed stupid. Can't you see that he's recognized me?'

At that every moment, the tiger growled once again, as if answering in the affirmative that he did indeed know Jack, 'Yes, yes, yes.'

Gingerly, using one hand, the guard opened the gates of the tiger's cage. In his other hand was a long iron rod which was used to train the animals. He clutched it tightly.

The minute the gates were opened, the crowd stepped back in fear. What if the tiger thought of enjoying a quick snack and pounced on one of them? But nothing happened as Billi was busy with his new friend and was quite oblivious to the world around him.

First, the tiger encircled Jack a few times, and then he began to lovingly rub his large head on his feet. Finally, he stood upright on his hind legs and put his front paws on Jack's shoulders. Jack took off his cap and tenderly placed it on the tiger's head. The crowd was amused. A few even smiled, for the tiger did look handsome. But there was more to come.

Jack took off the cap and whispered into the tiger's ears 'Billi, I hope you remember all that I had taught you. Now jump.'

Jack stretched out his hands high and the massive tiger jumped over it.

'Now return,' and the tiger jumped back. A very obedient student.

The guard was more than surprised. He could never make the tiger do any of these tricks. He asked Jack how he had managed to train the ferocious beast.

Jack answered with a smile, 'While we were travelling on the ship, I was the one responsible for feeding him. I can see that he has not forgotten that. Isn't it, dear Billi?'

The tiger grunted as if saying 'Of course not!'

'Okay, now sit down,' Jack said, and the tiger took a seat like any other domesticated cat.

Jack sat close to him, gently scratching his paws. He began

to sing. The tiger joined in too. The cage began to shake and rattle as Jack raised his tone and the tiger growled loudly in response, as if maintaining the same pitch. The windows of the performance room began to clatter. It would have continued for some time, but suddenly Jack saw the clock atop the nearby church tower. He had to catch a train as he was going to travel quite a distance. He had to leave immediately.

He bid adieu to Billi, but the latter simply refused to let him go. He walked along with Jack to the gate of the cage. But the second Jack tried to step out, the beast grabbed a corner of his coat with his teeth and began pulling him back. This happened thrice.

Now Jack was concerned, 'This is troublesome, my dear. I did not come here to stay, but merely came to pay you a visit.'

The guard was careful not to open the gates and began to get worried at the animal's behaviour. That's when an idea struck him. The cage had two rooms. In the front room, the tiger would display his tricks for the people, and in the adjoining room, he would sleep and eat. A gate separated both enclosures, which could be operated from the outside. The guard placed a large chunk of meat in the adjoining room, and the tiger immediately left his friend to munch on the treat. Immediately, the clever guard shut the gate. Jack was free and left at once.

THE WEAVER AND THE SEVEN GHOSTS

JOLA AAR SAAT BHUT

There was once a weaver, Jola, who loved to eat a sweet dish called pithey. One day, he asked his mother, 'I am craving for some pithey. Can you please make a few for me?' That day, Jola's mother prepared seven flat and thick, scrumptious, red and round, pithey for him. As Jola ate to his heart's content, he happily sang:

I ate one, I ate two,
all seven will I eat too!

Dancing, eating, and singing to himself, Jola kept walking and soon arrived at the weekly market. There, he stood under a large banyan tree and went on singing to himself:

I ate one, I ate two,
all seven will I eat too!

Now the banyan tree was home to seven ghosts. When they heard Jola singing the words '*All seven I will eat too*', they began to panic. Trembling in fear, they discussed amongst themselves, 'We are done for. Where did this monster come from? He says he'll eat all seven of us. Now what do we do?'

So they thought of a plan. They went to meet Jola with a magical clay pitcher. Then they requested him with folded palms, 'Forgive us, lord. Do not eat us. Instead, we will give you this pitcher. Take this, and please spare us.'

At that moment, forget about running for his life, Jola could barely move. Seeing seven ghosts before him, he stood petrified. What a remarkable sight they were. As tall as palm trees, as dark as night itself, ears as big as winnowing baskets, and teeth as enormous as radishes. Their eyes burned like clay ovens, and they spoke in the shrillest tone possible.

Jola gathered courage and asked, 'What will I do with a pitcher?'

The ghosts replied in unison, 'See, you can fetch anything from inside of it anything at any time. Whatever you wish.'

'Is that so?' Jola asked. 'Okay, I want to have some delicious payesh right now.'

Right at that moment, the sweet smell of freshly cooked payesh began to emanate from the pitcher. Neither Jola nor his parents or anybody else had ever tasted such a delectable preparation of rice pudding in their lives. Jola was extremely happy. He took the pitcher and merrily left for his home, while the ghosts thought to themselves, 'Uff! What a relief. We are saved.'

It was nearing noon. The sun was high up in the sky, and it was very hot that day.

'It is already so hot and sunny,' Jola said. 'Let me rest for some time at my friend's house which is nearby. I can resume my journey in the evening when it is cooler.'

Soon Jola arrived at his friend's residence, but unknown to him, the boy was a rogue. The minute he saw the pitcher, he asked Jola, 'Where did you find this?'

'Tell me what you would like to eat. I will fetch it for you from within,' Jola told him rather innocently.

So Jola's friend dictated a long list of sweetmeats: rabri, sandesh, rasogolla, shawrbhaja, malpua, pantua, kanchagolla, kheermohon, gawja, motichoor, jilipi, awmriti, borfi, chawmchawm....

Whatever the friend said, Jola put his hand inside the pitcher and brought it out. The boy became greedy, and decided to steal the special vessel. In an instant, his behaviour towards Jola changed. He began to pamper and spoil Jola silly. He made him sit comfortably, fanned him well, and even wiped his sweat with a gamchha. Then he finally said, 'You must be tired. You are sweating so much. Why don't you lie down for a while.'

Jola was very sleepy and asked his friend to prepare a bed for him. He was asleep in a minute. In the meanwhile, Jola's friend replaced the magical clay pitcher with a regular one that resembled it. Jola was completely unaware of the switch, and when he woke up in the evening, he started for home with the fake vessel. Upon reaching his home, he asked his mother what she would like to eat so he could take it out of the pitcher. But this is not the one the ghosts had given him. Jola looked like a fool in front of his mother, who scolded him for his tomfoolery.

Jola was livid. 'Those ghosts! Those rascals! It's all their doing.' Not even for a second did he think he had been cheated by his friend. So the next day, Jola was back under the banyan tree, singing:

I ate one, I ate two,
all seven will I eat too!

Once again, the band of ghosts quivered in fear. This time, they got a goat and pleaded before Jola, 'Sir, please spare us. Take this goat and do not eat us.'

'What can this goat do?' Jola questioned them.

'If you tickle him, he laughs out loudly and gold coins, mohurs, trickle out of his mouth.'

Jola decided to test the animal. He tickled the goat, and the second it laughed, mohurs fell out of his mouth. Jola was ecstatic. He immediately thought of showing this new goat to his friend.

That day, the friend took even greater care of Jola. He made him the best of beds, fanned him with the finest of hand fans, and Jola slipped into a deep slumber soon. It was then that his dishonest friend replaced the magical goat with an ordinary one.

Jola woke up to see that it was dark outside. He took the goat and hurried home to his mother, who was furious to see him walk in so late.

'Don't be angry,' he told his mother. 'You will be happy to see the magical powers of my goat,' and he sat down beside the goat and started to tickle him...*katu kutu, kutu, kutu, kutu.*

Nothing happened. The goat did not laugh, and neither did any mohur drop out of his mouth. Jola once again tickled the goat and said, '*Katu kutu, kutu, kutu, kutu.*' This time, it was too much for the goat to take. It became angry, bent his head, and butted Jola so hard that he fell down and cut himself badly. His nose bled profusely. To top it all, Jola's mother gave him the scolding of his lifetime. This time, Jola couldn't control his temper.

Angry, he reached the banyan tree soon and started to sing out:

I ate one, I ate two,
all seven will I eat too!

This time, he also added, 'You rogues. You cheated me twice and got me beaten up by a goat. I will not spare any of you this time.'

'What are you saying?' the ghosts replied as they appeared and surrounded Jola. 'When did we cheat you, and when did we cause you any harm with a goat?' The band of ghosts were most surprised.

'See for yourself. That goat butted me so badly; see my bruises. See what he has done to me. I will gobble all of you today.'

'That goat cannot be ours. Did you straight go home from here?'

'No. I visited a friend. There, I rested for a while at his house and then started for home.'

'That's it!' the ghosts exclaimed. 'Your friend stole your goat while you were sleeping.'

Finally, it was clear to Jola that the rogue had stolen his magical clay pitcher and his goat.

The ghosts gave him a fat stick and said, 'This stick will return your pitcher and your goat. Just instruct it by saying "Stick, start off" and you will see the fun. Even if one hundred thousand people gather all around, no one can beat this one. This stick will beat up everyone.'

Jola took the stick, tucked it under his arm, and reached his friend's home.

'My dear friend, do you want to see something funny?' Jola asked.

Like always, the nasty boy thought Jola had brought along something magical. But when Jola said, 'Stick, start off', he understood what kind of fun Jola was referring to. He had never experienced such 'fun' in his life. The stick beat him black and blue and was close to skinning him alive. He began running, but the stick followed him, dragged him back to the house, and continued beating him. He started sobbing and fell at Jola's feet, 'I beg of you, please take your goat and your pitcher, and spare me.'

'First, return my goat and my pitcher, only then will I let you go.'

What else could the friend do? He fetched the pitcher and the goat, all the while still getting beaten up.

Jola picked up the pitcher and said, 'Let some sweetmeat sandesh arrive.' Immediately, the pitcher filled itself with delicious sandesh. He then tickled the goat, and it laughed, some four hundred gold mohurs fell out of his mouth. Finally, Jola left with his stick, the pitcher, and the goat.

After that, Jola did not remain poor any more. He had a palatial house, cars, elephants, horses, and everything he ever desired. In fact, his entire demeanour changed, and he began to resemble the disposition of a king, including his walk and talk and the people he associated with. Even the actual ruler of the kingdom he lived in would often summon Jola and would always consult him before embarking on any important work.

Then one day, the kingdom was attacked by the ruler of a foreign land who went on a massive spree of pillage and plunder. The subjects were severely beaten up, and all of the king's soldiers were brutally assaulted. Only the king remained, anxiously awaiting his turn. He called for Jola and said, 'Brother, what do I do now? I fear they will arrive any moment to arrest me and capture me.'

'Do not fear, Your Highness,' Jola said reassuringly. 'You sit tight. Stay indoors, and let me handle things,' and saying so, he picked up his stick and sat right in front of the palace gates. The enemy king was coming that way. The ruckus of the accompanying soldiers, elephants, and horses was almost deafening. The loose dust from the thousands of footfalls brew up a storm which covered the sky. Jola didn't utter a word but kept a close watch.

The enemy king was riding a massive mount, as large as a mountain. He arrived first, while his entire troop followed, all with the sole intention of looting everything in sight.

The minute Jola felt the approaching enemy was close enough, he ordered, 'Stick, start off.' That was it. Immediately, one stick broke into a hundred thousand pieces, and each started to chase and beat up the king and his battalion. What severe thrashings they were! The boundless pain can only be described by the ones who received them.

Soon, the king began to plead, 'Spare us. We committed a blunder. We will immediately leave this country and return to our own.'

Jola still did not utter a word but stood there smirking. Then the enemy king added, 'I will return everything that I looted from this country. I will also give you my entire kingdom. Just spare us.'

Hearing this, Jola went to his king and said, 'Your Highness, the enemy king is ready to return everything and surrender his kingdom to you. He only wants to be spared. What should I do now? Please instruct us accordingly.'

At the king's request, Jola stopped his stick, and the defeated ruler fell at their feet. Pointing towards Jola, the king said, 'I will spare you, but on one condition. You must give half of your kingdom to this man and also have your daughter marry him.'

The king of the foreign land agreed immediately. After that, Jola ruled over half the kingdom and married the princess. What a splendid occasion the wedding was. The feast was so massive that I'm sure many could not finish eating. I think they are still eating even today. How I wish to go there to see it.

THE 'CLEVER' SERVANT

CHALAK CHAKOR

Once a judge, Kazi sahib, had a chakor, his servant, whose name was Buddhu. He was from a different region and was a little dim-witted too. This made Kazi sahib quite apprehensive all the time. Not aware of the local culture, Buddhu always failed to greet guests with a proper salaam upon their arrival. It would bother Kazi sahib even more when Buddhu would stare at all his guests with a gaping mouth. One day, Kazi sahib scolded Buddhu, 'If I catch you once again misbehaving or not properly greeting my guests, I'll teach you a lesson. You should behave well with all and also greet them well with a salaam. Just as I've taught you.'

Ever since, Buddhu started to do salaam to anybody he met on the road—a boy, an old man, or a cowherd...he excluded none. Once a man walked by with his donkeys. Buddhu did a salaam to the owner and then proceeded and generously greeted each donkey as well. The owner of the donkeys laughed at Buddhu and said, 'You imbecile. You don't need to do salaam to the donkeys. You just need to keep them on track by saying *hei hei*.' At a little distance, Buddhu saw a flock of birds and repeated the man's words. Now the birds were hovering around a hunter's net who was hiding silently in the nearby bushes. But Buddhu's *hei hei* chased them away, making the hunter livid.

Another day, Kazi sahib was invited to the house of a rich and elite man. Buddhu too tagged along. It was said that the family was related to the nawabs, and they had their special etiquette. While eating, a tiny grain of rice fell on the householder's beard. Immediately, a servant started to hum slowly to signal his master:

*'Under the flower, the fledgeling Bulbul lay,
make it fly away, make it fly away...'*

At once, the master understood the signal and waved his hand to remove the grain of rice caught in his beard.

Once they were back home, the Kazi sahib confided in Buddhu, 'Did you see their etiquettes? If anytime, you notice that a grain of rice has fallen into my beard, you too should remind me in such a manner.'

Soon after that, a great feast was held at Kazi Sahib's house. Amidst all the guests, he thought of testing Buddhu's skills. He dropped a few grains of rice on his beard and signalled his servant with his eyes.

Immediately, Buddhu started, 'Do you remember the other day in so and so's house, such and such a thing happened? Well, the same thing has happened to your beard as well. Fly away and fly away.'

Kazi sahib's guests erupted into laughter.

One day, Kazi sahib told Buddhu, 'You simply do not know how to cook steamed rice. You do not know how to properly discard the water once the rice is boiled, and the result is always an overcooked mess. When you cook rice today, call me when it starts to boil. I will teach you how to boil rice to perfection.'

That day, while the rice started to boil, Buddhu went to call his master. He stood outside the door of the room and began to silently signal Kazi sahib, who was sitting with his back towards the door, engrossed in his writing. Buddhu continued to signal him with one finger, and the noiseless gestures continued for a couple of hours. But the judge never looked up. Finally, when Buddhu was exhausted, he shouted angrily, 'How much longer do I need to call you? The rice is burned to a crisp by now.'

Kazi Sahib looked up and saw Buddhu standing behind him

and signalling him with one finger. Indeed, the rice was burned to a crisp.

One night, a thief entered Kazi sahib's house. Buddhu heard a *khawchh mawchh* sound and asked loudly, 'Who is it?'

The thief's reply was quite composed. 'Arey, I'm nobody. Just nobody.'

So Buddhu went off to sleep. The next morning, Kazi sahib was furious to see that the thief had escaped with all his possessions. When he asked Buddhu, the servant simply replied in a huff, 'What can I do? He said that he's a nobody. Now I can see that he was not only a thief, but a liar at that.'

One day, Kazi sahib was about to travel outside the city. While leaving, he instructed Buddhu, 'Keep a close eye on the front door. Do not go anywhere leaving the door, or else I will be robbed.'

After his master left, Buddhu sat with a stick to guard the main door. A couple of days passed. Then suddenly, on the third day, he heard that there was a play in town. He was desperate to watch a show, but what to do? An idea struck Buddhu. He unscrewed the bolts of the door and carried it on his shoulders to the venue. In the meanwhile, a thief came, entered Kazi sahib's house, and what he did did inside, you can very well understand. Kazi sahib returned to find everything wiped clean—the treasury where he stored his money, his almirah with all his prized things—everything was gone. Where was Buddhu? He was engrossed in the play, all the while carefully guarding his master's door.

THE DEMONS, PHINGEY AND KUNKRO

PHINGEY AAR KUNKRO

Once there was a demon named Phingey who roamed around with a massive staff made from the timber of a Sal tree, and this staff was two hundred and twenty-five feet long. There was another demon, whose name was Kunkro, and Kunkro was so mighty that his one punch could easily crumble an iron club.

Now it so happened that Kunkro was hunting for Phingey everywhere—across heaven and earth. He was roaming all over the regions, thrashing all demons. He had already beaten up everyone, and only Phingey remained. Scared to death, Phingey spent his days running here and there and wandering all across the lands, desperately trying to escape Kunkro's punches. Once Kunkro got to know that Phingey was hiding near the sea, and he reached immediately. Fortunately, by then, Phingey was out of sight and had run back home.

Phingey's house was on top of a mountain. It was so high that it took ten days to cover the length of that road that started at the peak and went all the way downhill. So Phingey thought if he would hide inside his home, Kunkro would never find him.

When Phingey arrived home in a hurry, his wife Una asked, 'What happened?'

Phingey pointed towards the sea and replied, 'There comes Kunkro! The rascal's one punch can easily crumble even an iron club. Now I am in trouble.'

Yes indeed Kunkro was on his way, but he was still quite a distance from Una and Phingey. It would take him another three to four days to finally reach their home. She told Phingey, 'You don't worry. Relax and sit tight. I will teach Kunkro a lesson.'

But Phingey remained anxious and spent his time fretting and in deep thought.

Meanwhile, Una approached every person in the village and collected various kinds of weapons, including broken knives, axes, sickles, hoes, hammers, door latches, and nails. Then she put everything in a sack and sat down to prepare a sweet dish called pithey. She continued to make them for the next two days and stuffed each one with a filling of the weapons that she had gathered. Phingey watched her with wonder and enquired from time to time about what she was doing.

'Let me do my work. You sit quietly,' Una answered.

After the pithey were ready, Una made three large buckets of cottage cheese. Then she gave specific instructions to Phingey and prepared him for everything that was to take place. Finally, the couple sat waiting for Kunkro.

Kunkro arrived the next afternoon. He entered shouting, 'Where is Phingey?'

Una started as planned. She said Phingey wasn't at home and that she's got to know about a young chap named Kunkro who was looking for her husband and was going around boasting that he had beaten him. So Phingey has left home to find that demon, and he has taken his famous stick along. Phingey would never spare Kunkro if he ever meets the chap.

Una's account greatly amused Kunkro. 'Lady, I am Kunkro,' he said. 'I have come to fight Phingey.'

Una laughed loudly at this. Finally, pretending to compose herself, she screwed up her nose and said, 'You are as thin as a lizard and just a young man. How do you propose to fight Phingey? Do not even attempt such a thing or you will lose your life. Listen to me, help me out instead. There is a very strong wind blowing. Why don't you twist the house and turn it around? Let me see if you can do it?'

'Goodness, is it true that Phingey turns around his house

if there is a gale?' Kunkro wondered. 'But now it will be quite embarrassing for me to decline the task.'

So the demon stretched and massaged the middle finger of his right hand. This was a magical finger and the key source of Kunkro's power and strength. He then tightly held Phingey's home and gave it such a strong twist that it turned around, along with the mountain peak.

And what was Phingey doing all this while? On Una's advice, he lay on his bed, nicely tucked in, and dressed like a baby. He could hear Kunkro, and it was enough to terrify him. He was sweating and trembling in great fear.

Suddenly, he heard Una telling Kunkro, 'You are such an obedient man. You deserve some sweetmeats, but there is not a drop of water at home. I wanted to serve you some sweets. How will I do that now? There is water at the very base of this mountain. If Phingey had been home, he would have removed the mountain and fetched us some water. But he's not there. What do we do now? Can you try?'

So once again, Kunkro stretched and massaged his middle finger and went to the foot of the mountain. There, he punched so hard that a massive lake was formed immediately.

This incident rather frightened Una and she was about to scream, but somehow composed herself and told Kunkro, 'Come, let me serve you some pithey.'

Una brought Kunkro inside and served him the pithey that she had prepared. Kunkro felt greedy. He took not one, but ten of them, and stuffed them in his mouth. Very soon, he spat them out with a loud shriek. Kunkro's mouth was bleeding, and he had broken a few teeth upon trying to greedily gobble the food he had been served. His screeches rang everywhere. In fact, if it had been a little louder, the house would have come crashing down.

'Don't shout so. My baby will wake up,' Una said. 'I thought you are a mighty man and you can easily stomach these pithey.

Both Phingey and my son love these.'

Immediately, the child's screams were heard from inside the house, 'Hungry. Eat. Pithey. I want to eat pithey.'

Hearing the infant's terribly monstrous voice, Kunkro jumped up in fright. Una, who had also prepared regular pithey alongside the ones stuffed with metal, served Phingey the first kind. Kunkro did not know this; all he saw was a 'baby', chomping on the same pithey which had left him with severe bruises and a bloody mouth. If the child possessed such strength, Kunkro began to imagine how mighty and strong Phingey, the baby's father must be.

Right at that moment, the baby said, 'Gib me stone. Will squeeze water.'

This time, Una gave Phingey a ball of cottage cheese and to Kunkro, a large piece of stone and said, 'My son keeps playing with this. It's his favourite game to squeeze out water from a stone. Why don't you do the same?'

But no matter how hard Kunkro tried, not a drop emerged from the stone given to him. At the same time, Phingey kept squeezing out water from the cottage cheese.

Now Kunkro trembled in fear. 'Baba go! I would like to see this baby's teeth, with which he can easily chew such dangerous pithey.'

Saying so, Kunkro put his right hand inside Phingey's mouth to feel his teeth. In one bite, Phingey cut off Kunkro's middle finger, which held the key to all his strength. The minute it was bitten off, he fell to the floor in the feeblest state. Immediately Phingey got out of bed, discarded his disguise, took out his stick, and gave Kunkro a firm thrashing. Phingey beat Kunkro black and blue and nearly broke all the bones in his body.

STORIES OF 'WISE' PANDITS

PANDITER KAWTHA

You know about that king, Hobuchandra Raja, and his minister, Gobuchandra Mantri? Well, Hobuchandra Raja also had a great scholar, a pandit in his court. The pandit possessed so much knowledge that to keep all of it inside of him, he would roam around with two pieces of cotton plugged into his nose and ears, just in case his intelligence escaped. Since he would walk around with the balls of cotton, what the villagers called 'tulor tipli', he earned the nickname of 'Tipai Pandit.'

One day, the fisherman of Hobuchandra Raja's kingdom had gone fishing in a murky old lake. Now from somewhere far off, a pig had come wandering and sat right in the middle of the dull water, hidden by a thicket of wild water plants. When a group of fishermen cast their net, they immediately caught the pig and brought it out. The sight of the animal amused them. Nobody in that kingdom had ever seen a pig before, and no one knew what kind of an animal it was. They had caught so many types of fish and even turtles, but they had never seen anything like the pig before. So they wrapped the animal in their nets and took it to the royal court.

The pig's loud grunts terrified Hobuchandra Raja. 'Baap re!' he exclaimed. 'What kind of an animal is this?'

Not a soul present in his court could reply. All the erudite scholars and advisors who sat there found themselves divided into two teams. They identified the animal through complicated Sanskrit names. One team identified the animal as a 'Gajokkhoy', which they described as an elephant that had shrunk in size to form such an animal. The other team said the pig was a 'Musha

Briddhi', a mouse which had blown up to form such an animal. Now who will decide which team is correct? Why? Of course, Tipai Pandit.

The king summoned Tipai Pandit, who arrived and after close inspection remarked, 'All of you are real fools. You know nothing. Take this animal and release him in the water. If he drowns and thrives, he is a fish. If he flies away, he is a black cormorant bird. And if he swims ashore, he is either a crocodile or a turtle.'

The court was very pleased with Tipai Pandit's answer and said, 'We are so fortunate to have someone so clever as him in our midst. Who else can solve such complicated riddles?'

When we were very young, we often heard the many stories of Tipai Pandit. There are many more such tales of 'erudite' pandits from many places in our country and also from far-off places. Let me share some of the stories of these 'great' pandits.

Tipai's son grew up to be an equally 'clever' pandit. If anyone in the village had a query about anything. he would definitely approach Tipai's son. One night, a massive elephant walked across a little road inside the village. In the morning, people woke up to see massive footprints in the mud. They were bewildered! Whose footprints are these? What will happen? Finally, they called Tipai's son. He arrived, inspected closely, and said, 'Oh, I get it now. This is the doing of a thief. That rascal came in the still of the night and had stolen someone's mortar. Since it was too heavy for him, he kept resting from place to place. These are the marks of that mortar.'

Towards Kashi, there is another bunch of stories revolving around a pandit named Laal Bujhhaggar. Once, on seeing the footprints of an elephant, he said:

'Laal Bujhhaggar sab samjhey, aur na samjhe koi,

chaar payr mein chakkar bandhke harna kude hoi.'

According to this riddle, no one apart from Laal Bujhhaggar understands it all and that these were the tracks made by a deer who had run past with a grindstone tied to its feet.

In Turkey too, there is a famous lore about a very 'wise' man. Once, someone asked him, pointing to a camel, 'What kind of an animal is this?'

The intelligent man replied, 'My God! Don't you know this? This is a rabbit who has aged a thousand years. Since he is very old now, he looks like this.'

Well, to some extent he is not wrong. If a rabbit does age a thousand years and if his nose and cheeks wrinkle and the face becomes a little protruding in the process, then of course, it would resemble a camel.

In Punjab, there are some stories about an 'intelligent' old man, a person we call a 'Buddhiman Buro'. He was the cleverest in the village and the rest were all fools. One night, a camel had passed through the main road of the village. In the morning, none could understand the marks left on the mud. Buro was summoned. He arrived at the spot, howled at first, and then suddenly burst out laughing: '*He he he he he!*'

Everyone was amused at his reaction. 'Why did you cry?' they asked.

'Why not? Hai hai. When I will not be around any longer, whom will you approach to find a solution to your many queries?' Buro replied.

To this, everyone said in unison, 'That is true. When you will no longer be around, who will help us? But we still don't understand why you laughed out loudly like that?'

'Why not? Ha, ha, ha, ha, aa, aa! I too could not understand what kind of marks are these. Ha, ha, ha, ha, ha, ha.'

Finally, I would like to narrate the tale of two brothers. In a particular village, there were many peasants. They had everything—land, money, everything—but none of them had ever received any education. So there was always a sense of sadness all around.

Then one day, they decided, 'Let us send two young boys to the city for education. They should go there, learn everything, and return as erudite pandits.' The village, of course, had no pandits. So, they decided to send the two boys to the head of the panchayat.

The two brothers set off, and on their way, began to memorize the names of everything that caught their eyes. They first saw a massive elephant tied to a tree near the road. Amused at the sight of the animal, they said, 'What is this?'

'This is an elephant.'

The two brothers were happy with the answer and started once again, mumbling all the way, 'Elephant, elephant, elephant, elephant.'

Nearing the city, they saw a temple, and asked, 'What is that?'

A passerby replied, 'That is a temple.'

Now the brothers mumbled, 'Temple, temple, temple, temple.'

Soon the brothers were passing through a bustling market. They knew almost everything that was there: fish, vegetables, grains, and pulses. But the only thing they did not identify was the potato. They stared at it for a while and finally asked the vendor, 'What are these?'

Irritated at such an obvious question, the vendor asked. 'What are you? Some kind of idiots? Don't you know that these are potatoes?'

The two brothers paid no heed to the abuse, and continued their journey, muttering, 'Potato, potato, potato, potato.'

Finally, they had begun to feel quite scholarly. The brothers discussed amongst themselves, 'People call themselves pandits after they learn one subject, but we have mastered three. What else is there to learn? Let us return to our home.'

Upon reaching their village, their entire demeanour changed. They walked around with an air of superiority and stopped travelling by foot. They never ventured out without a palanquin. The villagers would look at them in respect and say, 'Baap re! There go our three-faced pandits.'

A couple of years went by, and then one day, an elephant ventured into that village. Everyone fled immediately and took shelter anywhere they could find. They only peeped from a distance, but none could make out what kind of an animal it was.

Finally, they decided to call the pandits. A palanquin was sent. The brothers soon arrived, put on their spectacles, and carefully inspected the marks on the mud.

Finally, the older one said, 'This is a mandir.'

Immediately, the younger brother contested him, 'Brother, what are you saying? You have spent so much time learning and now you're saying that this thing is a temple? No, no. This is not a temple. This is a potato.'

BIG AND SMALL IMPOSSIBLE STORIES

GAWLPO SHAWLPO

1

Jodu was quite well-built, and he could eat a lot. When he was quite small, he was invited to a feast at a wealthy man's house. There were others present there, who were known to be connoisseurs of food. Luchi, the round, deep-fried puffy bread, and korma, the spiced, yoghurt-based curry, was served in plenty.

You see, foodies think that it is truly something great to be able to eat a lot. So after finishing their food, they began to discuss who had eaten the most during the feast.

'It's me,' one said.

'It's me,' said the other.

'No, it's me,' contested a third.

So it went.

Finally, a member of the staff who had been serving the food spoke up, 'It's none of you. The one who ate the most was that boy,' and they pointed at Jodu. 'He ate so many pieces of luchi and kofta from the korma.'

'Is it true that you ate so much korma and luchi?' those gathered asked Jodu.

'Of course,' he answered, 'I still can eat more.'

'Oh, is that true? Then bring more food. Let's see how much more can he eat.'

I've heard that after that, Jodu had eaten twenty-four pieces of luchi and eighteen pieces of korma. How much truth is there in all of this, God alone knows. You see, I hadn't been born.

Now don't think that he suffered from indigestion after

devouring such delicacies. He rode a horse, made from the branches of a betel tree, came home, climbed the jamun tree in his yard, and feasted upon many, many more juicy fruits.

2

This is a story from long ago. At that time, if you were considered quite a foodie, you would be respected. It was in this age that a Brahmin lost his life to eating too much.

You see, he would often be invited to a certain wealthy man's house to be fed generously.

One day, as he sat down to eat, the Brahmin announced, 'Today, I will only eat cottage cheese and sugar.' So, they were served. That day, he wiped clean seven seers of cottage cheese and earned a lot of accolades. Unfortunately, that very same night, he died of an overloaded stomach.

There was another man called Bhattacharjee Moshai, who was also famous for being a foodie. When everyone would be surprised to see him eat, he would tap his forehead and remark proudly, 'What are you staring at? Only this part is nireyt, the rest is all peyt...only the head is solid, the rest of the body is an empty stomach.'

3

There was once a good-natured but whimsical boy. One night, he went to watch a religious ceremony. While entering the venue, he left his shoes outside only to return and find them gone. This did not perturb him at all. In fact, he rolled with laughter.

'The rascal was rightly cheated,' he said. 'Those were such old shoes that he will not be able to wear them even for two months.'

He began the journey home barefoot and reached an area

called Hedo from where he needed to catch a tram. From Hedo his home was closer to the area called Potoldanga and was merely twenty-five minutes away. When a tram finally arrived, the boy thought to himself, 'Why will I pay six paisa for such a short distance and get cheated in the process? Let me walk to the area called Shyam Bazaar and catch a tram from there. That would be my money's worth.'

Now, the Shyam Bazaar area was even farther away from Hedo. The boy walked barefoot all the way over to the Shyam Bazaar tram terminus, only to find that no more trams were running that night. The one which he had seen near Hedo was the last tram for the day.

Once he managed to return home, he laughed so much that everyone who had gone off to sleep awoke in fright.

4

In Bengali, like in many other languages, one can directly write words from other languages, such as 'I go up', or someone's name like Lord Carmichael, James Watt, and so on. However, this is not the case with many other tongues. In the Chinese language, each alphabet denotes a word.

Once, a Bengali babu told a Chinese man, 'Can you write down my name in your language? My name is Dhruv.' The Chinese man thought for a long time and finally jotted down something which resembled scribbles. Then the text was shown to another Chinese man to read. He read it aloud and said, 'Here it is written "DuLufa".'

Once, a Japanese man was writing something about Trafalgar Square, but in his text, every time the word Trafalgar appeared, he wrote it in English. Someone asked him 'Why are you writing that specific word in English?' The Japanese man replied, 'I cannot write the word "Trafalgar" with our alphabets. The nearest that I can write down will be pronounced as "TraFaruGaru".'

5

Once, a foreigner wanted to learn Bengali. He appointed a pandit to teach him and began his tutorials. In the beginning, he was very excited, but as soon as the tough consonants started, it became greatly problematic for the man. He grew livid and thundered, 'What is this? One alphabet is on the shoulders of another. I have never seen such a strange language in my life. No sensible person can learn this language. Just like a person riding on another's shoulders, an alphabet rides on the back of another. This is only possible in your country.'

6

There was once a dim-witted farmer. As he set off for the fields, his wife tied up ten chapattis in a piece of cloth since he would be gone for long. The food was supposed to be his evening meal. However, the farmer who was a great foodie, was tempted to eat them the minute he had begun his journey. But he controlled his urges and decided to keep the food that his wife had packed for the evening.

A little while later, he thought, 'Uff, I am quite hungry. Let me have at least one. The remaining I will eat in the evening.'

But the minute he ate a single chapatti, his hunger seemed to grow. He thought to himself, 'Let me have another one.'

The more the farmer ate, his hunger seemed to double, and this continued until he had finished all eight. However, he was still hungry. Finally, he took out the remaining two and ate them as well. Lo and behold! His hunger was entirely satiated. At that point, the farmer began to think, 'I ate eight of them and nothing happened. Then I ate the last two and immediately my hunger went away. So why did I not eat the last two earlier?

My hunger would have been satisfied right at the beginning, and I would still have eight chapattis left. Indeed, I am such a fool.'

7

There was a feast going on in a house. Hearing about this, a band of liars came to join. On their way, one of them asked, 'Since we are going there, let me ask, how do you plan to enter? Their entrance is quite low.'

Hearing this, another person from the band began to crawl on all fours and replied, 'Why? This is how we will enter.' Following him, the rest joined, and they all started to crawl.

The minute the crawling band neared the front gate, four massive men, as large as the God of Death, picked them up by their necks. A member of the group, the one who had first raised the question about how would they enter the feast, said in a rather deep and serious tone, 'Now see. I told you. The entrance door is quite low. We'll be stuck.'

8

Translator's Note: The expenses mentioned in this text are in the present tense as it was written more than a hundred years ago, and the Indian economy was very different then.

༄

In one month, a student cannot survive with less than ten rupees for all his food-related expenses. When we were children, our servant was paid two paise. With that, he would feed us twice a day. But I am not here to write about the market calculations. Here, I want to write about that servant. His name was—well, we used to call him—Kaali, but behind his back, we would refer to him as 'Keley'. In two paisa, he would feed us a wholesome meal of rice, vegetables, and daal, and we would eat our heart's content. Keley would indeed feed us well, but would also make a profit out of that. His profit would often leave us hungry.

Irrespective of which fish would be available in the market, Keley would only buy the freshwater minor carp. A simple fish, about six fingers in length, he would cut its small body into two and serve one boy its tail, while the other ate its head. The one who got the tail still got to sample a bit of a fish, but the one who ate the head almost got nothing because of the presence of fish bones. So the latter would satiate their hunger by sucking at the bones.

The minute the food was served, all the boys would enquire amongst themselves to find out who was allotted which part of the fish. However, the question was never asked in Bengali because they were scared of Keley's bad temper and foul mouth. So the boys conversed in English and shouted out to each other, 'So, is it a "head" or a "tail"?'

One day, Keley had served one of the boys a portion of the tail, but mistakenly, he shouted out, 'Head!' Immediately, Keley retorted rudely, baring all his teeth, 'What? I just gave you the tail and you are saying that you got served a head?'

That day, once they had all eaten, the boys gathered for a meeting.

'Nah! We have to simply teach Keley a lesson. We speak in English, and within a couple of days, he's already learned the language. This will not do.'

Then it was decided that however less would be the quantity of the vegetable curry, the boys would eat copious amounts of rice to harass Keley.

Usually, the food was cooked for twelve. That night, the first five boys who sat down to eat finished off all the rice. They kept saying, 'Give us some more.' Keley was in trouble. His face had fallen. But what could he do? He had to feed all the boys well.

That night, he had to arrange for puffed rice and curd for some of the other boys because there was simply no rice left to serve.

The following night, Keley had cooked plenty of rice beforehand, but the boys said, 'We are not hungry today.' Keley suffered a significant loss. Three more nights went by like this. By now, Keley had realized that if he didn't keep the boys happy, his profit would continue to decrease. So Keley's behaviour changed, and suddenly, he seemed a much nicer and polite person.

WHAT HAPPENED AFTER THAT?

TARPOR

Once, there was a raja who liked nothing better than a nice story, but no one could narrate to him the exact kind of story which would make him happy. So one day, he announced, 'I promise to give away half of my kingdom to the person who can make me happy by telling me a story. But if he fails, he will lose an ear.'

Thus encouraged, several storytellers came from across many lands to meet the king. They were all renowned in their respective kingdoms and came prepared with great confidence. Sadly, none was successful, and each storyteller returned home with one ear chopped off.

You see there was a problem. The minute anyone would start with a story, the raja would interrupt and ask, 'Tarpor? And then?' After a very short while, he would ask again 'Tarpor?', and again, 'Tarpor?', and this went on until the poor man would give up out of sheer frustration. It went something like this:

'And the prince came back to life.'
'Tarpor?'
'And he returned to his kingdom with his beautiful wife.'
'Tarpor?'
'And everybody lived happily ever after.'
'Tarpor?'
'And my story ends here.'
'Tarpor?'
'And the Amaranthus plant went to sleep.'
'Tarpor?'

So it continued, but for how long can one endure this? Finally, the storyteller would say, 'I don't know what happened tarpor.' Or he would say, 'I cannot think of anything else.' Immediately, the king would order for the storyteller's ear to be chopped off. This way, no one ever received half of the kingdom, and the king never heard a story he loved. But in the process, several people lost their ears.

Now, in that kingdom lived an awfully lazy but equally shrewd Napit, a man who is a barber by profession. He thought of trying out his luck.

'Not bad if I can get half a kingdom. What else can go wrong other than losing one ear?' he thought.

So Napit arrived before the raja, dressed in his finest clothes, a large turban adorning his head, and a long tilak on his forehead. Saluting the king, he said, 'Long live our ruler. I want to tell you a story if you permit me.'

'Good, good, but do you know my conditions? If you make me happy, I will grant you half of the kingdom. If not I will cut off one of your ears.'

'But you must listen to my entire story. You cannot tell me to stop midway.'

'Well, absolutely. I want it that way too,' the Raja agreed.

Napit then went over to the servant's quarters, took a few puffs of tobacco, pulled up his chest once again, and finally arrived before the Raja. He began his narration in a serious tone:

'Your Highness, in a kingdom far, far away from here...'

Immediately, the Raja interjected, 'Tarpor?'

'Long ago, in that kingdom, there was a very famous raja—'

'Tarpor?'

'The kingdom was so large that it would take a month to travel from one end of the land to the other—'

'Tarpor?'

'The land had extremely fertile soil—'

'Tarpor?'

'In fact, the soil was so fertile that if one would plant a fistful of paddy seeds, it would yield ten maunds of paddy.

'Tarpor?'

'Since the Raja knew this, he instructed the farmers to plant seeds across all agricultural fields—'

'Tarpor?'

'So, you can imagine the copious quantities of paddy produced in just one harvest. A warehouse was prepared to store all of it—'

'Tarpor?'

'This warehouse was so large that if one stood at one end of the room, he could barely see the other end—'

'Tarpor?'

'A few lakh bullock carts arrived with all the unhusked rice. It was such a large storage area, yet it was filled to the brim with crops. It was about to burst—'

'Tarpor?'

'Then one day a band of locusts smelled all that unhusked rice and arrived. There were so many of them that the insects covered the sky. Everything became dark, the wind stopped, people began to inhale the swarming insects, and there was no air left to breathe—'

'Tarpor? Tarpor?'

'So the rascals came smelling the paddy, but the warehouse was quite sturdily built with no gap for them to enter from any side. You see, the raja had done an excellent job, and the locusts kept encircling the warehouse for days at a stretch, but could not make a hole to get inside—'

'Tarpor? Tarpor?'

'On the eleventh day, a cunning locust managed to locate a small opening. One could barely squeeze in through that—'

'Tarpor? Tarpor?'

'Then the leader said: "Listen you all, push me harder. Let me see if I can manage to enter this place—"'

'Tarpor?'

'Tarpor? Oh, what a massive push that was. Hundreds and thousands of locusts pushed their leader while chanting, "push, push, push"...'

'Tarpor?'

'Finally, he entered with great difficulty, but his body was severely bruised—'

'Tarpor?'

'Once inside, the leader picked up one kernel of unhusked rice in his mouth and then asked his band to pull him out—'

'Tarpor?'

'Oh! Now a massive action of pulling ensued. The leader was close to being spilt into two when he squeezed himself out of the hole with the kernel—'

'Tarpor?

'Then another locust came to the hole and wanted to go inside. Another round of pushing ensued. Once inside, he picked up a second kernel and was pulled out with great force—'

'Tarpor?

'Then another rascal went in—'

'Tarpor?

'Then another one—'

'Tarpor?

'Then another one—'

'Tarpor?

'Then another one—'

'Tarpor?

And, every time the king asked, 'Tarpor', Napit replied, 'Then another one...'

This continued for hours. The Raja was getting irritated, but as promised, he could not stop Napit midway. He had to listen to the entire story.

As evening fell, Raja Moshai could not take it any more and

said, 'How much longer? Is your story not over yet?'

Napit replied with folded palms, 'Your Highness, this is just the beginning. Till now, only a mere handful of locusts have come out with a mere handful of kernels. The warehouse is still full of grain and an entire band of locusts are still waiting, covering the whole sky.'

So the Raja continued listening to the saga of the locusts and the kernels of rice for two more days. Finally, he burst into tears and implored, 'Forgive me. I just can't tolerate this any more. You take half of my kingdom but spare me. I want to live.'

After that, it was a happy time for Napit indeed.

THE TALE OF BHUTO AND GHUTO

BHUTO AND GHUTO

Bhuto was short, and Ghuto was lanky. Bhuto was shrewd, and Ghuto was quite dumb. One day, both went to gather berries from a berry tree. Since Ghuto was tall, he could easily reach out to the branches, and since Bhuto was short, he was unable to fetch any for himself. So Bhuto stood under the tree and went on munching all the berries which Ghuto was plucking.

Once Ghuto was done, he looked down and asked Bhuto, 'Where are all the berries?'

'Finished. I ate all of them.'

'Really? Wait, let me fetch my stick,' Ghuto replied angrily.

Immediately, Ghuto went off to cut a branch. He was determined to make a good stick out of it to beat Bhuto. How did he dare to finish all the fruits and not even save one for Ghuto?

Watching Ghuto, the tree enquired, 'So Ghuto, how are you doing, and where are you off to?'

'I am here to cut a branch. I will make a stick out of that to beat Bhuto. Why did he finish off all the berries and not leave even one for me?'

'You want to cut my branch but with what? Where is your axe?'

Then Ghuto went to fetch an axe. The axe asked him, 'So Ghuto, how are you doing, and where are you off to?'

'I am here to fetch an axe. I will cut the branch of a tree, and beat Bhuto. Why did he finish off all the berries and not leave even one for me?'

The axe said, 'You want to use me, but how will you sharpen

my blade? Where is the stone for that?'

Ghuto left to fetch the stone. The stone said to him, 'So Ghuto, how are you doing, and where are you off to?'

'I am here to fetch a stone. I will sharpen the axe, cut the tree branch, make a stick out of it, and beat Bhuto. Why did he finish off all the berries and not leave even one for me?'

The stone said, 'You want to take me with you, but you need to dampen me first to sharpen the axe. Where is the water?'

Ghuto went in search of water. Then water said, 'So Ghuto, how are you doing, and where are you off to?'

Ghuto replied, 'I am here to fetch some water. I will dampen the stone, sharpen the axe, cut the tree branch, make a stick out of it, and beat Bhuto. Why did he finish off all the berries and not leave even one for me?'

Water said, 'If you want me, you need to get a deer and make it bathe in my waters. Only then can you take me with you.'

Ghuto then went to the deer. The deer said, 'So Ghuto, how are you doing and where are you off to?'

Ghuto replied, 'I am here to take a deer with me. It will help me to draw water, I will dampen the stone, sharpen the axe, cut the tree branch, make a stick out of it, and beat Bhuto. Why did he finish off all the berries and not leave even one for me?'

The deer then answered, 'If you want to catch me, you will need a dog. Where is your dog?'

Ghuto went to his pet dog, Bhola. Bhola said, 'So Ghuto, how are you doing, and where are you off to?'

Ghuto replied, 'I am here to fetch you, Bhola. You will help me to catch the deer, who will help me to draw water, then I will dampen the stone, sharpen the axe, cut the tree branch, make a stick out of it, and beat Bhuto. Why did he finish off all the berries and not leave even one for me?'

Bhola said, 'If you want me to catch the deer, I would need to put butter on my claws. Get me some butter then.'

Ghuto then set off to fetch butter. Butter said, 'So Ghuto, how are you doing and where are you off to?'

Ghuto replied, 'I am here to fetch some butter for my Bhola's claws. He will help me to catch the deer, who will help me to draw water, I will dampen the stone, sharpen the axe, cut the tree branch, make a stick out of it, and beat Bhuto. Why did he finish off all the berries and not leave even one for me?'

Butter said, 'Well, if you want to take a little of me with you, you need to get the cat. She will lick me out.'

Ghuto then went to his pet cat. She saw Ghuto and said, 'So Ghuto, how are you, doing and where are you off to?'

Ghuto replied, 'I am here to fetch you. You will help me to lick off some butter. Bhola will put that butter on his claws. He will help me to catch the deer, who will help me to draw water, I will dampen the stone, sharpen the axe, cut the tree branch, make a stick out of it, and beat Bhuto. Why did he finish off all the berries and not leave even one for me?

The cat said, 'If you want me to go with you, serve me some milk first. Let me drink it.'

Ghuto went to the cow. Upon seeing Ghuto, the cow said, 'So Ghuto, how are you doing, and where are you off to?'

Ghuto replied, 'I am here to ask you for some milk. I will feed that to my pet cat, who will help me to lick off some butter. Bhola will put that butter on his claws. He will help me to catch the deer, who will help me to draw the water, I will dampen the stone, sharpen the axe, cut the tree branch, make a stick out of it, and beat Bhuto. Why did he finish off all the berries and not leave even one for me?'

The cow said, 'Well! If you want milk, I must eat some hay first. Get me some.'

Ghuto went to the farmer, who said, 'So Ghuto, how are you doing and where are you off to?'

Ghuto replied, 'I am here to ask for some hay for the cow,

who will eat it and then give me some milk for my cat. My cat will help me lick off some butter. Bhola will put that butter on his claws. He will help me to catch the deer, who will help me to draw water, I will dampen the stone, sharpen the axe, cut the tree branch, make a stick out of it, and beat Bhuto. Why did he finish off all the berries and not leave even one for me?'

The farmer said, 'If you want hay, you must get me some flour. I want to make some delicious pithey first.'

Ghuto went to the grocer, who said, 'So Ghuto, how are you doing, and where are you off to?'

Ghuto replied, 'I am here to get some flour from you. The farmer will use it to make some pithey and then give me some hay. I will feed that to the cow, who will give me some milk for my cat. My cat will then help me to lick off some butter. Bhola will put that butter on his claws. He will help me to catch the deer, who will help me to draw water, I will dampen the stone, sharpen the axe, cut the tree branch, make a stick out of it, and beat Bhuto. Why did he finish off all the berries and not leave even one for me?

The grocer gave Ghuto a strainer and said, 'Go to the river and fill this up with water. Or else I will not give you any flour.'

Now no one can fill up a strainer with water. Ghuto dipped it into the water, but the minute he lifted the vessel, water dripped out of the little holes. All afternoon Ghuto continued trying but nothing happened. As evening fell, he panicked and thought to himself, 'Goodness, what do I do now?'

Suddenly, he saw a few ducks quacking nearby. '*Pyak, pyak, pyak*' went the ducks, and hearing them gave Ghuto an idea: 'I should apply some "paank" to the strainer!'

You see, in Bengali, the word 'paank' means the slushy mud found near riverbanks. So, when Bhola heard the ducks quack '*pyak*', he was struck by the thought of putting a layer of 'paank' on his strainer. 'This will help to cover all the holes, and I can fill it with water then,' he realized.

There was quite a lot of paank on the riverbank. Ghuto scooped a handful and applied a thick layer on the strainer, covering the holes. He was then able to fill it with water for the grocer.

With a broad smile, Ghuto returned to the grocer with a strainer full of water. The grocer was happy and gave him a large quantity of flour. He then took the flour to the farmer, who gave Ghuto some hay. This was fed to the cow, who gave Ghuto some milk. The cat drank the milk and immediately licked off some butter for Ghuto. The dog put the butter on his claws and ran off to catch the deer who jumped into the river to save itself. The wet deer shook off some water from its body which Ghuto then used to dampen the stone. This helped to sharpen the axe easily. Finally, Ghuto took the axe, chopped off a branch of the tree, and fashioned a sturdy stick out of it. Armed with his weapon, he ran at Bhuto.

Alas! Did you really think that Bhuto was still standing under the berry tree? He had run away long ago.

THE STRANGE SEA VOYAGE OF GILFOY SAHIB

GILFOY SAHEBER ODBHUT SAMUDRA JATRA

Do you all know where the United States of America is located? In a map of the world, the oval on the left-hand side is the new continent. America is there. The central part of this America is rather thin and looks like two countries. The northern part is North America and the southern part is South America. Among all the countries of North America, the United States is the largest.

Gilfoy Sahib was a resident of this very United States. A rather interesting man, Gilfoy Sahib, at the time of this story, was around thirty-three years of age. He had spent most of his life on a ship. He had travelled to many places on a ship and seen so many interesting things, but never in his life did he have an opportunity to cross the Pacific Ocean on a small boat. The thought of it often would make him sad. He once told a carpenter to make him a small boat. The carpenter did just that. The length of the boat was eighteen feet, its breadth was six feet, and its height was three feet. This boat was quite sturdy and could carry a weight of one thousand eight hundred and sixty-six kilograms. Sahib lovingly named his boat *Pacific* and said, 'I will now travel to Australia on this.'

Australia is located at a distance of around six thousand miles from America. Sahib gathered enough provisions to last for around five months. He loaded everything onto the boat, and finally on 19 August 1882, Gilfoy Sahib set off for Australia. The first week went off quite smoothly and without any hassle. The only problem was that since the boat was rather shallow, the food would get drenched easily because of the spray of seawater. Then came the little problems of sailing, and those lasted for a month. On some days, there was a pleasant wind, while on others, there was no wind at all. On such days, shoals of fish and bales of turtles would often gather around the static boat just to look on. With no wind and no movement of the boat, Sahib realized that it was not conducive to eat regularly as he did not have enough supplies left. Now, sitting in one place and eating less resulted in the death of Sahib's appetite. But this helped him in the voyage. He had developed a habit of sleeping for a couple of hours before sunrise, but suddenly that sleep started to be disturbed by a strange *thak thak* noise rising from the bottom of the boat. Upon close inspection, Gilfoy Sahib found that several smaller fishes, in an attempt to survive the onslaughts of a massive shark, would flee towards the boat and often would come and bump against the bottom, causing the *thak thak*. So Sahib decided to drive the shark away.

You all must have seen a long rod with a harpoon-like tip held by boatmen. Sahib owned one such apparatus. He held it low as he sat steering his boat and would hit the shark with it the minute it swam towards him. The band of sharks did get scared, but it was only as long as he was awake. So, he devised another plan, making a mannequin out of a flowy pheran and putting it in his place. This would resemble a human and easily fooled the predators, keeping them at bay, while he had his nap. Finally, the *thak thak* noise stopped.

On 10 November, Sahib saw a ship passing by and managed to gather adequate provisions from the crew. After that, a strong wind blew continuously for many days. This helped Sahib cover one hundred and six miles in just a day. On 14 November, there was a massive, violent storm that completely toppled Sahib's boat. He swam for a long time before grabbing hold of the ropes of the anchor. For an hour, he struggled to upturn his boat. Alas, it was overturned once again. The second time, Sahib struggled a little less to make the boat straight and also was careful while bailing out the water. However, in the midst of all of the chaos, Sahib lost his compass and his watch. A while later, a swordfish bore a hole in one side of the boat. Sahib didn't realize it until much later when he saw water trickling into the boat and all his things floating in that. He soon had the hole padded up.

Soon it was a new year. On 7 January, a bird came and sat on the boat. Sahib hunted and ate it. On 11 January, he hunted another bird. At times, a shoal of flying fish would zoom by. Sahib caught a few and ate them. On 16 January, the oars broke. He made another set . After that, he managed to hunt a bird only once, and by 21 January, he was starving. He had grown emaciated by then. One day Gilfoy Sahib found several oysters stuck on the sides of the boat and he sucked on a few of them. Then one day, he hunted another bird with his gun, but since it fell into the water, he was unable to fetch it. On 30 January he hunted another bird and roasted it in the meagre fire of a matchstick. By then, he was so weak that he could barely ascertain which direction his little boat was headed towards. One day, as he sat with a forlorn face, contemplating his fate, he suddenly saw an approaching ship. The vessel noticed Gilfoy Sahib stranded in the water and took an about turn. The minute he stepped on board, he pleaded for some food. After a hearty meal that restored his energy, the sailors gathered around to listen to his incredible journey. He had written everything down in a notebook. This story was published in an English newspaper from the pages of that notebook.

THE MAN WHO LOVED TO CRITICIZE

KHUNT DHORA CHHELEY

Once, in a foreign land somewhere, four brothers sat chatting about who would grow up to do what in their respective lives. All of them wished to be a prominent 'someone', but since all their wishes were not the same, each brother spoke about being something different.

One said, 'I want to do a business of bricks. I will become wealthy, and from the same bricks, I will build a home for myself.'

Another replied mockingly, 'Truly you cannot think bigger. I have a grand plan in mind. I want to be an engineer. Many people will come to get their homes designed by me. Soon I will become a prominent name and rise to the ranks of the ten most admired people of the region. You wait and watch, I am sure there will be a road named after me soon.'

The third brother answered, 'A builder, contractor, and engineer all are quite useless. I will be something useful. Why will I run around doing someone else's work? I will use my mind for my work. I will construct everything as per the latest designs. The designs of those houses would be such that no one would have ever seen anything like that before.'

Finally, the last brother replied 'Whatever you all do will have to involve me. It will be a perfect arrangement because whatever all of you will do, I will find a mistake within those. I will sit and criticize. That way, I will never be out of a job in my life.'

Over time, all brothers became exactly what they had desired. One of them started a business dealing with bricks and made quite a lot of money from that. He built a home for himself. Incidentally, he also built a home for a poor old woman using his bricks and money. The brother who became a contractor, did well for himself. He pulled a few strings at the municipality and had a road named after himself. The third brother was unfortunate. He died, buried under his own house. The newly designed house could not sustain itself and came crashing down. The fourth one, however, was the luckiest of them all. Such was his focus that there was never any dearth of things to criticize. So, he continued his work, with elan, till the day he died.

After death, he reached the gates of heaven. What a magnificent gate that was, made of glass with glistening diamonds fashioned into doorknobs. The gate had been designed by God Vishwakarma himself, the deity of craftsmen. So you can imagine how beautiful it was. Next to it, sat the god who guarded the gates of heaven. He was sitting on a stool made of gold, resting his hand on the diamond doorknob, and napping. The massive glass gate meant that one could easily see who was approaching heaven. But these days there was hardly a crowd outside because no one was fortunate enough to reach heaven. With no work to do, the guard had nodded off, but was rudely awoken when he heard a knocking at the gate, *karat karat*. The god who guarded the gates woke up to the sound of a voice from the other side.

'Kind sir, I would request you to allow me inside. Well, the gates are not bad, but why are they shut? The gates of heaven should never be shut. In fact, they should be larger.'

'Who are you? A mortal? And why are you incessantly talking?'

'Why are you so angry? I want to enter heaven.'

'Really? What have you done in life?'

'I spent my life finding mistakes in other people's works, and I have always criticized them. All my criticisms of all my three brothers are written in a notebook. I have carefully jotted down the details. Say, just the other day, if my brother had baked the brick a little less, then it would have been easier for the workers at the kiln to pound it. The other one, who had a road named after him, was so thin that he never needed to name such a wide avenue after himself. The one who died, buried under his own house was...'

'Stop, stop,' the guard cut him short. 'What kind of work is this? What did you really achieve in life with your own two hands?'

'I wrote down all my criticisms as notes with my own two hands.'

'Get lost. That means that you have never done anything in life. Simply sitting around and insulting the work done by others is no work at all.'

'But all of my criticisms were published in the newspaper named *Smriti*.'

'Leave this instance. You are not allowed in here,' and with that, the guard began humming a song: '*Aau pacharib kanku, jaganatthanku....*'

Now since our protagonist always engaged in criticism or 'somalochana', let us call him Mr Samalochak. At the behaviour of the god at the gates of heaven, our Mr Samalochak was livid. All that he had spent to reach heaven, including railways and four-wheelers, had been a waste. He thought about writing his thoughts on the matter in a newspaper column and naming his piece, 'One Is Not Welcome in Heaven.'

Now, the ride back home was long to come, so Mr Samalochak decided to spend his time noting down the faults he had found in the gates of heaven. Once he was finished writing about the gates, he had just started to write about everything that was wrong with the god who guarded the gates when suddenly he saw a poor old woman approaching the gates. It was the same old lady for whom his brother had once constructed a house.

Surprised at seeing her, Samalochak asked her, 'How come you are here?'

'I do not know myself how come I am here. I am only a poor, unfortunate woman. I have not done anything in life to deserve to come here.'

'Did you not do anything at all? Well, at least I have done criticisms throughout my life.'

'I cannot remember anything, but I do recollect that one day, there was a frozen pond in front of my house. A lot of people had gathered there to have fun. Most of them met me on the way and even said a few nice things to me. I was very ill and weak and could barely get up. Suddenly, I saw a dark cloud gathering at one corner of the sky. I had seen similar colossal, ferocious cloud only once before in my life. It had gathered above a river and I remembered that within seconds, it had caused the frozen river to burst open. Everything had been drowned in its wake. Seeing a similar cloud again, I was frightened but was too frail to either shout for help or leave my house to warn the others who were playing on the ice. All I could think about was how many people would perish in a matter of minutes if the frozen river would burst open. With much difficulty, I pulled myself up, came out, and set my house on fire. Everyone who was playing or had gathered around the frozen lake came running towards my house, thinking that I would die in the fire. So, the crowd moved away from the frozen lake. That's all, I do not remember anything else. Much later, I did ask someone if everybody was safe. They all were saved; by the time the ice had collapsed, the visitors had left the vicinity of the river and had headed towards my house. But I don't remember anything else. Then I saw someone bringing me here.'

Listening to the old woman's story, the god at the gates of heaven informed the central quarters and several gods appeared to greet her. Welcoming her warmly, they said, 'Come, please come inside.'

Just as the old woman was being ushered in through the gates, she began sobbing, looking at Mr Samalochak, 'His brother had built a house for me with his own money as I had no place to stay. Yet he has to return with a sullen face, and I will be going through these beautiful gates. How is that possible? Please do not take me inside heaven. This man here will be very sad.'

Then all the gods rebuked Samalochak, 'You good-for-nothing, lazy fellow. It is only to honour this old woman's wishes that we are accepting you into heaven. You spent your entire life doing samalochana. You never did anything good. Till today, there is not a single person such as yourself who has been accepted by us to live in heaven.'

As the gods grudgingly dragged Mr Samalochak along with themselves, he continued his criticisms, 'I think none of you can pull well. I can see that you are not being able to do your work properly. No one pulls like this.'

Do you know what a dhenki is? It is a mortar and pestle that is operated manually to pound something or to separate grains from the chaff and amidst its many uses, it is frequently used to separate rice kernels from their husk. Wherever you keep it, the dhenki would continue doing its job. Our Mr Samalochak was something like that. The minute he reached heaven, he began criticizing. What else could he do? That was all he had done throughout his life.

Like him, many amidst us only sit and criticize. Instead, they should concentrate on improving and completing their work and not spend their energies trying to assess others.

NEW STORIES

NUTON GOLPO

There was once a raja, who had three sons. The elder one was good-for-nothing and had an affliction for intoxicants and the middle one would roam around with a stick in one hand, showing off his might. It was only the youngest one, who would sit along with his father to look after the daily activities of the kingdom. This made his elder brothers very jealous.

The raja had a wish. He wanted all his sons to get him a 'tree made of gold, with leaves of silver, and a nest of a white crow on its branches'.

The three brothers set off, wandering far and wide, but were unable to find such a tree. They never returned and I don't know what happened to them. Soon, the youngest son set off too and reached a palace after a while. But he was surprised to see how empty it was. Only in one room, a girl lay sleeping. She had a stick made of silver kept near her head and one made of gold close to her feet. Quietly, the youngest son exchanged their positions.

Immediately, the girl woke up and upon seeing the prince, started to lament loudly, 'Hai re! You are the son of a human. Why did you come here? This is the house of a rakkhosh, a terrifying monster, and he will eat you up the minute he sees you. He has eaten my entire family, including my parents, and two other princes who had come earlier looking for the "tree made of gold, with leaves of silver, and the nest of a white crow on its branches". I don't know how the rakkhosh has spared me till now.'

The prince immediately understood that the princess was talking about his elder brothers. They became friends, and he discovered many things about the rakkhosh. The prince got to know that the only way the monster could be slayed was if someone went into the depths of a nearby pond and hauled out in one breath, a hidden marble pillar from its very bottom. Then one had to break it open and kill the bumble bee which lay hidden within it. The rakkhosh had also preserved the bones of his victims. After killing him, if someone took the gold and silver sticks, washed them well, and sprinkled that water on the remains of all those who had been killed, they would once again come back to life. The young prince carefully heard everything. Then, one day he did exactly what was required. His actions slayed the rakkhosh and saved the lives of many, including that of the princess.

Now here's another story I have heard. Once a king's daughter passed away when she was very young. A sage arrived to meet the king and said, 'I am here to bring her back to life. Give me a large vessel, a table, a knife, a little water, and some fire.'

The king provided everything. The sage took the daughter's corpse and boiled it in the vessel. Then he took her bones, put them on the table, and sprinkled water on them, all the while chanting a mantra. In an instant, the bones came together to form the princess. She was alive once again.

A GHOST STORY

BHUTER GOLPO

I love a good ghost story.

If the five of you gather around and decide to sit for a session of ghost stories that will last for five hours, I can easily sit alongside all of you. There is a certain fun in it. When you sit through one ghost story, you feel like listening to another. Finally, when all the stories are over, I am scared to step out of the room by myself. I do not know if there are more people like me among you, but I am sure there are. So today, while I felt like changing the English names of the story into Indian ones, I soon realized that it wouldn't bring out its true essence. Thus, I am reproducing the exact story below, which I have read elsewhere.

If you closely observe the map of Scotland, you will see that there are a bunch of smaller islands on its left. The one on the top is called North Uist, and the one on the bottom is called South Uist. In between, there are several smaller islands. This is a story from a time when there was no steam engine or even the telegraph. My paternal grandfather, Thakurdada, used to work in one of these islands as a school teacher.

Since the population was sparse, the lives of the people inhabiting the islands were rather simple and centred around harvesting only a few crops. This was enough to help them survive and lead a basic life. The soil was very unproductive, so one had to be content with what one produced, and the food was divided amongst all. From that handful of grains, they would also pay their taxes to the landlord, the zamindar. But despite the hardships, the people were quite brave and smiled through all the odds of life.

On the island, there lived a man named Allen Cameron. His house was a mile away from the village. He was quite close to my grandfather, the Master Moshai, and they had a great friendship. The duo would often sit and chat. One day, Cameron fell sick and passed away from his illness a few days later. He had no next of kin, so his assets were sold. But since no one wanted to buy his house, it remained just as it was.

A few months later, a young shepherd named Donald Mclean was passing by. Suddenly he noticed the silhouette of Allen Cameron at one of the windows of the old house. Half dead with fright, Donald was unable to move. Goosebumps broke out all over his body. His mouth was parched, and his throat went dry.

After a while, when he had managed to calm himself, he ran for his life. In such a situation, who would want to stay back and enquire after such a ghastly spectre? From Cameron's house, Donald headed straight to Master Moshai's residence where he narrated the incident. Now Master Moshai was a man of logic and never believed in the supernatural. Hearing everything, he mocked Donald and then advised him that such things are figments of one's imagination and one should not believe in such nonsense. Nevertheless, Donald didn't stop at that. He started going around narrating his experience to the rest of the townsfolk. Soon, the entire island knew the story. Everyone began to talk about it, especially the elderly, who had an opinion about everything, and saw this incident as an ominous sign for the island's future.

On that island, only Master Moshai received the newspaper. It arrived once a month and all the townspeople would visit him so they could hear him read it aloud. It was a particularly joyous occasion, and the villagers would look forward to it. Everyone would gather around the large hearth in Master Moshai's kitchen and deliberate upon everything in the newspaper, from the advertisements to the publisher's information about the press where the paper was printed; such information had become familiar to everyone who came to listen to Master Moshai read.

This gathering was interestingly a myriad one and included people from various walks of life, including farmers, shepherds, the young padre of the church, and many others. The cobbler called Rori also would be present at the gathering. He was quite a stubborn man and would not let go of a discussion until he was satisfied with gathering every possible detail about it.

One day, soon after the incident of Donald Mclean, people had gathered at Master Moshai's place and a discussion was underway, when another woman claimed she too had witnessed the spectre of Allen Cameron. She saw his ghost in the same place as Donald. Moreover, both Donald's and the woman's description of the ghostly figure was identical.

This greatly upset Master Moshai and once again, he mocked them. At once, Rori objected in his usual adamant manner, and so began an argument with Master Moshai, while the rest of the audience looked on. The heated quarrel steered from a general discussion about spirits to the ghost of Cameron's.

'I bet you my new pair of boots, Master Moshai,' Rori spoke out excitedly. 'I challenge that you will not be able to visit the place this midnight.'

Everyone clapped in anticipation. The challenge seemed to be an interesting one. Master Moshai wanted to wish it away, but the obstinate cobbler was not ready to budge. Rori even convinced the audience that since Master Moshai did not believe in any of the stories, it was necessary for him to show that things could be otherwise.

Master Moshai was in trouble, but he realized that it was impossible to back out in such a situation. In a bid to save himself from humiliation, he assented, 'Of course I will go, but let me add, even if I return alive, it will never change your beliefs.'

'Well, we will see that later,' Rori answered.

'Well! So, what am I expected to do there?'

'You will stand near the front door and say aloud "Is Allen Cameron there?" three times,' Rori instructed. 'If you do not receive any reply, you may return. In that case, I too will never believe in ghosts again in my life.

Master Moshai smiled, 'Let me also tell you that, if Allen is there, he will surely answer. We were great friends.'

Some from the audience added, 'If you happen to meet Allen, do remind him that Rori owed him money,' and everyone burst out laughing at this, while Rori looked a little unsettled.

The banter and laughter continued till it was time for Master Moshai to leave.

Rori looked at the clock and remarked, 'It is only twenty minutes to twelve. You should leave right now if you have to reach the spot by midnight.'

Master Moshai dressed in warm clothes, took his walking stick, and started. The audience decided to stay back at his place to see what happened that night.

It was a full moon night, and the sky was clear enough. But just as Master Moshai had left for Allen Cameron's house, a bunch of black clouds covered up the moon. The audience, who had remained in the house, began discussing Master Moshai's journey and whether he would be brave enough to endure it all. The young padre guessed that in all probability, Master Moshai would return midway and narrate a story which he would have conjured. If that happened, no one was in a position to say anything. Rori felt troubled. He did not want to part with his new pair of boots so easily. Finally, someone suggested that it was important for Rori to also follow Master Moshai and witness the entire event with his own eyes and also to make sure that the teacher did reach the house.

Rori disliked the idea at first, then agreed and prepared to leave. The audience cautioned him, telling him to be careful so that Master Moshai did not spot him.

Soon Rori noticed Master Moshai at a distance. He continued to follow him, all the while maintaining a safe distance. It was difficult to be stealthy as it was a marshland, and there were no trees nearby for Rori to hide behind just in case Master Moshai turned to look.

Finally, when Master Moshai reached Allen Cameron's house, Rori took a turnaround, found a barbed wire fence, and lay down behind it.

Although Rori was entrusted with keeping an eye, in reality, he was terrified to death. If Master Moshai was not there, he would have screamed his heart out in fear. He managed to lay still, waiting for the teacher to shout three times as decided. Rori had made up his mind that the moment he would hear Master Moshai's shouts, he would run for his life.

Soon, the church clock struck twelve. Rori could see Master Moshai near the main door.

Master Moshai stood at the spot, cleared his throat, and said aloud, 'Is Allen Cameron there?'

No reply.

He took a few steps back, and repeated himself, 'Is Allen Cameron there?'

Once again, no reply.

Then, Master Moshai retreated to the main road and shouted for the third time, 'Allen Cameron are you there?' and then he ran at a breakneck speed in the direction of his house.

Rori was completely taken by surprise. He had thought of joining Master Moshai on his way home, but now he had to travel all alone. What if the ghost was lurking around? Terrified, he barely managed to get up from his hiding place behind the fence before sprinting behind Master Moshai all the while uttering a strange '*goooon, goooon*' sound in fear. Finally, he started to scream, 'Wait Master Moshai, wait.'

The teacher heard Rori's voice and mistook it for Cameron's ghost. His speed doubled. At the same time, poor Rori tried his best to keep up with him and began to run in a frenzy, frightened that he was being followed by the ghost. Finally, when exhaustion overcame and Master Moshai realized that he couldn't run any longer, he gathered all his strength and turned to face the spectre. He raised his walking stick in the air and brought it down with full force, hitting the ghost's forehead: '*Shawpaat!*'

Oh, what a blow that was!

Master Moshai felt relieved when he was not able to spot the ghost. Whatever he had hit had disappeared within seconds. He resumed his journey back home, walking briskly. Finally, when he could see the lights of the village from a distance, he wiped the sweat off his forehead and calmed himself. When he entered his house, he pretended as if nothing had happened and told his audience:

'As I said before, there is nothing called a ghost.'

Those who had gathered told Master Moshai that Rori too had stepped out soon after he had left. They kept waiting for him to return. When more than half an hour had passed and there was still no sign of Rori, everyone began to worry. Soon, it was one o'clock. Scared, thinking about what might have happened to Rori, they confided in Master Moshai about where the cobbler had gone.

Master Moshai screamed, picked up the lantern, and rushed out, motioning the rest to follow him. Nobody understood anything and thought the teacher had lost his mind. But they still rushed out and followed him.

The dogs barked at the crowd, and their noises awoke the rest of the village. Everyone wanted to know what the matter was.

In the meantime, Master Moshai ran through the marshes.

He could not think of anything else, other than the police, the magistrate, and the jury. As he ran, the rest followed him closely, asking and enquiring all along the way. Soon everyone could hear a strange sound, like someone was whining in the field. Then everyone spotted a man sitting next to the marshes. It was Rori.

Poor chap. He was sitting, holding his head with both hands, whining and cursing Master Moshai. Everyone heard Rori's story and finally went to inspect Cameron's house. It was then that things became clear. There stood a large tree in front of the window next to the door whose shadow would be reflected on the wall inside the house on a full moon night. Nevertheless, what was quite strange was to see how much the silhouette of the tree resembled the figure of Cameron. Since the clouds had covered up the moon that night and there was no moonlight, Master Moshai could not see any silhouette.

WHY IS SEAWATER SALTY?

SAGAR KENO LONA?

Translator's Note: This is a story from Norse folklore and continues to be famous as a part of modern northern European folklore.

⌒

Once, there was a king called Frodi, and he owned a mill called Grotti. This was no ordinary mill as it could churn out almost anything that one wished for. But the question was who would work that mill? It was larger than a mountain. None of the raja's servants could ever get it to work, and even the young men in Frodi's kingdom failed miserably to get that mill to work. The raja, who had always dreamt of extracting large quantities of precious and semi-precious stones from the mill, remained miserable as he realized it was just not meant to happen.

Time passed by and one day, the raja went travelling to a foreign land. There, he saw two giant sisters—Menia and Fenia. They were so mighty that the earth shook when they walked, and there would be a deep depression on the ground wherever they sat down. He immediately thought, 'Now I have found someone suitable to work my mill.'

The raja bought Menia and Fenia as slaves, took them to his mill, and instructed the sisters: 'Push, push, push. Let silver and gold come out. Push, push.'

Menia and Fenia began pushing the lever of the mill while singing:

'Come gold, huin re haan!
Come silver, huin re haan!

*Come to Frodi's home, huin re haan!
Fill up his chest, huin re haan!'*

Soon, Frodi's palace was filled with silver and gold, yet he shouted incessantly, 'Push, push, push.'

After days and days of never-ending work, Menia and Fenia were exhausted. Their backs ached and their hands became numb with pain. But the greedy king's instructions never ceased. The sisters continued to push the mill.

As the king's slaves, Menia and Fenia had no power to refuse any command, but now they were getting angry. So one day, while the raja was sleeping and Menia and Fenia were hard at work, they thought of teaching the Raja a lesson. They began humming another song:

*'Come dacoits, huin re haan!
Thousands and thousands, huin re haan!
Beat beat, huin re haan!
Start a fire, huin re haan!'*

Their song reached the ears of dacoits all over the kingdom. Known as bombeytey, these dacoits were ferocious, invincible plunderers who would travel across lands and water to rob people.

While the king slept, these robbers looted everything. They pillaged all. Unfortunately, they also captured Menia and Fenia and took the mill as well. Finally, they boarded everything on their ship.

'Wah, what an excellent mill,' the leader of the dacoits exclaimed. 'We can get anything we want from it. We already have lots of money and luxuries. The only thing missing is salt. Now we need not worry any more. Push, push, push. Let the salt come out, salt, salt.'

Menia and Fenia kept working at the mill, and soon, the

ship was full of salt. But it could no longer take the weight of the massive mounds of salt, and the ship drowned, along with the terrifying band of dacoits.

It was quite a scene to behold when that large mill went down. A massive sinkhole was formed around which a great whirlwind was created, and it is said that this whirlwind has yet not stopped.

And what happened to those great quantities of salt? Well, all of it was dissolved into the sea. The giant sisters had managed to produce so much salt from the mill that it was enough for all the water in all the seas and oceans of the world. So this is why sea water is salty. If you don't believe me, you may taste it for yourself.

THE TIMID BOY NAMED KAMA

BHITU KAMA

Note from the author: this is a story of Zululand.
Translator's Note: the home of the Zulus was also referred to as the Zulu kingdom. Founded in 1816 and dissolved in 1897, this was an indigenous region in the northeastern part of present-day KwaZulu-Natal, formerly the Natal province of South Africa.

⁓

There was once a boy named Kama. He was rather small, had a large tummy, and his limbs were rather thin and wriggly. He would often be bullied by others. You see, he was quite weak and had no strength to sit up and fight. He would desire to do work of great might, but since he was so feeble, he could do nothing.

Kama was given a nickname by the people of his village. They called him Bhitu Kama, or the timid Kama. The villagers wanted their boys to grow up to become big and strong. So when their leader noticed how weak Kama was, the poor boy was driven away.

Kama was in trouble. Where would he go? Where will he stay? He thought of going to the mountains where a community of fairies lived. He thought of asking them if they would permit him to stay with them.

In that kingdom, the fairies lived around a round mountain. Nobody dared to venture into that territory. Kama trembled out of fright but carried on. When he reached their home, several small fairies surrounded him. They had thin, delicate, and small wings like that of a grasshopper's, and each was carrying a shield and a spear. They became angry when Kama entered their home in the mountains. Their raja said, 'How dare you enter our mountain? We will kill you right away.'

Kama shuddered even more and pleaded before the king, 'Forgive me, Your Majesty, please spare my life. I am Bhitu Kama. I mean no harm, and you will gain nothing from killing me.'

'Is that so? You are Bhitu Kama. Well, I have heard about you. You are a rather weak person, but you are strong at heart. Now stop trembling like that. Let me turn you into a mighty, brave man.'

The raja took a mat made from the skin of a lion, put it on the ground, and instructed Kama, 'Lie down here and sleep for a while.'

Kama did as he was told. He lay down on the mat and dozed off. After a while, when he awoke, he noticed his limbs were not thin and wriggly any more. They were big, strong, and muscular. He felt that he possessed enough strength to kill an elephant with just a single slap. Suddenly, Kama realized that he was all alone atop that mountain. None of the fairies could be seen. They had disappeared but left for him a large shield and a sharp spear.

Kama took the weapons and started for his village. Within a short distance, he saw a massive lion charging towards him. But he was not scared any more. He killed the lion with his spear. Then he flung the dead animal on his shoulders and continued. Soon, he reached his village, where people stood stupefied on seeing Kama and the lion. They tried to pull at the lion, or the shield, or the spear, but nothing would budge. The leader who had once driven him away busied himself welcoming Kama home. He arranged for a house for Kama and also gave him several buffalos.

Now Kama was happy. He lived in his new home with his mother. And all those who once called him Bhitu Kama? They had a new name for him: 'Kama Palowan', meaning Kama the wrestler.

THE MOTHER KITE

CHEEL MA

Once, there was a young daughter-in-law in a big family, who had a lovely baby daughter, Khuki. This baby was just a wee toddler. One day, as the woman sat cutting vegetables in her kitchen, Khuki crawled up to the terrace where she was snatched away by a large kite. Her mother did not get to know anything about it at all.

The kite took Khuki to her nest in the depths of the jungle. There, Khuki began to grow up. She would play inside the nest with the kite, smile and laugh and hide her face in between the kite's wings. The bird loved her too. She would travel across kingdoms and bring her the choicest of food. When it would rain, she would shelter Khuki with her strong wings.

Days passed and Khuki grew into a lovely young woman. She was so beautiful that she looked like the daughter of a god. The kite had fetched her a spinning wheel from somewhere, and she would play with it all day long.

Now one day, the raja of the kingdom came hunting in the part of the jungle where the kite had built her nest. He was accompanied by a retinue of royal staff. They all sat hiding in different parts of the forest to help the king hunt a deer. While searching for the animal, the king's men came close to the tree which housed the kite's nest. They heard the sound of the spinning wheel and remarked, 'This is strange. How come we can hear such a sound coming from a kite's nest?' Curious, they climbed the tree and were just about to peep into her nest when the kite swooped in and attacked them furiously with her beak and talons. The bruised and wounded men fell to the ground and ran to inform their raja, 'Your Majesty, we have never heard of something like this. Someone is sitting and working at a spinning wheel inside a kite's nest. This is unbelievable. We went to have a look and see, what the bird did to us.'

This time, the raja arrived at the tree, but seeing him, the kite flew away. He climbed inside the nest and discovered a very pretty girl, as beautiful as a fairy, sitting right in the middle of it.

The raja forgot all about hunting and brought the maiden home. Soon, the priest was called for, the palace was decorated with bright lights, there was music all around, and everyone sat smiling and laughing and in between all this celebration, the king married Khuki. Everyone said, 'What a beautiful queen, a pretty rani indeed.'

Now, the raja already had six wives, and they grew jealous of this new queen. They began enquiring about her family and where she came from. Unfortunately, Khuki, who was now Chhoto Rani, the youngest queen in the palace, could not provide any answer to their questions. So the six queens went to the king and complained, 'What kind of a person have you brought into this house? She cannot even say who her father is or where she comes from?'

'How will she?' the king contested. 'She was raised by a kite. She hardly remembers her parents. Just have a look at her, and you will understand if you feel that she comes from a lowly background.'

This made all the queens even more jealous, and so began their schemes against Chhoto Rani.

One day, the king announced to all the seven queens, 'Arrange and decorate all your rooms. I would like to see how each one of you goes about it and who is the best.'

The six queens, haughty as they were, thought that Chhoto Rani would fail miserably. How can a girl who grew up in a kite's nest know anything about decorating a palatial room? She would fail miserably and look like a fool before the king.

The six queens ordered very expensive items: chandeliers, lanterns, curtains, fringes, carpets, and many other things. Now what would Khuki do? She stood sobbing in her veranda, humming to herself:

> *'You pull one thin frond and the whole palm tree moves you see,*
> *Mother Kite, Mother Kite, come flying to me.'*

Immediately, the kite came flying to her daughter and asked, 'What happened, dear? Why are you calling for me?'

Chhoto Rani said, 'The king has instructed us to decorate our rooms. All the other queens have already completed the task wonderfully. I do not know anything, mother. How will I go about it?'

'So that's it? Don't worry, dear. You sit and wait for a while. I will soon return,' and so the kite flew away and within a short while, she came back with the branch of a tree. She gave this to Chhoto Rani and instructed, 'Rub the leaves of this branch all over your room, everywhere, on the walls, the door, the terrace, the floor, and also on all the things in your room. That's all. You need not worry any more.'

The kite left and Chhoto Rani did as she was told. As soon as she rubbed the branch all over the room, everything turned into gold—the walls of the room, the bed, the blankets, mattresses, the duvet, the pillows, and even the mosquito net.

Having toured the rooms of the six queens, the Raja happily set off for Chhoto Rani's room, all the time thinking, 'The Chhoto Rani must not have been able to do anything.'

But what the king saw left him with a gaping mouth. He had never seen a room more beautiful than the golden one before him. He immediately called for the other queens and said, 'See for yourselves. You all doubted her upbringing. Can this be the work of someone with a lowly way of life?'

The six queens were left speechless. They simply had nothing to say.

Then another day, the Raja called for all his queens once again and said, 'Do cook for me and my men. I will visit each of you so you can serve us what you have prepared.'

This time too, the six queens were certain Chhoto Rani wouldn't be able to cook like them. True indeed, all the six queens were excellent cooks. The Raja along with his men visited each queen's quarters and every time they all left saying, 'Wah! What a delectable meal that was.'

At a loss for what to do, Chhoto Rani went to her veranda and stood there sobbing and humming again:

> 'You pull one thin frond and the whole palm tree moves, you see,
> Mother Kite, Mother Kite, come flying to me.'

Immediately, the kite came flying to Chhoto Rani and asked, 'What happened, dear? Why are you calling for me?'

'The Raja will visit tomorrow along with his men. I have to cook and serve everyone. but I do not know anything. What will I do?'

'Do not worry, dear,' the kite answered. 'You sit for a while. I will be back soon,' and she flew away, only to shortly return with a small clay pitcher. She handed this over to Chhoto Rani and instructed her, 'Put this on the clay oven and ask for anything you want to eat. This pitcher will produce all of it and even if you feed a hundred thousand people, there will be enough for everyone.' Saying so, the kite flew away.

The next morning, Chhoto Rani shut her kitchen doors, put the pitcher on the oven, and quietly sat next to it. Finally, she sent for the Raja and his men for lunch. Once they had seated themselves, Chhoto Rani served the choicest of dishes from her pitcher: pulao, mutton curry, luchi, sandesh, payesh, and many different kinds of food. Their delicate aroma filled the room. And their taste? It was so wonderful that I cannot describe it in words. None of the men had ever had such a feast in all their lives.

Right after finishing his meal, the overjoyed Raja appointed Chhoto Rani as his Paat Rani, chief queen and the most powerful queen of the kingdom who sat next to the Raja's throne in court.

This made the six others livid and they decided to do away with Chhoto Rani once and for all. So one day, when she went to bathe in the river, they pushed her. Khuki lost her balance and fell into the river while the others returned and told the Raja that she had drowned in the river.

But you see, Chhoto Rani did not die. Her mother, the kite, had seen everything. She flew down and saved her daughter, then took her away to a lovely place in the middle of the jungle. There Khuki, the Chhoto Rani, and her kite mother began to live peacefully. Khuki's days of suffering were over; the kite fed her well and took great care of her.

Days passed. Then one day, the king returned to hunt and found her. He was overwhelmed, and tears of joy rolled down his cheeks. Soon he found out what had happened. He brought Khuki back to his home and immediately called for the ministers. As ordered by the raja, the ministers instructed the royal guards to fetch the six nasty queens. Their heads were shaved, whey poured on their bald heads, and a drum tied around their necks. In that terrible condition, they were banished from the kingdom forever.

www.ingramcontent.com/pod-product-compliance
Lightning Source LLC
Chambersburg PA
CBHW060416100426
42812CB00037B/3483/J